James E Howl
1/1975

ESTHER

THE ANCHOR BIBLE is a fresh approach to the world's greatest classic. Its object is to make the Bible accessible to the modern reader; its method is to arrive at the meaning of biblical literature through exact translation and extended exposition, and to reconstruct the ancient setting of the biblical story, as well as the circumstances of its transcription and the characteristics of its transcribers.

THE ANCHOR BIBLE is a project of international and interfaith scope: Protestant, Catholic, and Jewish scholars from many countries contribute individual volumes. The project is not sponsored by any ecclesiastical organization and is not intended to reflect any particular theological doctrine. Prepared under our joint supervision, THE ANCHOR BIBLE is an effort to make available all the significant historical and linguistic knowledge which bears on the interpretation of the biblical record.

THE ANCHOR BIBLE is aimed at the general reader with no special formal training in biblical studies; yet, it is written with the most exacting standards of scholarship, reflecting the highest technical accomplishment.

This project marks the beginning of a new era of co-operation among scholars in biblical research, thus forming a common body of knowledge to be shared by all.

William Foxwell Albright
David Noel Freedman
GENERAL EDITORS

THE ANCHOR BIBLE

ESTHER

INTRODUCTION, TRANSLATION, AND NOTES
BY
CAREY A. MOORE

Doubleday & Company, Inc.
Garden City, New York
1971

Dedicated to
Patty
Kathy, Stephen
David, and Bruce

PREFACE

Like Odysseus steering a middle course between Scylla and the equally dangerous Charybdis, the translator of a biblical book must steer a course between the rocks of literalism and the whirl-pool of paraphrase. Unlike Odysseus, I can claim neither the help nor hindrance of the gods, but I must admit to being guided by the work of scholars, past and present, as well as urged on by colleagues and friends. Where possible, I have tried to indicate my indebtedness to scholarly articles of the past; and, like all students of the Book of Esther, I am especially indebted to the standard works on the subject.

To Professor Wilfred G. Lambert, now of the University of Birmingham, England, who first introduced me as a graduate stu-dent at The Johns Hopkins University to a serious study of Esther, and to Professor Jacob M. Myers of the Lutheran Theological Seminary at Gettysburg, who much earlier introduced me to the Hebrew language and the fascinating field of biblical studies and who graciously consented to read the manuscript and make numer-ous suggestions, I am far more indebted than either of them realizes. Like all former students of Professor William F. Albright, I grate-fully acknowledge all his past and present inspiration and help. I am also very much indebted to Professor David Noel Freedman, without whose suggestions this volume would be far less acceptable. Nor can I forget Sallie Waterman and Robert Hewetson of the Doubleday staff for their cordial co-operation and many helpful sug-gestions.

Nor am I unmindful of my debt to those things we so impersonally characterize as "institutions," namely, to Gettysburg College for a year's sabbatical in 1967–68, to Hebrew Union College of Cincinnati and Jerusalem for a most generous study grant, and to École Biblique of Jerusalem for the use of its superb library. To an accurate typist, Mrs. Mary Miller, who faithfully reproduced everything I wrote except my errors, I express my thanks. My wife Patty did not prepare an index or check the references; rather hers was the most precious gift: she provided a happy and loving home in which a man can work. But after getting all the help and advice I could, I, like Odysseus, had to chart my own course— for weal or woe.

C. A. Moore

Gettysburg, Pennsylvania

CONTENTS

INTRODUCTION

X CONTENTS

ESTHER

APPENDIXES

LIST OF ILLUSTRATIONS

1. Gate of King Xerxes at Persepolis. From *The Arts of Ancient Iran* by R. Ghirshman, figure 203. Source: Noel Ballif

2. Darius and his son giving audience before two fire altars (sixth–fifth century B.C.). Courtesy of the Oriental Institute, University of Chicago

3. Symbol of the Persian god Ahuramazda, from the east door of the Tripylon at Persepolis (sixth–fifth century B.C.). Courtesy of the Oriental Institute, University of Chicago

4. Stone relief showing a Chorasmian with his horse, from the east stairway of the apadana at Persepolis. From *The Arts of Ancient Iran* by R. Ghirshman, figure 231. Source: Antonello Perissinotto

5. Stone relief of Persian and Medean guards, from the stairway of the Tripylon at Persepolis. From *The Arts of Ancient Iran* by R. Ghirshman, figure 236. Source: Antonello Perissinotto

6. Gold drinking cup in the form of a winged lion (fifth century B.C., Achaemenian). Courtesy of the Metropolitan Museum, New York

7. Gold ring, with antelope, found at Persepolis. Courtesy of the Oriental Institute, University of Chicago

8. Aerial view of Susa. Courtesy of the Oriental Institute, University of Chicago

9. Aerial view of Persepolis. From *The Arts of Ancient Iran* by R. Ghirshman, figure 199. Source: Photo Vahé

10. Plan of Persepolis, from the original plan in *Moyen Orient* (Guide Bleu, 1965 edition). Courtesy of the Librairie Hachette, Paris

11. Illustrated *Megillah* scroll of the Book of Esther, from Prague ca. 1700. Courtesy of the Jewish Museum, New York

MAPS

PRINCIPAL ABBREVIATIONS

1. PUBLICATIONS

AfO   Archiv für Orientforschung
ANET   *Ancient Near Eastern Texts,* ed. J. B. Pritchard*
ArOr   Archiv Orientální
BASOR   Bulletin of the American Schools of Oriental Research
BDB   F. Brown, S. R. Driver, and C. A. Briggs, eds., *A Hebrew and English Lexicon of the Old Testament**
BH³   *Biblia Hebraica,* ed. Rudolph Kittel, 3d ed.*
BJRL   Bulletin of the John Rylands Library
BZ   Biblische Zeitschrift
ET   Expository Times
GHB   *Grammaire de l'Hébreu Biblique,* by Paul Joüon.* References are to sections
GKC   *Gesenius' Hebrew Grammar,* ed. by E. F. Kautzsch and rev. by A. E. Cowley.* References are to sections
HPE   *The History of the Persian Empire,* by A. T. Olmstead*
HTR   Harvard Theological Review
HUCA   Hebrew Union College Annual
IB   The Interpreter's Bible
IDB   The Interpreter's Dictionary of the Bible
JBL   Journal of Biblical Literature and Exegesis
JNES   Journal of Near Eastern Studies
JQR   Jewish Quarterly Review
JTS   Journal of Theological Studies
1QpHab   Qumran Pesher on Habakkuk
OTTV   *The Old Testament Text and Versions,* by B. J. Roberts*
PAAJR   Proceedings of the American Academy for Jewish Research
RB   Revue Biblique
RHA   Revue Hittite et Asianique
SEÅ   Svensk Exegetisk Årsbok
VBW   *Views of the Biblical World,* ed. Benjamin Mazar*
VT   Vetus Testamentum

* For complete reference, see Bibliography, Other Books.

VTS   Vetus Testamentum Supplements
WZKM   Wiener Zeitschrift für die Kunde des Morgenlandes
ZAW   Zeitschrift für die alttestamentliche Wissenschaft
ZDMG   Zeitschrift der deutschen morgenländischen Gesellschaft

2. VERSIONS

AT   Greek "A-text," the so-called Lucianic recension of Esther
LXX   The Septuagint, or B-text
  LXX^A Codex Alexandrinus
  LXX^B Codex Vaticanus
  LXX$^\aleph$ Codex Sinaiticus
OL   The Old Latin
Vulg.   The Vulgate

AB   The Anchor Bible, 1964–
KJ   The King James or Authorized Version of 1611
RSV   The Revised Standard Version, 1953

3. OTHER ABBREVIATIONS

Akk.   Akkadian
Ar.   Arabic
Aram.   Aramaic
Assyr.   Assyrian
Bab.   Babylonian
Gr.   Greek
Heb.   Hebrew
MT   The Masoretic Text
OT   The Old Testament
Pers.   Persian

INTRODUCTION

INTRODUCTION

No other book of the Old Testament has received such mixed reviews by good, God-fearing men as the Book of Esther.[1] It has had the unique but dubious distinction of frequently being praised by many Jews and ignored and disliked by even more Christians. So appreciative of the book was the great Jewish scholar Maimonides (1135–1204 A.D.) that he ranked it after the Pentateuch; Martin Luther, on the other hand, voiced the sentiments of many Christians in declaring, "I am so hostile to this book [II Maccabees] and to Esther that I could wish they did not exist at all; for they judaize too greatly and have much pagan impropriety."[2] This radical difference of opinion concerning the book's worth is not a medieval phenomenon alone but goes back at least to the time of the book's canonization at the Council of Jamnia in A.D. 90, and possibly even back to the time of its composition.

RÉSUMÉ OF THE STORY OF ESTHER

Before going further, we should summarize the story which has raised so much controversy.

One day, during one of his lavish drinking parties, King Xerxes was feeling high and ordered Queen Vashti to appear before his guests, so that he might show off her much rumored beauty. When she refused, the king deposed her immediately (ch. i). Later he launched a large-scale search throughout the kingdom to find someone suitable to replace her. Among the many attractive candi-

[1] In addition to the specialized studies on Esther, the interested reader should consult the treatment of Esther in the standard general introductions to the literature of the Old Testament, including the works of Aage Bentzen, S. R. Driver, Otto Eissfeldt, W. O. E. Oesterley and T. H. Robinson, and R. H. Pfeiffer. [For more complete reference, see Bibliography, Other Books.]

[2] *Table Talk,* XXIV.

dates taken to his bed—but only after a year of extensive beauty preparations—was the Jewess Esther, the niece and adopted daughter of Mordecai the Jew. A beautiful and shapely girl, Esther was quite popular among all who knew her at the palace, and not surprisingly, the king chose her as his queen.

Some time after this Mordecai learned about a court intrigue against the king; he told Esther, who in turn warned the king in Mordecai's name but without revealing that she herself was a Jewess. As it turned out, Mordecai's good deed was officially recorded although he was not rewarded at the time (ch. ii). Later on, Mordecai refused to bow down to the king's prime minister, Haman, because he was an Amalekite and thus the mortal enemy of all Jews. In revenge for this disrespect, Haman persuaded the king to approve a pogrom against the people who were the principal obstacle to the success of all his plans for the empire. These "enemies" were, of course, the Jews. Nevertheless, Haman succeeded in getting the pogrom accepted without identifying them by name. Thus an edict was sent throughout the empire, declaring that on the thirteenth day of the month of Adar, all Jews, including women and children, were to be wiped out and their possessions plundered. Dictated by Haman but written in the king's name and sealed with the king's signet, the edict was irrevocable (ch. iii).

As soon as Mordecai heard about the edict, he ordered Esther to intercede for her people. Reluctant to approach the king unsummoned for fear of being summarily executed, Esther was finally persuaded by Mordecai to take the risk. To improve her chances of success, she insisted that all the Jews in Susa, herself included, observe a strenuous three-day fast, after which she would appear, unsummoned, before the king in her most fetching attire (ch. iv).

When Esther approached the throne three days later, the king received her most cordially, assuring her that her request would be granted no matter what it was. But instead of interceding for her people then and there, Esther invited the king and Haman, her greatest enemy, to dinner. At that time the king repeated his sweeping promise to grant her almost any request, but she asked only that the king and Haman come again for dinner the next day; then, she assured him, she would ask her favor. Haman, of course, went away jubilant, flattered that only he had been invited to the queen's dinner with the king. The taste of victory and joy turned to ashes in his mouth, however, when he noticed Mordecai sitting at the gate, acting as if nothing had happened to him or his people, and still refusing to bow down! Haman controlled himself until he got home, where after boasting to his wife Zeresh and friends of all his accomplishments and honors, he admitted to being robbed of any joy and self-respect by Mordecai's continuing contempt for him. When someone suggested he ask the king's permission to hang Mordecai, the idea struck him as perfect; and he ordered a seventy-five-foot gallows constructed outside his home (ch. v).

That night, when the king could not sleep, he had his journal read aloud. In this way he was reminded of how Mordecai had saved his life by uncovering the assassination plot against him. Embarrassed to realize that Mordecai had never been rewarded, the king determined to remedy the matter right away, and on learning that his prime minister was waiting in the outer court, asked that he come in. Without indicating the particular person he had in mind, the king asked Haman what should be done for someone he especially wanted to honor. Unable to recognize anyone's merits but his own, Haman assumed that the king wanted to honor *him;* he therefore advised that a royal robe and horse be given to that man, and that a high-ranking official of the court go before him throughout the city, crying, "This is what is done for the man whom the king especially wants to honor!" One can imagine Haman's surprise and dismay on learning that Mordecai was the man to be so honored and that he, Haman, would be the high-ranking official to wait on Mordecai and walk before him. Returning to his home mortified and seeking solace, Haman was cautioned by his wife and friends that if Mordecai really was Jewish, then Haman would never get the better of him (ch. vi).

If Haman left home for the queen's party hoping to forget his humiliating experience and have his ego bolstered, he was rudely disappointed. During the party the king reaffirmed, for the third time in two days, that he would grant Esther virtually any request. Realizing that it was now or never, Esther asked that she and her people be saved from destruction, arguing that she would not have bothered the king if they were only to be made slaves. When the king demanded that she identify her enemy, she pointed to Haman as the one who had abused his position of power and the king's friendship. So surprised and incensed was the king that he bolted from the room. Haman, left behind, begged Esther to intercede with the king on his behalf. As Haman begged Esther for his life, and possibly even touched her as she lay upon her dinner couch, the king returned. For this serious violation of decency and harem etiquette Haman was sentenced to death on the spot. When Harbonah, one of the eunuchs attending the king, informed him that Haman had constructed a gallows for Mordecai, the king ordered Haman to be hanged on it himself (ch. vii).

As compensation for Esther's suffering, the king awarded her Haman's estate, which she, in turn, gave to Mordecai; the king also appointed Mordecai Haman's successor. Unable to revoke Haman's letter instituting the pogrom against the Jews on the thirteenth of Adar, the king did the next best thing: he granted Mordecai full authority to compose a letter, in the king's name and sealed with the king's signet, granting Jews the right to defend themselves that day and, more importantly, encouraging all public officials to aid them. Mordecai hoped that this letter, copies of which were sent throughout the empire, might counteract the potential evil of Haman's letter; but although the letter may have had its intended effect on many, it did not deter all (ch. viii).

When the thirteenth of Adar arrived, the enemies of the Jews were still so numerous that the Jews that day killed five hundred men in Susa and seventy-five thousand elsewhere. But although granted specific permission to plunder, the Jews did not do so. Throughout the empire they celebrated their victory on the fourteenth of Adar with feasting and the exchanging of gifts, but their enemies were still sufficiently strong in Susa for Esther to request permission to fight there the next day as well, and to expose the corpses of Haman's ten sons killed the day before. Permission was granted, and so the Jews in Susa fought also on the fourteenth, killing three hundred people but not taking any plunder. Thus they celebrated their victory on the fifteenth of Adar, instead of on the fourteenth with the rest of the Jews throughout the empire (ix 1–19).

Mordecai kept a record of these things, and later wrote to all the Jews, commanding them to continue to observe Purim on the fourteenth and fifteenth of Adar (the holiday being named after the pur, or "lots," which Haman had cast to determine the propitious day for the pogrom) as the days of salvation and deliverance, and to observe them with feasting and gladness. Later on, to re-enforce

Mordecai's command, Esther used her authority as queen and as the people's heroine to write a letter to the Jews throughout the empire, encouraging them to observe forever both days of Purim (ix 20–32). With Mordecai as his prime minister, the king's fortunes and programs prospered; Mordecai himself grew in power and influence among the Persians and in the affections of the Jews (ch. x).

As the résumé indicates, it is a simple plot. The story is effectively told in the Hebrew, with emphasis more upon action than character study. The author was ever mindful of little ways to increase the reader's interest or suspense (see pp. LV–LVI and NOTES *passim*). Concerned primarily with telling an interesting story which, in turn, would provide the "historical" basis for the festival of Purim (see p. LIII), he spends little time on details or the motives of his characters (see NOTES *passim*). There is much justification for Shemaryahu Talmon's view[3] that the characters of the story are stereotyped representations of people seen as typical by the Wisdom school, that is, Mordecai and Esther as the righteous wise struggling against the cunning schemers, Haman and Zeresh, for the favor and support of the powerful but witless dupes, Xerxes and Vashti.

The Greek translation has six major additions which are scattered throughout the canonical portions of the Greek Esther (see Appendixes I and II). Additions B and E purport to be the texts of the letters sent by Haman and Mordecai, respectively. Addition C contains the prayers of Mordecai and Esther preparatory to Esther's going unsummoned to the king, while Addition D is a dramatic expansion of her audience with the king. Addition A is the dream of Mordecai which "predicts" his confrontation with Haman, while Addition F is the detailed explanation of that dream in retrospect. These Additions, which have no basis in the Hebrew (see pp. LXIII–LXIV below) serve either to increase the story's religious character (Additions A, F, and C), dramatic interest (D), or its authenticity (B and E). While translated in Appendix I of the present volume, the Additions will be given extensive treatment by the present writer in one of the volumes of the Anchor Bible Apocrypha.

[3] VT 13 (1963), 441.

THE CANONICITY OF THE BOOK OF ESTHER

As noted earlier, quite contradictory opinions on the religious worth of Esther go back at least to the Council of Jamnia in A.D. 90. "Jamnia in A.D. 90" is, of course, a convenient phrase or symbol to mark the closing of the Jewish canonization process rather than a definitive date. For as F. P. W. Buhl[4] observed some eighty years ago, the decisions at Jamnia did not settle all doubts about the canonicity of some Old Testament books;—indeed there is not even an accurate record of exactly what was determined there.

Among the Jews

Evidently Esther was not regarded as canonical by the Essene community at Qumran, which dated from the second century B.C. to about the first century A.D.[5] As is well known, Esther is the only OT book not represented among the Dead Sea scrolls. Since the Essenes did include in their liturgical calendar festivals not provided for in the Pentateuch, the non-Mosaic origin of Purim (see Lev xxvii 34) cannot be the reason for Esther's rejection. Some scholars have argued that its absence from Qumran is an archaeological accident, that is, that the book existed there even though no fragment has been found. Paul Winter[6] and Ruth Stiehl[7]

[4] *Canon and Text of the Old Testament*, tr. by J. MacPherson (New York: Scribner, 1892), pp. 24–25. Studies on the process of canonization since Buhl have confirmed his observations and shown that decisions of the Pharisee schools at Jamnia were "unofficial" and only gradually became the accepted positions throughout Judaism; see especially Albert Sundberg, *The Old Testament of the Early Church*, Harvard Theological Studies, XX (Cambridge, Mass., 1958), 113–28; and Samuel Sandmel, *The Hebrew Scriptures* (New York: Knopf, 1963), p. 14.

[5] For excellent introductions to Qumran studies, see F. M. Cross, Jr., *The Ancient Library at Qumran and Modern Biblical Studies*, New York: Doubleday, 1958; and J. T. Milik, *Ten Years of Discovery in the Wilderness of Judaea*, tr. by John Strugnell, Studies in Biblical Theology, Vol. 26, Naperville, Ill.: A. R. Allenson, 1959.

[6] *The Jewish Chronicle*, July 5, 1957, p. 16.

[7] Franz Altheim and Ruth Stiehl, "Esther, Judith, und Daniel," in *Die aramäische Sprache unter den Archaemeniden*, I, p. 201. [When publication data—city, publisher, year—are not included in footnote, they are provided (when known) in the Bibliography.]

regard its absence from Qumran as proof that the book did not exist until late in the Hasmonean Age (see Appendix IV). But closer to the truth are H. L. Ginsberg[8] and Hans Bardtke, who contend that Qumran rejected the book for theological reasons. Perhaps the Essenes resented the absence of any explicit mention of God in the book; or possibly they did not consider Esther a "good" Jewess because she failed to observe the laws of kašrût (see fn. 32) and was evidently at first not willing to help her own people (iv 10–14). (In the Hebrew version, at least, Esther seems to be Jewish in a sense more ethnic than religious.) In any case, since the Essenes at Qumran did not include the festival of Purim (or Hanukkah) in their liturgical calendar, they had no need for a book which had the establishing of Purim as its raison d'être.

There is, however, no reason to doubt that Esther was regarded as canonical by the Council of Jamnia in A.D. 90;[9] Esther appears as one of the twenty-four books of the Jewish canon in the oldest list, Baraitha in Baba Bathra 14b–15a, a Talmudic work of the second century A.D. Earlier, Josephus (A.D. 37–100)[10] had said

---

[8] "The Dead Sea Manuscript Finds," in Israel: Its Role in Civilization, ed. Moshe David (New York: Harper, 1956), p. 52; see also Bardtke, p. 257, n. 12. [For works cited only by author's last name—as Bardtke here—see Bibliography.]

[9] But see Solomon Zeitlin, who, on the basis of the second-century A.D. Megillat Taanit XII ("The 13th [of Adar] is the Day of Nicanor. The 14th and 15th are the Days of Purim. Fasting is forbidden"), argues that "if the Book of Esther was already canonized in the year sixty-five, it would have been unnecessary for the author of Megillat Taanit to state that on the day of Purim fasting is prohibited" (PAAJR 3 [1931–32], 132).

[10] Flavius Josephus, or Joseph ben Mattathias, is our principal ancient source for Jewish history from the Maccabean Period to his own day, that is, from ca. 167 B.C. to A.D. 73. A Hasmonean born of a priestly family, he had "tried" all three types of the major Jewish sects of his day before he was nineteen, namely, the Pharisees, the Sadducees, and the Essenes. Even though as a youth he invested three years of his life living in the desert with the Essene Bannus, he finally settled on being, he says, a Pharisee. (His numerous critics would have said, at their kindest, "a Roman collaborator.") Josephus visited Nero in Rome in A.D. 64 to intercede for certain Jewish priests sent there by the Palestinian procurator Felix; and it was probably then that his lifelong respect and affection for "things Roman" became firmly fixed. Nevertheless, when the Jews of Palestine revolted against Rome the following year, Josephus sided with his countrymen to the extent that he became a commander of Galilean forces in A.D. 66–67. When only he and one other Jewish soldier survived—under most suspicious circumstances—the terrible forty-seven-day Roman siege of Jotapata (A.D. 67), and he was taken before the victorious general Vespasian, Josephus predicted right away that

there were twenty-two books in the Jewish canon,[11] but unfortunately he did not enumerate them. There can be no doubt, however, that Josephus himself regarded Esther as canonical; for, on the one hand, he paraphrased Esther in *Jewish Antiquities* XI, and, on the other hand, Esther purports to have been written during the time of, or shortly after, Xerxes (see NOTES on "exact account" in x 2), a Persian king who lived in a period when, according to Josephus, canonical works were still being composed.

Grounds for the book's claim to canonicity at Jamnia are easily surmised: (1) the book claimed to be an accurate historical account

---

the general would very soon become emperor. This prediction was fulfilled in A.D. 69, and Josephus enjoyed the emperor's patronage in that he became a Roman citizen, was permitted to adopt Vespasian's surname Flavius, and received a generous pension.

From this point on until his death Josephus resided in Rome, where in his writings he devoted himself, on one hand, to interpreting the Jews and Romans to one another and, on the other hand, to justifying himself to both. By relying on well-educated Greek secretaries, by copying the dramatic style of Thucydidean speeches, and by utilizing both famous and little-known histories, including *The Life of Herod* by Nicholas of Damascus, Josephus wrote several works of major importance. Historians disagree on the sequence of his writings, in part because some of them, such as his *History of the Jewish War against Rome*, underwent several revisions; composed originally in Aramaic, these revisions were later translated into Greek and then expanded. In any case, his *Jewish Antiquities* (ca. 93–94), modeled after the *Roman Antiquities* by Dionysius of Halicarnassus, is his most important work for biblical scholars; it tells the history of the Jews from the time of the Patriarchs to Josephus' own day, often paraphrasing, as in his account of Esther, the Septuagint. (He did not, however, confine himself to paraphrasing his Hebrew or Greek biblical text; in a number of instances from Genesis through Esther he added Haggadic materials as well as his own views.) To the *Antiquities* he appended his *Vita*, or "autobiography," an account of his six-month command of Galilean forces, in which he denies the charges brought against him by Justus of Tiberias that he had been responsible for the revolt of that city against Rome. His *Against Apion* was a defense of Jewish culture and morality against the slanderous charges and rumors of the Greco-Roman world in general, and Apion's charges in particular. (Apion was a Greek pedagogue, resident in Alexandria, given to complaints against the Jews—he once, in A.D. 38, headed a deputation that protested against them before Caligula. More attractively, Apion is the original source of the story of Androcles and the Lion.)

For additional material on Josephus, see article in IDB, II, pp. 987–88; and H. St. John Thackeray, *Josephus: The Man and the Historian,* New York: Jewish Institute of Religion, 1929.

[11] See *Against Apion* I. 38–41. "Twenty-two" corresponds to the number of letters in the Hebrew alphabet. It is generally believed that Josephus counted Judges and Ruth as one, and Jeremiah and Lamentations as one. Thus he could have included Esther in his list of twenty-two canonical books.

of a time when the Jews were saved from almost certain extinction, and (2) the book provided the *raison d'être* for a popular religious festival. Moreover, by the time of the Council of Jamnia the Jews, with Jerusalem destroyed by the Romans in A.D. 70 and their people even more scattered about than before, had good cause to find consolation in the hope that another Esther or Mordecai would rise up.

But whether or not opposition to Esther continued or arose *after* Jamnia,[12] it is clear that the book was disputed by some Jews and rejected by others a couple of centuries later. Melito, the bishop of Sardis (fl. A.D. 170), records in a letter to a friend the canonical books of the Jews in the East;[13] Esther alone of the current Hebrew canon is omitted. One might argue that its omission was just a scribal error but for the fact that two passages in the Talmud[14] clearly indicate that long after Jamnia some Jews did not regard Esther as canonical, literally "as defiling the hands."[15]

We read in *Megilla 7a:* "Rab Judah said in the name of Samuel: (the scroll of) Esther does not make the hands unclean. Are we to infer from this that Samuel was of the opinion that Esther was not composed under the inspiration of the holy spirit? How can this be, seeing that Samuel has said that Esther was composed under the inspiration of the holy spirit?— It was composed to be recited (by heart), but not to be written."[16] Both Samuel ben Judah and Rab Judah were rabbis of the third century A.D.[17] This passage shows that Esther was not regarded by all as sacred scripture; moreover, it tries to save Samuel's reputation by harmonizing his unorthodox opinion in this matter with the "official" view of Jamnia.[18]

The second Talmudic passage is even more illuminating: "Levi ben Samuel and Rabbi Huna ben Ḥiyya were repairing the mantles

---

[12] So Jack Lewis, "What Do We Mean by Jabneh?" JBR 32 (1964), 130.

[13] For the Greek text, see H. E. Ryle, *The Canon of the Old Testament,* 2d ed. (London: Macmillan, 1909), p. 298.

[14] For a brief article on the "Talmud," see IDB, IV, pp. 511–15.

[15] "All the Holy Scriptures render the hands unclean," *Yadaim* III 5, in *The Mishnah,* tr. and ed. by Herbert Danby, Oxford University Press, 1933.

[16] *Megilla,* tr. by Maurice Simon, in The Babylonian Talmud, ed. Isidore Epstein (New York: The Soncino Press, 1938), pp. 35–36.

[17] See *The Index* for The Babylonian Talmud, ed. Isidore Epstein (New York: The Soncino Press, 1952), pp. 716, 678.

[18] So G. F. Moore, *Judaism in the First Centuries of the Christian Era, the Age of the Tannaim,* 3 vols. (Harvard University Press, 1926–30), III, p. 69.

of the Scrolls of Rabbi Judah's College. On coming to the Scroll of Esther, they remarked, 'O, this Scroll of Esther does not require a mantle.' Thereupon he reproved them, 'this too savours of irreverence.' "[19] Rabbis Levi and Huna belong to either the third or the fourth century A.D.[20] Whatever their reason may have been, it is clear that neither Levi nor Huna believed that the Scroll of Esther "defiled the hands."

Among the Christians

If the Jews could not be unanimous about the canonical status of Esther at first, neither could the Christians. To determine Esther's canonicity in the Christian Church is not easy, but H. B. Swete[21] has assembled much of the relevant evidence by printing full lists of the canonical books of Church Fathers, Councils, and Synods. A study of these book lists permits the generalization that in the West Esther was nearly always canonical, while in the East very often it was not. (See following page for map showing Esther's canonical status in various centers of the early Christian Church.)

Among the Christians in the East, especially those in the area of Anatolia and Syria, Esther was often denied canonical status. It was completely omitted from the list of canonical books by Melito of Sardis;[22] Gregory of Nazianzus (329–390) in Cappadocia; Theodore of Mopsuestia (350?–428) in Cilicia; Junilius (fl. 542); Leontius (485?–?543), who was at first a Nestorian; and Nicephorus (758?–829), a patriarch of Constantinople. Greek manuscript 58 in the Larger Cambridge Edition of the Septuagint has as its inscription "Esther: not canonical." While denying Esther's canonical status, Athanasius (295–373) did include it with Judith, Tobit, and others as "edifying reading"; and Amphilochius (d. 394), bishop of Iconium, observed that it was "accepted only by some." Even among those Fathers who accepted the book as canonical it still occupied a somewhat precarious position, being listed as *the last* book of the canon on

[19] *Sanhedrin*, tr. by H. Freedman, in The Babylonian Talmud, ed. Isidore Epstein (New York: The Soncino Press, 1935), II, p. 677.
[20] See *The Index* for The Babylonian Talmud, pp. 685, 657.
[21] *An Introduction to the Old Testament in Greek*, 2d ed. rev. by R. L. Ottley, pp. 200–14.
[22] For very brief introductions to the Church Fathers cited here, see Berthold Altaner, *Patrology*, tr. by H. C. Graef, Edinburgh-London: Nelson, 1960.

MILES

0   100   200   400   600   800

ITALY

Rome ✝

MEDITERRANEAN

Hippo ✝   Carthage ✝

SICILY

GREECE

Map illustrating
the canonical status of Esther
in the early Christian Church

✝ CANONICAL   ■ NOT CANONICAL

the lists of Origen (185?–?254); Epiphanius (315?–403), bishop of Constantia in Cyprus; the Anonymi *dial. Timothei et Aquilae,* where it is preceded by Judith; and John of Damascus (675–745). Esther was also accepted by Cyril of Jerusalem (d. 386); Ebedjesu, who listed it right after Judith; the Laodicene Canons (343–381); the Apostolic Canons (ca. 380); and the Synod of Trullo (692) at Constantinople.

In the West, on the other hand, Esther was nearly always regarded as canonical. Clement of Rome (30?–?99) alluded to Judith and Esther as examples of brave and godly women in *First Epistle of Clement* LV, but whether this necessarily implies canonicity is uncertain (Jude's use of Enoch i 9 in vss. 14–15 is certainly comparable). In any case, by the fourth century the Western Church clearly regarded Esther as canonical: for so it was accepted by Hilary (315–367), Ruffinus (345–410), Augustine (354–430), Innocent I (401–417), Pseudo-Gelasius, Cassiodorius (478–573), Isidorus (560–636), the Cheltenham List, the List in *Codex Claromontanus, Liber sacramentorum* (6th–7th century), as well as by the councils of Hippo in 393 and of Carthage in 397. Since the Latin Church knew the Old Testament only through the Septuagint, it could more easily be ignorant of problems posed to those Christians in the East who lived in greater proximity to Jewish centers.[23]

In many of the lists mentioned above, Esther is closely associated with Judith and Tobit,[24] two apocryphal works.[25] Significantly, the three earliest allusions to the Book of Esther among the Fathers are intimately tied up with the story of Judith, namely, in *First Epistle of Clement* LV, dating from the first century; *Stromata* IV. 19 of Clement of Alexandria who died before 215; and the *Constitutions of the Holy Apostles* V. iii 20 (ca. 380). In all three of these works allusions to the bravery of Judith and Esther are mentioned in the same breath. In other words, the

---

[23] For the original texts of the Church Fathers, see J. P. Migne, *Patrologiae cursus completus,* Series *Graeca* and Series *Latina.*

[24] For a translation of the text, see *The Book of Tobit,* ed. C. C. Simpson, in *The Apocrypha and Pseudepigrapha of the Old Testament in English,* ed. R. H. Charles, 2 vols. (Oxford University Press, 1913), I, pp. 202–41; for introduction and commentary, see the standard general introductions to OT literature such as those by Eissfeldt and Pfeiffer.

[25] Augustine lists Tobit, Esther, and Judith side by side; so do Innocent I, Pseudo-Gelasius, Cassiodorius, Isidorus, the Cheltenham List, the List in *Codex Claromontanus,* and the Council of Carthage in 397; so also LXX[BA].

canonical status of Esther was certainly not strengthened by the book's frequent association with the Book of Judith, a work which did not enjoy canonical status among the Jews.

That Esther should have been so frequently associated with the Book of Judith is not surprising, given the similarity of theme and spirit in the two books.[26] Judith was, of course, a very beautiful and religious widow who rigorously observed the Jewish law, fasting and praying continually. When Holofernes, the commander of Neb-uchadnezzar's army, besieged her town of Bethulia, near Esdraelon, and had the town's water supply cut off for thirty-four days, she asked the Jewish community to fast and pray for her while she, in her finest, visited the camp of the enemy and through God's help delivered them. Her beauty and eloquence captivated all who saw her, and especially Holofernes; when she confided to him that her countrymen would be delivered into his hands because they had disobeyed their God by eating the first fruits and tithes which properly belong to him, the general believed and trusted her com-pletely. He even permitted her to leave camp each evening to go and pray to her God. On the fourth night of her stay she was invited to Holofernes' tent, where she drank his wine but ate only her own kosher food. Late in the evening, finding herself alone with the king in a drunken stupor, she cut off his head with his own sword. By bringing Holofernes' head in a sack to her countrymen, she inspired them to attack the next day. The Jews were completely successful, and Judith lived to the ripe old age of 105.

Although the themes of Judith and the Hebrew version of Esther are similar—the delivery of the Jewish people through a brave and beautiful woman—the parallels between Judith and the Greek version of Esther (which the Christians knew) are considerably greater, primarily because of the spirit and theology of the Ad-ditions in the Greek Esther. (This similarity will be treated by the present writer in his "The Additions to Esther" in a volume of the AB Apocrypha.)

---

[26] For a translation of the text, see *The Book of Judith*, ed. A. E. Cowley, in *The Apocrypha and Pseudepigrapha of the Old Testament in English*, I, pp. 248–67; see also article on the book itself in IDB, II, pp. 1023–26, and Otto Eissfeldt, *The Old Testament: An Introduction*, pp. 585–87. Claus Schedl argues for a core of historicity to Judith in the days of Darius; see his "Nabuchodonosor, Arpakšad, und Darius," ZDMG 115 (1965), 242–54.

Esther's Place in the Canon

As the lists below suggest, Esther occupies various locations in the Hebrew, Greek, and English texts, depending upon whether the particular compiler or copyist arranged his canon along chronological, logical, or theological lines.

MT (Len. B 19ᴬ)	Baba Bathra 14b	LXXᴮ	KJ, RSV
Minor Prophets	Minor Prophets	Job	Chronicles
Psalms	Ruth	Wisdom of Solomon	Ezra
Job	Psalms	Wisdom of Sirach	Nehemiah
Proverbs	Job	*Esther*	*Esther*
Ruth	Proverbs	Judith	Job
Song of Solomon	Ecclesiastes	Tobit	Psalms
Ecclesiastes	Song of Solomon	Minor Prophets	Proverbs
Lamentations	Lamentations	Isaiah	Ecclesiastes
Esther	Daniel	Jeremiah	Song of Solomon
Daniel	*Esther*	Baruch	Isaiah
Ezra	Ezra	Lamentations	Jeremiah
Nehemiah	Nehemiah	Epistle of Jeremiah	Lamentations
Chronicles	Chronicles	Ezekiel	Minor Prophets
		Daniel	Daniel

Virtually every Hebrew and Greek recension has its own peculiar canonical sequence, for example, even codices Vaticanus, Sinaiticus, and Alexandrinus do not completely agree with one another.

OPPOSITION TO THE BOOK OF ESTHER

Christian

It is not difficult to guess why many Christians were uncertain as to Esther's divine inspiration. The simple fact that some Jews were opposed to it would have been adequate reason for the tradition among some Christians that Esther was not canonical. Moreover, with or without the Additions (see pp. LXIII–LXIV below), the book's *raison d'être* was meaningless for Christians, that is, the book provides the "historical" basis for a Jewish festival which, unlike Passover and Pentecost, found no counterpart in the Christian calendar of that day. And while the story of Esther was understandably comforting to its Jewish readers, providing as it did assurance that God ever looks after them and delivers them from their enemies, some Christians, then as now, found the Greek version not only excessively nationalistic and bloodthirsty but also somewhat anti-Gentile (see especially Addition F). Significantly, Esther is not even alluded to in the New Testament, nor was a Christian commentary written on the book until Rhabanus Maurus' work in 836; even casual references to the work are quite rare among the Church Fathers.[27]

And finally, if Christians knew the Greek version without the Additions, which may very well have been true in the Eastern Church (see p. xxv above), the book might have seemed too anthropocentric since it does not even mention God. Moreover, apart from fasting, no distinctively religious practices or concepts seem to be in the canonical version. Perhaps the difference in Esther's canonical status between East and West stems from the fact that the West knew Esther only in the Latin translation of the Septuagint while the East knew the Septuagint itself, and was in greater proximity to the Jews and their Hebrew version.

Jewish

The Jewish opposition to Esther is, however, the really crucial and basic question. In the absence of more concrete information from the Talmud (see, however, below), we are forced to conjecture why the book was rejected by some Jews. Three rather likely objections immediately suggest themselves; they will be treated briefly here and dealt with more extensively elsewhere in the Introduction and NOTES. These three difficulties may be characterized as theological, historical, and textual.

Before examining these three problem areas, we should realize that long ago G. F. Moore[28] may have pointed out a very simple and obvious answer to our problem: the principal objection to Esther, according to the *Jerusalem Megilla 70d,* was that the keeping of Purim conflicts with the principle in Lev xxvii 34, that is, that only Mosaic laws and festivals should be observed by Jews. Tempting though Moore's theory is, it is probably not adequate since Hanukkah[29] was accepted by Jews as a religious festival even though it was not Mosaic.

[27] For details on the use of Esther by some Church Fathers (A.D. 300–850), complete with their Latin text or a German translation of the Latin or Greek text, see Bardtke, pp. 258–60; for details on Jewish and Christian commentaries from the Middle Ages to 1908, see Paton, pp. 104–18; for important works since then, see Bibliography.

[28] *Judaism,* I, p. 245.

[29] For a discussion of Hanukkah (literally "Dedication") as the celebration of the liberation of the Second Temple, see IDB, I, s.v. "Feast of Dedication."

The Absence of Religious Elements in the Book of Esther

In the MT's present state many, if not most, of the distinctive religious features of biblical Judaism are missing. The most conspicuous of these is, of course, Yahweh himself. The king of Persia is mentioned 190 times in 167 verses, but God is not mentioned once. Neither Law nor Covenant, two key concepts running throughout the entire Old Testament, is so much as alluded to, let alone acknowledged. Because of the story's Persian setting, it is not surprising that neither sacrifice nor the temple of Jerusalem is mentioned, for since the Deuteronomic Reformation[30] sacrifices could not be performed outside of Jerusalem. On the other hand, the Persian setting makes all the more puzzling the absence of any allusion to angels or afterlife,[31] two concepts which Judaism may very well have borrowed from Iranian religions of Persia. But regardless of physical setting, one would have expected *some mention* of prayer, for unlike the Song of Solomon, in Esther the perilous situation of the Jews demanded it. Finally, some Jews and Christians would argue that the OT virtues of love, kindness, mercy, and forgiveness are also conspicuously missing from the book, while a vengeful, bloodthirsty, and chauvinistic spirit is only too prevalent. In fact, the only OT religious practice or idea explicitly mentioned in Esther is a comparatively unimportant one, namely, fasting (iv 16).

Although God is not mentioned in the MT, the crucial question is whether he was left out of the Hebrew version originally or edited out later. Since the oldest extant Hebrew text of Esther dates back only to the Middle Ages (see p. LIV below), any generalization about the earliest Hebrew text must be quite tentative. Nevertheless, judging from both internal and external evidence, we may say that most, if not all (see NOTES *passim*), of those instances where God is mentioned in the Greek represent additions to the Hebrew text; they do not witness to Hebrew readings which have dropped out of the MT or have been deliberately taken out. As for such extended additions in the Greek as Addition C (The Prayers of Mordecai and Esther), which not only present a clearly defined concept of God but also have definite references to election, re-

---

[30] See John Bright, *A History of Israel* (Philadelphia: Westminster Press, 1959), pp. 295–302.
[31] See articles in IDB, I, s.v. "Angel," and II, s.v. "Immortality."

demption, *kašrût*,[32] and prayer (see Addition C 28), there is no evidence that either Addition C or Additions A, D, or F is a survival in the Greek of passages originally in the Hebrew version (see p. LXIV below). On the contrary, these Additions were created later to make Esther more "historical" (Additions B and E), more dramatic (D), or more "religious" (A, F, and C).

On the other hand, even in the MT's present form certain religious concepts are presupposed, though not explicitly mentioned. There is, for instance, faith in the concept of Providence, or the hand of God in history (see NOTE on iv 14 and COMMENT on § 5), as well as faith in the efficacy of fasting and, by implication, of prayer (see NOTE on iv 16 and COMMENT on § 5). That the MT does not state these religious concepts more clearly adds substance to the view of Paton (p. 95) and others who, pointing to the ruling in the Mishnah that Jews are to drink while celebrating Purim until they are unable to distinguish between "Blessed is Mordecai" and "Cursed is Haman" (*Megilla 7b*), argue that the boisterous and joyous manner in which Purim was to be celebrated required that the book contain nothing which could be accidentally profaned by an overly enthusiastic or inebriated Jew hearing the story read aloud. Thus some of the distinctly religious elements were deliberately kept out.

Tempting though this theory is, it is probably not correct. It may well explain the absence of God's name in Esther, but not the absence of law, convenant, dietary regulations, prayer, angels, or afterlife. In one of the few genuinely original articles on Esther in the last fifty years, Talmon[33] offers a convincing explanation for our problems: Esther is *"a historicized wisdom tale . . . an en-*

---

[32] *Kašrût*, "legitimacy," is used here in the popular sense, that is, denoting permitted or *kosher* foods. In the Old Testament certain foods were *kosher* or clean, for example, all plant products, the flesh of all quadrupeds which have cloven hoofs and which chew their cuds (Lev xi 2–8), the flesh of all fish that have fins and scales (Lev xi 9–12), and all clean birds (Deut xiv 11). On the other hand, quadrupeds either lacking the cloven hoof or not chewing their cuds, "fish" lacking either fins or scales, certain birds and insects, and all reptiles were unclean (Lev xi 13–44). In Talmudic Judaism there was much discussion and expansion of these dietary laws in such Mishnaic tractates as *Ḥullin*, for example, "you shall not boil a kid in its mother's milk" (Exod xxiii 19) becomes the basis in *Ḥullin* 8 for the separation of meat and dairy products at a meal. For a brief discussion of dietary laws in the Bible as well as the more technical aspects of *kašrût*, see IDB, II, s.v. "Clean and Unclean."

[33] "Wisdom in the Book of Esther," VT 13 (1963), 419–55.

actment of standard 'Wisdom' motifs";[34] and the characters in Esther are the typical stereotypes found in Wisdom literature. Because the author of Esther was a student of the Wisdom school,[35] he naturally did not emphasize the usual elements of Jewish piety, for example, dietary laws, covenant, and the immanent God who is easily accessible in prayer and who personally acts in Jewish history. In this respect, Esther is not unlike other Wisdom books such as Qoheleth, or Ecclesiastes, where God is only rather dutifully and perfunctorily acknowledged (cf. Eccles xii 13) and cultic acts are virtually ignored; or the Book of Job and many passages in Proverbs, where God is quite remote and such concerns as dietary laws and Sabbath observances are also ignored. (If the Council of Jamnia considered Esther to be of the same literary genre as Qoheleth, that is, Wisdom literature, then Esther may have entered the canonical list on the coattails of Qoheleth, itself a controversial book which purported to be of Solomonic authorship.) According to Werner Dommershausen, Esther is "veiled Wisdom Theology"; the word "veiled" is descriptive, but it is neither explanatory nor helpful in understanding Esther.

THE HISTORICITY OF THE BOOK OF ESTHER

As already noted, Esther may have been rejected by some Jews because Purim, the book's *raison d'être,* was not a Mosaic festival

---

[34] *Ibid.*, p. 426. But see J. L. Crenshaw's rather unconvincing efforts to disprove Talmon's thesis in "Methods in Determining Wisdom Influence upon 'Historical Literature,'" JBL 88 (1969), 129–42.

[35] The Wisdom school is not to be understood here in the sense of a formal, structured institution of learning but of a particular perspective or viewpoint. Though many definitions of "wisdom" (ḥokmâ) have been offered by scholars, that of Gerhard von Rad would be acceptable to many, namely, "a practical knowledge of the laws of life and of the world, based upon experience" (*Old Testament Theology*, tr. by D. M. G. Stalker, 2 vols. [Edinburgh and London: Oliver & Boyd, 1962], I, p. 418).

Like law and prophecy, Wisdom did not originate with the Israelites but had its roots in the Egyptian and Mesopotamian civilizations where, primarily concerned with happiness and success in this world, it tended to be prudential, pragmatic, non-cultic, and detached in spirit. In its earliest stages Israelite wisdom was probably not appreciatively different from Canaanite or Egyptian wisdom, but with the passing of time it did become more Yahwehistic, especially in the post-Exilic period. For brief introductory statements on Wisdom, see IDB, IV, pp. 852–61; Walter Baumgartner, "The Wisdom Literature," in *The Old Testament and Modern Study*, ed. H. H. Rowley (Oxford University Press, 1956), pp. 210–35; and von Rad, *Old Testament Theology*, I, pp. 418–59.

or because the book had what some regarded as grievous religious "deficiencies" (pp. XXXII–XXXIII). A third possibility is that the book's ancient critics, like the majority of nineteenth- and twentieth-century scholars, questioned the complete historicity of the events it narrated. To pose the problem somewhat differently, did the events narrated in Esther actually happen, or is the entire story just a fictitious account, invented to provide a "historical" basis for an originally pagan festival?

Support for Its Historicity

On the face of it, the story seems to be true. Apart from the supposed irrevocability of Persian law (see NOTE on i 19) and perhaps the battle fatalities for the thirteenth of Adar in ix 16, nothing in the book seems improbable, let alone unbelievable, especially since the plot centers around court intrigue and ethnic prejudices. Moreover, the author, who begins his work in the manner typical of biblical histories (see NOTE on i 1), encourages his readers to confirm the details of his account for themselves by referring them to an accessible and well-known historical record (see NOTE on x 2). Only a writer acting in good faith would dare extend such an invitation to his readers.

Then too, the book itself abounds in evidence that the author knew much about the time, place, and setting for his story. Although, with the possible exception of Mordecai (see p. L), the only indisputably historical figure in the story is King Xerxes, much that the author says about Xerxes seems to be quite compatible with what we know of him from other literary and archaeological sources.

Xerxes (486–465 B.C.) was, of course, the fourth king in the Achaemenian Period (550–331 B.C.) of Persian history (see Appendix IV). Apart from the Achaemenian founder, Cyrus the Great (550–530 B.C.), who has always been regarded quite rightly as a great benefactor of the Jews living in the Babylonian Golah ca. 539–537 B.C.,[36] Western readers for some two thousand years have seen the Achaemenian kings through the sharp but admittedly

---

[36] Not only was Cyrus responsible for bringing to an end on October 13, 539 B.C., the dynasty of Nebuchadnezzar, the Babylonian king who had taken the Jews into exile in 586 B.C.; he even encouraged the Jews' return to Jerusalem (see Ezra i 1–4, vi 3–5; Esdras ii 3–7; Josephus *Antiquities* XI. 1–7; for a discussion of details, see J. M. Myers, *The World of the Restoration*, pp. 50–54).

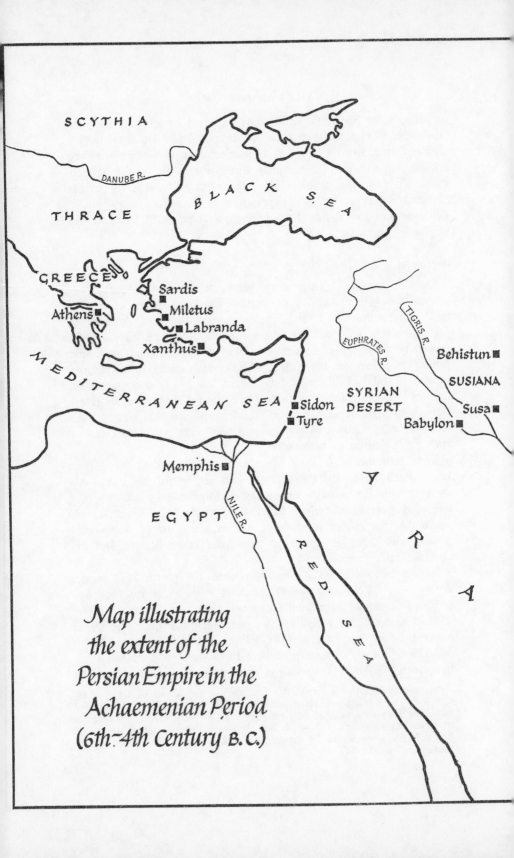

Map illustrating
the extent of the
Persian Empire in the
Achaemenian Period
(6th–4th Century B.C.)

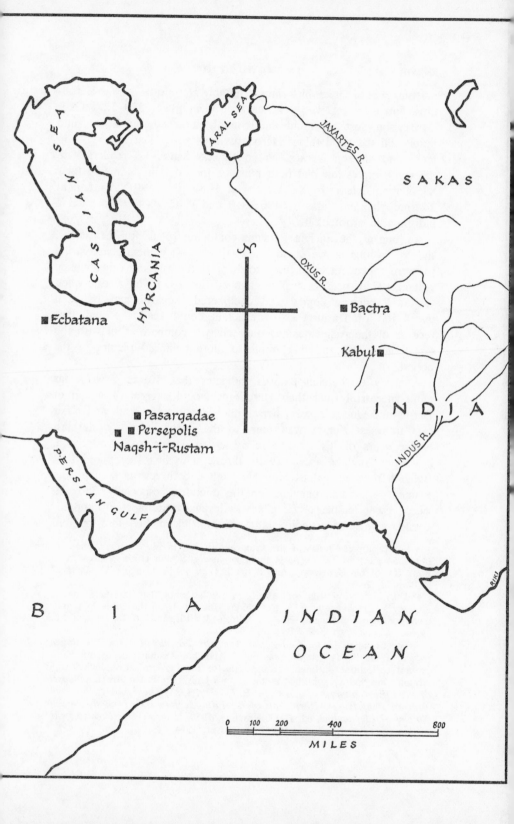

CASPIAN SEA

ARAL SEA

JAXARTES R.

SAKAS

HYRCANIA

OXUS R.

■Ecbatana

N

■Bactra

Kabul■

■Pasargadae
■Persepolis
Naqsh-i-Rustam

I N D I A

INDUS R.

PERSIAN GULF

B   I   A

INDIAN

OCEAN

R.IKI

0   100   200   400   800

M I L E S

partisan eyes of Greek historians,[37] notably Herodotus. It was Herodotus, for instance, who told us that Cambyses (530–522 B.C.), Cyrus' son, lost his mind and committed suicide in Egypt; and despite all the good things Herodotus says about Darius (522–486 B.C.) and his son Xerxes, he nonetheless leaves his readers with the vivid impression that both must be judged failures in life, their humiliating defeats by the Greeks at Marathon (490 B.C.) and at Thermopylae and Salamis (480 B.C.) and Plataea (479 B.C.) being indisputable proof of it.

As long as the ancient Persians could not speak for themselves, that is, as long as we could not read what they themselves wrote, we were dependent upon the records of Herodotus and other classic writers. That was radically changed in 1854, however, when G. H. Rawlinson copied and deciphered the trilingual Behistun inscription of Darius.[38] Now scholars could read the abundant records of the Achaemenians themselves,[39] compare them with the Greek accounts, and thus obtain a more balanced picture of the period.

A study of Persian records indicates that Xerxes was a far more successful ruler than Herodotus would suggest. The son of Darius and Queen Atossa, herself the daughter of Cyrus and sister of Cambyses, Xerxes was born to the purple, and for the last twelve years of his father's reign served as viceroy of Babylon. No sooner had he ascended the throne than first Egypt and then Babylon rebelled against him. He quelled both revolts quickly and exacted very harsh penalties on the offenders, especially Babylon, whose great temple of Esagila was leveled and its eight-hundred-pound, eighteen-foot gold statue of Marduk melted into bullion.

---

[37] For example, Ctesias of the fifth century B.C. in his *Persica;* Xenophon (430–354 B.C.) in his *Anabasis* and *Cyropaedia;* Strabo (63 B.C.–A.D. 21) in Book XV of his *Geography;* and Plutarch (A.D. 46–120) in his "Artaxerxes" in *Parallel Lives.*

[38] This inscription was for cuneiform studies what the Rosetta Stone of Ptolemy V Epiphanes was for Egyptology; for details on the Behistun monument and its decipherment, see A. T. Olmstead, HPE, pp. 116–18, especially n. 39.

[39] For example, G. G. Cameron's *Persepolis Treasury Tablets.* The *lingua franca* of the Persian empire was not Persian but Aramaic; hence other important collections of linguistic materials for the Persian period include the Aramaic inscriptions published by the Oxford University Press: *Aramaic Papyri of the Fifth Century,* ed. and tr. A. E. Cowley, 1923; *The Brooklyn Museum Aramaic Papyri: New Documents of the Fifth Century B.C. from the Jewish Colony of Elephantine,* ed. E. G. Kraeling, 1954; *Aramaic Documents of the Fifth Century B.C.,* ed. and tr. G. R. Driver, 1954.

With this background, he was well equipped on the death of his father to take over Darius' two unfinished tasks: the conquest of Greece and the completion of the royal palace at Persepolis. As everyone knows, Xerxes failed completely in the first; even though he devoted the first eight years of his reign to the invasion of Greece, he was no more successful than Darius. A number of reasons may be offered for his failure, but organizing his armies along national lines and not according to types of weapons was certainly a factor. But as only too few general readers know, Xerxes was highly successful in his second task: the building of Persepolis. A devout worshiper of Ahuramazda, Xerxes never mentioned other gods by name in his inscriptions; he even went so far as to prohibit the worship of *daevas,* or demons.[40] It was in honor of Ahuramazda and himself that Xerxes used the fabulous wealth of his empire to build the most magnificent structure of Achaemenian times, the palace of Persepolis, the epitome of Achaemenian art. Only pictures can adequately suggest the extent and majesty of the palace complex.[41] Xerxes spent the last thirteen years of his reign creating this testimony to Achaemenian greatness. He did, of course, also build at Susa, but that site is not well preserved today, partly because so much of the building material was wood[42] and mud brick rather than stone, and partly because the site was so poorly excavated by M. A. Dieulafoy in the early days of Near Eastern archaeology. The floor plan of Susa, unlike that of Persepolis, is therefore difficult to determine.[43] Some idea of Susa's design and materials as well as the international character of its workmen is hinted at by a clay tablet in Persian cuneiform, pre-

[40] In spite of Xerxes' undeniable devotion to Ahuramazda, neither he nor Darius was a true Zoroastrian; for from certain treasury tablets it may be inferred that "in the worship carried out at the court, the cult of the haoma, originally a feature of the Mithra community, together with the libation-pourers of the Magian priesthood and the sacred fire, played a full and prominent part" (Cameron, *Persepolis Treasury Tablets,* p. 9).

[41] See Plates; and especially the magnificent photographs in Roman Ghirshman, *The Arts of Ancient Iran,* in The Arts of Mankind Series, ed. André Malraux and Georges Salles, pp. 155–209. As our NOTES (*passim*) will indicate, many reliefs at Persepolis well illustrate various scenes and sayings from the Book of Esther.

[42] Susa was badly burned during the reign of Artaxerxes I (465–424 B.C.); see F. H. Weissbach, *Die Keilinschriften der Achämeniden* (Leipzig: J. C. Hinrisch Buchhandlung, 1911), pp. 122–25.

[43] See aerial photograph of Susa, Plate 8; and diagram of palace of Persepolis, Plate 10.

served as a foundation record, dating from the time of Darius and reading as follows:

This is the *hadish* palace which at Susa I built. From afar its ornamentation was brought. Deep down the earth was dug, until rock bottom I reached. When the excavation was made, gravel was packed down, one part sixty feet, the other thirty feet in depth. On that gravel a palace I built. And that the earth was dug down and the gravel packed and the mud brick formed in molds, that the Babylonians did. The cedar timber was brought from a mountain named Lebanon; the Assyrians brought it to Susa. Teakwood was brought from Gandara and from Carmania. The gold which was used here was brought from Sardis and Bactria. The stone—lapis lazuli and carnelian—was brought from Sogdiana. The turquoise was brought from Chorasmia. The silver and copper were brought from Egypt. The ornamentation with which the wall was adorned was brought from Ionia. The ivory was brought from Ethiopia, from India, and from Arachosia. The stone pillars were brought from a place named Abiradush in Elam. The artisans who dressed the stone were Ionians and Sardians. The goldsmiths who wrought the gold were Medes and Egyptians. Those who worked the inlays were Sardians and Egyptians. Those who worked the baked brick (with figures) were Babylonians. The men who adorned the wall were Medes and Egyptians. At Susa here a splendid work was ordered; very splendid did it turn out. Me may Ahuramazda protect, and Hystaspes, who is my father, and my land.[44]

An elaborate building program such as Xerxes undertook at Persepolis required adequate financial resources. Satraps continued, of course, to provide predetermined tribute, and there were gifts brought from other peoples, but Xerxes also extended and improved upon the money-economy introduced by Darius. From the Treasury Tablets of Persepolis we know that his workers there were often paid in money rather than in kind; moreover, tribute brought in kind was often expressed in monetary equivalents.

According to A. T. Olmstead, "the fine promise of Xerxes' younger years had not been fulfilled. Failure of the European adventure opened the way to harem intrigues, with all their deadly consequences."[45] (One particularly nasty harem intrigue involved Xerxes' affair with the lovely Artaynte and, subsequently, the horrible mutilation of her mother by the vengeful Queen Amestris.[46]) Assassinated in his bedroom by a conspiracy led by his uncle Artabanus and his

[44] Quoted by Olmstead, HPE, p. 168.
[45] HPE, p. 266.
[46] Herodotus *History* IX. 107 ff.

grandson Megabyzys, Xerxes was buried in a magnificent royal sepulcher close to Darius at Naqsh-i-Rustam.[47]

As was noted earlier, the author of Esther says much which is consistent with what we know about Xerxes from non-biblical sources. For example, Xerxes' empire did extend from India to Ethiopia (see NOTE on i 1, as well as NOTES on verses cited below), and Xerxes did have a winter palace at Susa (i 2), which had features not incompatible with the architectural details given in i 5–6. Famous for his lavish drinking parties (i 4–7) and his extravagant promises and gifts (v 3, vi 6–7), Xerxes also had, on occasion, a nasty, irrational temper (i 12, vii 7–8).

Moreover, the author of Esther shows awareness of certain features of Persian government, such as the seven princely advisers (i 14) and the very efficient postal system (iii 13, viii 10); he is also familiar with certain practices of Persian court life, including doing obeisance to the king's high officials (iii 2) and the recording and rewarding of the king's "benefactors" (ii 23, vi 8). The author is also aware of various details and Persian customs, among them hanging as a form of capital punishment (ii 23, v 14, vii 10); the observance of "lucky" days (iii 7); royal horses with crowns (vi 8); eating while reclined on couches (vii 8); and the headpiece known as a "turban" (viii 15). And finally, the author uses a number of Persian nouns, including the following: part^{e}mîm, "nobles," i 3; bîtān, "pavilion," i 5; karpas, "cotton," i 6; dāt, "law," i 8; keter, "turban," i 11; pitgām, "decree," i 20; '^{a}ḥašdarp^{e}nîm, "satrapies," iii 12; g^{e}nāzîm, "treasury," iii 9; patšegen, "copy," iii 14; '^{a}ḥašt^{e}rānîm, "royal horses," viii 10 (see NOTES for details).

But taken together the arguments outlined above provide, at best, only evidence for the author's familiarity with Persian history, customs, and vocabulary; they do not establish the essential historicity of his entire story, especially since there is some evidence to the contrary. Before examining that evidence, however, we must first consider the problem of personal names in Esther.

A priori, one would expect the successful analysis of the many person names in Esther to provide crucial evidence for determining the time and place of the story as well as its possible authenticity. Successful analysis of personal names presupposes, however, their reasonably accurate transmission. The following chart, listing the

[47] For a fuller account of Xerxes' life, see HPE, pp. 214–88.

English	MT	LXX	z^{48}	AT	Josephus	OL	Vulgate
Major Characters							
i 1 Xerxes	'ăḥašwērōš	artaxerxēs	artaxerxēs	assuēros	artaxerxēs	assuerus	asuerus
ii 5 Mordecai	mordŏkay	mardochaios	mardochaios	mardochaios	mardochaios	mardochaeus	mardocheus
ii 7 Esther	'estēr	esthēr	esthēr	esthēr	esthēr	hester	hester
iii 1 Haman	hāmān	aman	aman	aman	amanes	aman	aman
Minor Characters							
i 9 Vashti	waštî	astin	ouashein	ouastin	aste	vastis	vashti
ii 8 Hegai	hēgay	gai	gōgaiou	(gōgaiou)		oggeo	aegaeo
ii 14 Shaashgaz	ša'ašgaz	gai	sasagazi				sasagazi
ii 15 Abihail	'ăbîhayil	ameinadab	ameinadab			abiel	abiahil
ii 21 Bigthan	bigtān	(gabatha	gabbathan	(astaou	bagathoou	bartageus	bagathan
Teresh	tereš	tharra)	tharas	thedeutou)	theodestou	thedestes	thares
iii 1 Hammedatha	hammedātā'	amadathou	amadathou	amadathou	amadathou		amadathi
Agagite	hā'ăgāgî	bougaion	gōgaion	bougaion	amalekiten	bagogeum	agag
iv 5 Hatak	hătāk	achrathaios	athak		achratheon	aetac	athac
v 10 Zeresh	zereš	zōsaran	zōran	zōsaran	zarasas	zosarram	zares
Seven Eunuchs in i 10							
Mehuman	mᵉhûmān	aman	maouman			mayma	mauman
Biztha	bizzᵉtā'	mazan	zabatha			narbona	bazatha
Harbona	ḥarbônā'	tharra	arbōna			nabatha	arbona
Bigtha	bigtā'	bōrazē	bagatha			zathi	bagatha
Abagtha	wa'ᵃbagtā'	zatholtha	abagatha			cedes	abgatha
Zethar	zētar	abataza	zarath			tharas	zarath
Carcas	karkas	tharaba	acharbas			tharecta	carchas

Seven Princely Advisers in i 14

Charshena	karšᵉnā'	arkesaios	charsan		mardochaeus	charsena
Shethar	šētār	sarsathaios	asatha		sarothas	sethar
Admatha	'admātā'	malēsear	ramatha		pabataleus	admatha
Tarshish	taršīš				malesatha	tharsis
Meres	meres		maros			mares
Marsena	marsᵉnā'		marsana			marsana
Memukan	mᵉmûkān		mamouchan	mouchaiou	mucheas	mamucha

Ten Sons of Haman in ix 7-9

Parshandatha	paršandātā'	pharsan-nestain	pharsendatha	pharsan	pharsandatha
Dalphon	dalphôn	delphôn	adelphon	adelphon	delphon
Aspatha	'aspātā'	phasga	aeiphatha	pharna	esphata
Poratha	pôrātā'	pharadatha	phouratha	gagaphardatha	phorata
Adalia	'ᵃdalyā'	barsa	adalia		adalia
Aridatha	'ᵃridātā'	sarbacha	aridatha		aridatha
Parmashta	parmaštā'	marmasima	pharmostha	marmasaima	ephermesta
Arisai	'ᵃrîsay	rouphaion	arisai		arisai
Aridai	'ᵃrîday	arsaion	aridai		aridai
Vaizatha	wayzātā'	zabouthaion	ouaizatha	izathouth	vaizatha

⁴⁸ The symbol z is given by the Larger Cambridge Septuagint to the Greek manuscript 93 of Holmes-Parson, a manuscript which was strongly influenced by Origen's Hexapla.

personal names as they appear in various versions, is graphic illustration of the formidable difficulties confronting the scholar who would try to establish their origin and meaning.

Even a cursory study of this chart raises certain inescapable, and perhaps unanswerable, questions about the Hebrew consonantal text and vocalization. To be sure, some of the discrepancies between the Greek and the Hebrew may be attributed to either the misdivision of words (see NOTE on ix 7, § 11) or the inadequate representation in Greek of certain Hebrew sounds, such as sibilants or gutturals; but short of being arbitrary and dogmatic, one cannot assume that where the Greek and the MT disagree, the MT necessarily preserves the better spelling. Unfortunately, we do not have for Esther what we have for many other books of the Old Testament: an old Hebrew manuscript from Qumran or the Hexaplaric transliteration into Greek of the Hebrew.[49] Not only must we have reservations about the Hebrew consonantal text of Esther, we must also question its vocalization, since it is well known that for other OT books the Greek sometimes preserves the original vocalization of personal names better than does the Hebrew.[50] In fact, in Esther itself the Gr. *mardochaios* is certainly more accurate than the MT's *mordᵃkay* (see NOTE on ii 5).

Fully cognizant of the above difficulties, a few scholars have devoted much time and ingenuity to this problem, and the interested reader should consult in detail the older as well as the more recent treatments of the subject.[51] Although each scholar seems convinced that he has successfully established his own argument for the origin and meaning of various names, the only safe and probably valid generalization is that, apart from the names of Mardochai and possibly Esther (see NOTE on ii 7), most of the personal names are probably Iranian in origin (see NOTE on i 10). From exactly where the author took his names and whether they represent actual persons, excluding Xerxes of course, is impossible to say. But even if tomorrow all these names were definitely proved to be Persian, it would not necessarily prove the historicity of the Esther story.

[49] See B. J. Roberts, OTTV, pp. 128–33.
[50] OTTV, pp. 108–10.
[51] Peter Jensen, WZKM 6 (1892), 47–70, 209–26; Haupt (*passim*); Paton, pp. 66–71; Gehman, pp. 321–28; Jacques Duchesne-Guillemin, *Muséon* 66 (1953), 105–8.

Evidence against Its Historicity

The story as it stands contains certain statements which, while possible, seem most improbable. Among these are the following: the feast given by the king for the leaders of his empire lasting one hundred and eighty days (i 1–3); Vashti's refusal to obey the king's command (i 12); the king's ridiculous letter ordering all men throughout his empire to be master in their own homes (i 22); the appointment of non-Persians to the all-important post of prime minister (iii 1, viii 2, x 3); the letters sent out in all languages of the empire, instead of Aramaic, the official language of the Persian empire (i 22, iii 12, viii 9); the king's permission —granted a full year ahead of time (iii 12–13)—for an entire people within his empire to be wiped out and their possessions plundered (iii 8–15); and the king's sanction of fighting everywhere, even within the palace complex itself (ix 11–15). Though improbable, these things may of course still have been true.

Even more serious are certain statements in Esther which seem to contradict extrabiblical sources whose basic accuracy in the matter is not suspect. Some of these discrepancies or "contradictions" are quite minor, such as the one hundred and twenty-seven provinces in the empire mentioned in i 1, in contrast to Herodotus, who said there were twenty satrapies;[52] Esther's arrival at the court

[52] As the reader will soon discover, Herodotus *History of the Persian Wars* is not only a principal source for the present-day historian's knowledge of much ancient Persian history and culture but also a major criterion by which the possible historicity and authenticity of numerous "facts" in Esther are to be judged (see NOTES *passim*).
    Born of Greek parents in Halicarnassus in Asia Minor ca. 484 B.C., Herodotus came to Athens in 454. Although the details of his life and travels are much disputed by scholars, it seems he resided in Athens until ca. 464 B.C., when for the next seventeen years he traveled throughout the Near East, visiting such places as Crete, Rhodes, Anatolia, Cyprus, Phoenicia, Egypt, and Babylon, thereby covering a latitude of some 1,700 miles. After his travels he returned for a brief stay in Athens, and then in ca. 445 B.C. went to the newly founded Athenian colony in Thurii, Italy, where he died and was buried in ca. 424 B.C.
    Presumably it was in the later years of his life, after his travels, that he wrote his book. Although its title is *The History of the Persian Wars*, it is both much more, treating as it does peoples, incidents, and places not at all relevant to the Persian wars, *and* much less, since he is ultimately interested in the great Persian invasions of Greece under Darius and Xerxes, and not in other Persian wars.
    Wherever Herodotus visited, he studied the place and its people with

of Susa in 480 B.C. (ii 16), a time when, according to Herodotus, Xerxes would still have been away fighting in Greece; and Mordecai as part of Nebuchadnezzar's deportation of 597 B.C. (ii 6), which would make him, and especially Esther, far too old to have accomplished everything attributed to them. Other contradictions are of a much more serious nature: according to ii 16 and iii 7, Esther was queen between the seventh and twelfth years of Xerxes' reign, but according to Herodotus,[53] Amestris was queen then; moreover, again according to Herodotus (III. 84), Persian queens had to come from one of seven noble Persian families, a custom which would have automatically ruled out an insignificant Jewess.

Taken individually, few, if any, of these improbabilities and contradictions are sufficiently serious to undermine the essential historicity of Esther, since errors in detail can easily occur in an essentially true historical account. These objections are ultimately important only because they tend to support two more serious objections: (1) the recognition that a number of elements in the story of Esther bear striking resemblance to certain legendary stories of the ancient Near East, such as A Thousand and One Nights, and (2) the legitimate suspicion that Purim is in its origin a pagan festival adopted at some period somewhere along the line by the Jews.

THE NON-JEWISH ORIGINS OF PURIM

Esther's canonical status may have been opposed by those Jews who saw the book as a defense for a Jewish festival which, as its very name suggests ("the pûr [that is, the lot]", iii 7; see also ix 26), was non-Jewish in origin. Certainly modern scholars have felt the explanation for Purim's name in ix 26 to be strained and

---

an appreciative but critical eye, gathering geographical, cultural, historical, and literary "facts" about them from whatever sources he could, whether from his own observations, the eyewitness accounts of others, oral traditions, written sources, or the like. Given the variety and nature of his sources, we should not be surprised to learn that present-day scholars differ greatly in assessing his objectiveness and trustworthiness as a historian. But none would dispute his greatness as a consummate storyteller and literary writer who, although writing in Ionic prose, reaffirmed the epic traditions of Homer. And few would dispute the encomium offered by Cicero who called him "The Father of History" (Laws I. 1).

[53] Herodotus VII. 114, IX. 112.

unconvincing. Moreover, the "secular" character of the feast suggests a pagan origin, that is, no prayers or sacrifices are specified, but drinking to the point of excess *is* permitted in the Talmud, *Megilla* 7*b*. The problem of identifying the pagan origins of Purim has been complicated by the possibility that *pûrîm* is itself a corrupt Hebrew form and not the original Hebrew transliteration. This possibility is suggested by the fact that the LXX has in ix 26 *phrourai*, which would not be significant except that it is also supported by Josephus,[54] who knew the festival well. Paul A. de Lagarde once argued that *pûrîm* was a more corrupt form of the A-text's *phoudaia*, the latter being an inaccurate transliteration of *farvardīgān*, the Persian Festival of the Dead; the *phrourai* of the Septuagint in turn reflected imperfectly an older spelling, *fravardīgān*.[55] Julius Lewy saw in *phrourai* the aramaized form of the Bab. *purruru*, "to destroy."[56]

In any case, *pûr* has been "traced" to many languages, including the Heb. *pûrā*, "wine press" (J. D. Michaelis); the Old Pers. *pûrti* "portion" (cf. *mānôt* in ix 19, 22; so Haupt); the Pers. *behâr* "Spring" (E. Meier); the Bab. *puḫru* "assembly" (F. Hommel), and the Assyr. *pûru* "stone," "lot."[57] Julius Lewy[58] ended all debate on this particular point by showing clearly that the Bab. *pûru* does mean "lot" and, secondarily, "fate." That *pûrîm* is a hebraized form of a Babylonian word does not, however, necessarily mean that the festival was Babylonian in origin or that Esther originated there.[59]

Efforts to identify Purim with an earlier Jewish or Greek festival have been neither common nor convincing,[60] and ever since the 1890s, when Heinrich Zimmern and Peter Jensen equated Mordecai

[54] *Phrouraious* in Josephus *Antiquities* XI. 295.

[55] *Purim: Ein Beitrag zur Geschichte der Religion* 34, Abhandlungen der Gesellschaft der Wissenschaft zu Göttingen, 1887. J. von Hammer first proposed identifying Purim with Farvardigan (*Wiener Jahrbücher für Literatur* 38 [1872], 49). See, however, C. C. Torrey, HTR 37 (1944), 7, who argues that *phourdaia* was originally a scribal error for *phouraia*, the first *a* being read as *d*, these two uncial letters being graphically similar in the Greek alphabet.

[56] HUCA 14 (1939), 139. But see T. H. Gaster's criticisms of this in his *Purim and Hanukkah in Custom and Tradition*, p. 11.

[57] W. F. Albright, BASOR 67 (1937), 37.

[58] RHA 5 (1939), 117–24.

[59] But see Augustin Bea, *"De origine vocis pûr,"* Biblica 21 (1940), 198–99.

[60] For very detailed discussions of various theories of Jewish, Greek, Persian, and Babylonian prototypes for Purim up to his own day, see Paton, pp. 77–94.

and Esther with the Babylonian gods Marduk and Ishtar, and Haman and Vashti with the Elamite gods Humman and Mashti, a Babylonian origin for Purim has been popular. Though scholars like Jensen, Zimmern, Hugo Winckler, Bruno Meissner and others have each picked a different Babylonian myth or festival as the prototype for Purim, namely, the Gilgamesh Epic, the Babylonian Creation Story, the Tammuz-Ishtar Myth, and the Zagmuk Feast, respectively, they all agreed in seeing Esther as a historicized myth or ritual.

More recently, however, a Persian origin for Purim has been gaining support among scholars. Citing ancient and modern parallels in rites and ceremonies from various parts of the world, T. H. Gaster[61] has tried to establish a phenomenological agreement between New Year festivals in general and the Purim story in particular. Thus he finds the prototype for Purim in the Persian New Year,[62] and the story of Esther is "simply a Jewish adaptation of a popular Persian novella" (p. 35). Justifiably critical of Gaster's highly eclectic phenomenological argument, Helmer Ringgren, who has analyzed various Persian stories and practices, concludes by seeing in Purim "*a connection with* [italics added] the [Persian] New Year festival."[63] "It is not impossible," he concludes, "that at a certain New Year festival there had been an outbreak of hostility against Jews which was successfully warded off and that the institution of Purim festival had something to do with those events. . . . [This however] does not alter anything in the fact that Purim is essentially derived from a certain form of Persian New Year ceremonies."[64] Gunkel (p. 115) suggested that Purim is a Jewish imitation of the Persian festival identified by Herodotus in III. 68–79 as "Magophonia," a festival commemorating the slaughter of magi.

Julius Lewy,[65] taking his clue from the gentilic endings -*aios* in *Mardochaios* and *Bougaios* (the Greek translation[?] of *h'ggy* in iii 1), argues that *mrdky* and *h'ggy* are *Nisbe*-formations (see GKC, § 86*h*, *i*) meaning "Mardukian" or "worshiper of Marduk," and "Bagaian" or "worshiper of Mithra." Haman, he notes, is in some way to be associated with *hoama*, the sacred drink of Mithra worship.

---

[61] *Purim and Hanukkah in Custom and Tradition*, p. 14.
[62] For a discussion of New Year's Day at Persepolis, see Olmstead, HPE, pp. 272–88, and especially Ghirshman, *The Arts of Ancient Iran*, pp. 154–222.
[63] SEÅ 20 (1955), 23.
[64] SEÅ 20 (1955), 24.
[65] HUCA 14 (1939), 127–51.

"Hadassah" was not Esther's Hebrew name but an epithet, being the Aramaic form of *hadašatu,* "bride," the equivalent of the Bab. *kallātu,* the frequent epithet of Ishtar goddesses; hence, he argues, we never get in Esther *hmlkh 'str* but always *'str hmlkh.*[66] Thus the historical basis for Esther would go back to a conflict between those worshipers of Marduk, associated with the Ishtar temple at Susa, and the devotees of Mithra and Anahita, around the time of Artaxerxes II (404–358 B.C.);[67] this background for the story would help to explain, he rightly notes, the absence of Yahweh in Esther.

Scholars have suggested much but proven very little about the probable origins of the festival of Purim, the major reason for this being the inadequacies of our present sources.[68] But the problem is also rooted in the very nature of any popular festival, which is "a dynamic, not a static thing, and there can be perforce neither constancy nor permanence in either its form or meaning."[69] Given the Persian setting of Esther, we believe that a "Persian" origin for the festival is probable but not provable, and that the name "Purim" is secondary, "lots" being a folk etymology supplied by Babylonian Jews some time later. It is significant that, apart from Esther itself, the earliest allusion to the events of Purim is in II Macc xv 36, where the thirteenth of Adar is identified not as "the day before Purim" but as "the day before Mordecai's day."[70] Called *phrouraious* by Josephus around the end of the first century A.D., *pûrîm* is not specifically so called in extrabiblical sources until *Megillath Ta'anith XII,* which dates from the second century A.D.

Certainly no opprobrium should be attached to the suggestion of a pagan prototype for the festival of Purim. Like Christianity, whose two great festivals of Christmas and Easter contain pagan elements,[71] Judaism has survived partly because of its ability to adopt pagan ideas and institutions by which it found itself surrounded, and to adapt them to its own distinctive purposes.

[66] But see Dommershausen, p. 140, who convincingly argues that the author of Esther regularly wrote *hmlk 'hšwrwš,* "King Xerxes," but *'str hmlkh,* "Esther the Queen," to emphasize that Xerxes was *king* while Esther was only one of his wives.

[67] See also Olmstead, HPE, p. 47.

[68] See Bardtke, pp. 247–48.

[69] Gaster, *Purim and Hanukkah in Custom and Tradition,* p. xiv.

[70] The parallel account in I Macc vii 49 does not have this phrase.

[71] According to Bede (*De temporum ratione* xv), our English word "Easter" goes back to Ostara, the Teutonic goddess of spring; and as is well known, the pagan Roman Saturnalia, celebrated December 19–25, had certain customs and attitudes not incompatible with Christmas.

ORIGINS AND *Gattung* OF ESTHER

If Purim was adapted from a pagan festival, what does this say about the story which purports to explain its origin? Three possibilities immediately suggest themselves: the story is essentially fact (so Hoschander, Schildenberger, and Barucq), fiction (Haupt, R. H. Pfeiffer, T. H. Gaster), or a combination of both (Julius Lewy, Ringgren, Bardtke, and others). At the turn of the century the "fiction theory" was in clear ascendancy among scholars; today, the "combination theory."

To the present writer, the contradictions, exaggerations, and inconsistencies of Esther (see pp. XLV–XLVI) argue against the story being taken at face value. On the other hand, Mordecai may very well have been a historical personage. The name itself is certainly genuine enough, appearing as *mdrk* in an Aramaic letter[72] and as *mar-du-uk-ka, mar-duk-ka, and mar-du-kan-na-ṣir* in Treasury Tablets found at Persepolis.[73] More importantly, in an undated text coming probably from either the last years of Darius or the first years of Xerxes, there is mention of a *Mardukâ,* an accountant who was a member of an inspection tour from Susa.[74] We do not know how common the name *Mardukâ* was at that particular time and place, but Arthur Ungnad is probably justified in saying that "it is improbable that there are two Mardukas as high officials in Susa."[75] The question, then, is which part of Esther may be fact and which fiction, and how to distinguish between the two.

Like a number of scholars at the turn of the century, many scholars today, including Lewy, Gaster, Ringgren, and Bardtke, rightly regard (see NOTES *passim*) the story of Vashti (i 1 – ii 14) as more fiction than fact, especially since it bears resemblance to such harem stories as those found in *A Thousand and One Nights.*[76] Henri Cazelles[77] opened up a new line of investigation by suggesting that Esther is a conflation of two texts, the evidence for his theory being the common phenomenon in Esther of "twoness,"

---

[72] Driver, *Aramaic Documents of the Fifth Century B.C.*, p. 20, n. 2.
[73] In Tablets 1 and 84 in Cameron, *Persepolis Treasury Tablets,* p. 84.
[74] Arthur Ungnad, ZAW 58 (1940–41), 244.
[75] ZAW 59 (1942–43), 219.
[76] See Emmanuel Cosquin, "Le Prologue-cadre des Mille et une Nuits. Les legendes perses et le Livre d'Esther," RB 18 (1909), 7–49, 161–97.
[77] "Note sur la composition du rouleau d'Esther," *Lex tua Veritas,* pp. 17–29.

namely, two banquets (i 3, 5); two lists of seven names in i 10, 14, the one list being in reverse order of the other;[78] "the second house" of ii 14; the second contingent of candidates in ii 19; Esther's two dinners in v 5 and vii 1; Haman's two discussions with Zeresh and his friends in v 14 and vi 13; Esther's twice risking her life by appearing before the king unsummoned in v 2 and viii 3 (for an alternative explanation of the last reference, as well as for some of the others, see NOTES ad loc.). The one text, Cazelles argues, is "liturgical," centering around Esther, the provinces, and non-Jews near the time of a new year, and so Purim is to be identified with a bacchanalian type of Persian festival called the Sakaea.[79] The other text is "historical," centering around Mordecai, court intrigues, and a persecution of Jews in Susa.

Taking his clue, perhaps, from Cazelles, Bardtke (pp. 248–52) has advanced the theory that the author of Esther drew his material from a Jewish midrashic source containing stories of various Jewish heroes, heroines, and persecutions; and that he combined into one story three separate and unrelated stories: (1) the Vashti story, which could have been an apocryphal harem story originally; (2) the story of Mordecai, which concerned court intrigue, jealousy, and persecution in Susa; and (3) the story of Esther,[80] which told about a young Jewess who, after becoming a favorite of the king, prevented a certain persecution of her people. In perfect innocence and good faith, the author of Esther identified Hadassah, Mordecai's daughter in one tradition, with Esther, the Jewess in the other tradition. (On the basis of his literary analysis, Dommershausen [pp. 15 f.] also sees Esther as written by one author who used several sources.)

Bardtke's theory has much to commend it. Certainly the first candidate for such a "Jewish midrashic source" as he has hypothesized is that work mentioned in x 2 of Esther, namely, the *Annals of the Kings of Media and Persia,* which the author of Esther invites his readers to double-check for themselves (see NOTE ad loc.). In passing, it is worth noting that the *Annals* in x 2 mention Mordecai rather than Esther, just as the earliest reference to the events of Purim outside Esther itself mentions Mordecai,

[78] Cazelles bases this view on the findings of Duchesne-Guillemin in "Les noms des eunuques d'Assérus," *Muséon* 66 (1953), 105–8.

[79] For detailed information on the *Sakaea,* see Paton, pp. 92–93.

[80] '*Str* has often been equated with the Babylonian name Ishtar, the goddess of love, but it can just as easily be equated with the Persian word for "star"; see A. S. Yahuda, "The Meaning of the Name Esther," *Journal of the Royal Asiatic Society* (1946), pp. 174–78.

not Esther ("the day of Mordecai" in II Macc xv 36). Moreover, in *Megilla* 7b, the phrase "Let Haman be cursed" is juxtaposed
to "Let Mordecai be blessed," not "Let Esther be blessed." All
this early emphasis on Mordecai rather than Esther gives greater
credence to the actual existence of Mordecai, a priori the less
likely of the two Jewish heroes in Esther to have been fictional.
Between Mordecai and Esther the greater hero in the Hebrew is
Mordecai, who supplied the brains while Esther simply followed
his directions; it is in the Septuagint that Esther steals the show
from Mordecai, especially in Addition D.

The "midrashic source" may reflect an actual event. There is nothing improbable about Jews in Susa experiencing discrimination, persecution, and even death in the traditionally tolerant Persian empire.
To be sure, no extrabiblical evidence of such a Persian persecution
exists, but this may only reflect the incompleteness of our sources
for the Eastern Diaspora from the fourth to the second century
B.C.; after all, we would have known nothing about Egyptian
hostility to the Jews at Elephantine in the fifth century B.C. had it
not been for the chance find of the Elephantine Papyri.

The Jewish *midrash* hypothesized here was certainly not the
only source used by the author of Esther. The Scriptures were
also a source of information and inspiration. Whether or not
Daniel and Judith were available to him is a moot question
(see below), but he was undeniably influenced by the story
of Joseph in Genesis.[81] That he also had access to Herodotus'
History of the Persian Wars is quite possible but not too likely;
if he had, one would have expected to find far fewer contradictions
between its account and Esther (see NOTES *passim*).

Thus when all the evidence is taken together, we conclude that
Esther is neither pure fact nor pure fiction: it is a historical novel.
Such a characterization is hardly new, but as J. M. Myers has
recently written of Esther with some justification, among scholars

[81] See L. A. Rosenthal, "Die Josephsgeschichte, mit den Büchern Esther und
Daniel verglichen," ZAW 15 (1895), 278–84; 16 (1896), 182; 17 (1897),
126–28; and more recently, Moshe Gan, "The Esther Scroll in the Light of the
Story of Joseph in Egypt" (in Hebrew), *Tarbiẓ* 31 (1961–62), 144–49.
The view of von Rad that the Joseph story is "a wisdom story throughout"
(*Old Testament Theology*, I, p. 432) provides additional support for the view
of Talmon (VT 13 [1963], 419–55) that Esther is also a Wisdom tale. See
also Gerhard von Rad, "The Joseph Narrative and Ancient Wisdom," in
Congress Volume: Copenhagen, 1953, VTS, I [Leiden: Brill, 1953], pp. 120–
27); the article is reprinted in his *Problem of the Hexateuch and Other Essays*,
tr. by E. W. Dicken (New York: McGraw-Hill, 1966), pp. 292–300.

"perhaps the emphasis has fallen too much on the noun rather than the adjective."[82] Comparisons with a pearl are possible. A lustrous pearl consists of a hard core of sand around which successive layers of colorful foreign substance have accumulated. Similarly, the Book of Esther has a historical core—the story of Mordecai, and possibly even the story of Esther—to which have been added legendary and fictional elements, notably the story of Vashti. Whether the festival of Purim was also a very early part of the historical core is impossible to say: certainly the book's concern to harmonize the different dates for observing Purim is a later feature, probably Hellenistic. Exactly when Mordecai's struggle with Haman occurred cannot be proved, but it may very well date to the time of Xerxes. That the story in its final form is later than either the time of Xerxes (so MT) or Artaxerxes (so LXX), however, is highly probable.[83]

THE AUTHOR'S INTENT

There is always considerable danger in assuming one knows an author's intent, for unless he himself has explicitly stated it, it can only be inferred. Nonetheless, as indicated on p. xx above, the author of Esther was primarily concerned with telling an interesting and lively story which would provide the "historical" basis for the festival of Purim. His emphasis was on plot and action, not character or personality. Thus, more often than not he simply states what was said or done (see NOTES *passim*), without saying why or how (see NOTES on ii 22, iii 3, iv 1). His major characters are so superficially drawn that it is difficult to identify very long or intensively with either the book's villains or heroes. Neither Vashti nor Zeresh is a believable life-and-blood individual; they are simply tools the author uses to construct his story (see NOTE on vi 13). And while the character and personality of Xerxes do emerge rather clearly, it is at least questionable whether his characterization in Esther conforms with the real Xerxes (see pp. XXXV–XL, above). As for Haman, he lacks the stature and humanity of an Oedipus by too much to deserve our pity. And it is certainly in the Greek rather than the Hebrew version that one can better identify with the wise Mordecai and the courageous Esther, thanks

[82] *The World of the Restoration,* p. 92.
[83] For a brief but very sound analysis of the origins and *Gattung* of Esther, see Roland de Vaux, *Ancient Israel,* pp. 516–17.

primarily to Additions C and D, which introduce the reader to their inner thoughts and feelings. In the Hebrew version it is more asserted than illustrated that Mordecai was wise and good; while beautiful and courageous, Esther nonetheless seems to be almost two-dimensional, lacking in depth. Despite the insistence of ii 20 that Esther concealed her identity as a Jew because Mordecai had so instructed her, the impression remains that Esther's Jewishness was more a fact of birth than of religious conviction. (That Esther in the Hebrew account seems more of a Jewish nationalist than a follower of the Jewish faith may have been one of the obstacles to the book's attaining canonicity among very pious Jews.) Finally, in structuring his plot the author was influenced by his love of irony, especially as it illustrated the principle of retributive justice (see p. LVI below for some examples).

SYNTAX AND STYLE

Any discussion about the date of Esther's composition must involve an analysis of the book's syntax and style as based upon the oldest extant manuscript, the *Leningrad MS. B. 19*[4], an eleventh-century text of the Tiberian masorete Ben Asher.[84] A far cry from the purity of Classical Hebrew, the Hebrew of Esther is closest in its vocabulary and grammar to Chronicles, Ecclesiastes, and Daniel (see NOTES *passim*), and even contains Mishnaic vocabulary and grammatical constructions,[85] not to mention a number of Persian and Aramaic words (see p. XLI above and NOTES *passim*). Significant for purposes of dating, Esther, like Chronicles and Ecclesiastes, contains no Greek words, a fact which clearly points to a pre-Hellenistic date (see p. LVII).

The author of Esther was no master of the Hebrew language, writing timeless prose. Even though the vocabulary and syntax of Esther must be termed "literary" rather than "vernacular," as Hans Striedl has pointed out,[86] the Hebrew vocabulary is scarcely what might be called "rich"; in 167 verses *mlk,* "king, to rule," occurs approximately 250 times; *'śh,* "to do, make," 87 times; *ntn,* "to give," and *dbr,* "word, thing, to speak," 40 times; and *bw'* "to come," 35 times. The word order of sentences in Esther is

---

[84] For a helpful introduction to the Masoretes, see P. E. Kahle, *The Cairo Geniza,* pp. 57–109, and Roberts, OTTV, pp. 40–74.

[85] See NOTES *passim,* and Paton, pp. 62–63.

[86] Striedl, pp. 73–108.

more characteristic of Aramaic than of Classical Hebrew, namely, subject–verb–object. The author's preference for the imperfect tense (160 times in 167 verses) may be part of his attempts at archaizing,[87] but it also contributes effectively to the life and movement of his story.[88]

Despite the poverty of his vocabulary, the author of Esther was nonetheless a poet who wrote, in the case of Esther, a poetic prose account. More than any other scholar, Dommershausen (see pp. 138–52) has called attention to the poetic features of Esther, including alliteration, assonance, parallelism, rhythm, symmetry, hendiadys, hyperbole, and especially chiastic constructions. Whereas Striedl was often content to describe sentence structure, Dommershausen tries, sometimes with good effect, to show the specific literary function or psychological effect of the syntax (see NOTES passim). Moreover, utilizing the well-known analytical tools of Formgeschichte,[89] Dommershausen has profitably analyzed the Book of Esther into such component parts as "Speech" (ii 1–4); "Notice" (ii 5–7); "Report" (ii 8–14); "Brief Report" (iv 1–3); "Narrative" (iv 4–17); "Short Narrative" (v 9–14); "Narrative with Report" (viii 1–8); "Decree with Short Report and Description" (viii 9–17); "Report with Notice" (ix 1–10); "Decree" (ix 20–28), etc. In some instances these designations are both accurate and suggestive; for example, i 10–22 is called "Wisdom Narrative" while vi 1–14 is "Narrative with Wisdom Speech." In other instances the assigning of a Gattung helps little; as Goethe's Faust long ago observed, to name a thing is not necessarily to explain it.[90]

Even though the style of Esther is admittedly "awkward and laboured" (so Paton), the story is nonetheless told in a clear and interesting way. Since the author was writing a historical novel and could have far greater freedom with his sources than, say, the authors of Genesis who had to operate within well-established traditions, he had virtually a free hand in structuring his plot. For example, the story of Vashti was probably an unrelated harem tale which the author adopted (and adapted) because, in addition to explaining how and why Xerxes deposed his first queen and began looking for another, it also provides a colorful and interesting

---

[87] Striedl, p. 74.
[88] So Dommershausen, see especially pp. 138–43.
[89] For an introductory article on "Form Criticism," see IDB, II, pp. 320–21.
[90] For a more detailed appraisal of Dommershausen's monograph, see the present writer's review of it in the Catholic Biblical Quarterly 31 (1969), 250–52.

introduction to Xerxes and his court (see especially COMMENT on § 1). The author is free enough to make even Zeresh, the wife of Mordecai's sworn enemy, the spokesman for his own Jewish ethnic pride (vi 13).

The plot is skillfully constructed, with due attention given to increasing suspense and the reader's interest. For example, Esther, under pain of death, goes unsummoned to the king (iv 11–v 2); on two separate occasions she *refuses* to state her petition to the king in spite of his promise to grant her any request (v 4, 8); and the king asks Haman how he should honor the very man Haman plans to hang the next day (v 14, vi 6).

The author is especially interested and effective in his use of irony. For example, Vashti was deposed for being disobedient once (i 17–19)—Esther was disobedient twice and yet was rewarded (v 1–2, 8); Haman obeyed the king's command, humiliating though it was (vi 11–12)—Mordecai deliberately disobeyed a royal command, yet was handsomely rewarded (iii 2, viii 1–2); the city wept while the king and Haman drank (iii 15); Haman, thinking that he was prescribing royal honors for himself, was actually prescribing them for Mordecai, his bitter enemy (vi 6–9); Haman was hanged on the gallows which he had intended for Mordecai (vii 9–10).

While chapters i–ii and viii–x are reportial or descriptive in character, chapters iii–vii are quite dramatic, in part because of the author's effective use of irony (see above) and direct address (see iii 3, 8–9, 11, iv 11, 13–14, 16, v 3–5, 6–8, 12–14, vi 3–11, 13, vii 2–6, 8–10).

There are very few really puzzling passages in the book, in part because the author, or an early glossator, explains many of the foreign words and practices; for example, see NOTES on i 13, 19, ii 12, iii 7, viii 8, and ix 26. Repetition, *the* characteristic literary weakness of the book, is also one of its strengths: this very frequent repetition in the form of identical or synonymous words, phrases, and even entire sentences makes for greater clarity (see NOTES *passim*). The Greek translator of Esther was a sophisticated stylist who so disapproved of these redundancies and repetitions that he deliberately omitted them (see p. LXI below).

Esther's great and lasting popularity among Jews is certainly a witness to the book's acceptable, if not eloquent, style. Once its canonicity was no longer questioned, the book became exceedingly popular, so much so that it had many *midrashîm*,[91] or commentaries, based on it, and alone of all the books of the Prophets and The Writings had *two* Targums (Aramaic translations, with expansions). In addition, there are more extant medieval manuscripts of Esther than of any other Old Testament book. (Doubtless the brevity of the book, in contrast, for instance, to the books of the Pentateuch, as well as the fact that it was prescribed reading for the popular festival of Purim, helps to explain the great number of medieval manuscripts.) For a brief discussion of illustrated Esther scrolls, see Appendix III.

DATE OF COMPOSITION

In fixing the date for Esther's composition one must distinguish between its first and "final"[92] versions. Virtually all scholars agree that the final edition took shape sometime in the second century B.C. (see below), but great uncertainty surrounds the *terminus a quo,* or oldest date, for the book's composition.

When Striedl concluded in 1937[93] that on the basis of syntax and style Esther could not have been written earlier than 300 B.C., scholars tended to agree with him. Today that date has fewer supporters for several reasons. First, we now have a sizable mass of literary Hebrew of the second century B.C. from Qumran, and as D. N. Freedman observed to the present writer, "Esther's Hebrew has practically nothing in common with it; that alone would rule out a second-century date for Esther, and make a third-century date unlikely." Second, there is a total absence of Greek vocabulary in Esther, a fact which has been long recognized but insufficiently appreciated until recently. And, finally, as the dates for the composition of those Old Testament books having literary and linguistic affinities with Esther have been moved back in time rather than forward, so must the date for the first version of Esther. For example, the Hebrew of Esther is most like that of The Chronicler (see NOTES *passim*), which is now being dated to ca. 400 B.C.;[94] the date for Ecclesiastes is being moved back to the fourth or pos-

---

[91] See IDB, III, s.v. "Midrash."

[92] By "final" is meant that Hebrew text closest to the completed text which the rabbis ultimately approved in the second century A.D. and from which our present MT presumably descends.

[93] ZAW 55, 81.

[94] See J. M. Myers, *Ezra · Nehemiah,* AB, Vol. 14 (1965), pp. LXVIII–LXX.

sibly the fifth century B.C., thanks to the efforts especially of W. F. Albright and Mitchell Dahood who have disproved the book's so-called "Greek influences." Daniel, of course, continues to be a problem, but one should probably distinguish between the stories (Dan i–vi), which go back to the fourth century B.C., and the visions (vii–xii) which certainly date from the second century B.C.; in other words, while the final version of Daniel dates from ca. 165 B.C., the first edition of Daniel, or the stories, goes back to the Persian Period. Something similar must be said for the Book of Esther: the first edition probably goes back to the fourth century, or Persian Period, and the final edition appeared in the Hellenistic Period.

Ruth Stiehl[95] would lower the *terminus a quo* for Esther to 190 B.C., because neither Mordecai nor Esther is mentioned by Ben Sira in his "Praise of the Fathers" (Wisdom of Sirach xliv–xlix) dating from ca. 190 B.C. The only difficulty with her view is that —whatever the reason may have been—Ezra the Scribe was also excluded by Ben Sira, yet Ben Sira knew of him. Possibly Esther and its festival of Purim were regarded by Ben Sira as too worldly to be included.[96] Nor are other "arguments from silence" any more decisive, that is, those concerning Qumran (see pp. XXI–XXII above) or Philo.[97]

On the basis of II Macc xv 36, Bardtke and others have argued for 50 B.C. as the *terminus ad quem* for Esther's composition, forgetting that the phrase "day of Mordecai" says only that the *festival* of Purim was known in 50 B.C., not necessarily the book itself. Nonetheless, the latest possible date for Esther is much earlier, being either 114 B.C. (so Benno Jacob) or 78 B.C. (E. J. Bickerman), these being the two most probable dates for the Greek translation of Esther (see Appendix II).

Basing her arguments on both linguistic and archaeological evidence, Ruth Stiehl (pp. 203–13) insists on a composition date between 165 and 140 B.C. The linguistic evidence consists, she says, of the presence in Esther of Persian *and Elamite* names,[98]

---

[95] Altheim and Stiehl, *Die aramäische Sprache unter den Achaimeniden*, I, p. 202.

[96] So Bardtke, p. 252.

[97] Philo (ca. 25?B.C.–A.D. 40) does not mention Esther; but neither does he mention Ruth, Ecclesiastes, Song of Solomon, Lamentations, Ezekiel, or Daniel.

[98] See also Rudolf Mayer, "Iranischer Beitrag zu Problem des Daniel-und Esther Buches," in *Lex tua Veritas*, pp. 130–35, who finds Vaizatha in ix 9 to

thereby reflecting a political and cultural situation that did not exist from fifty years after the beginning of the Achaemenian empire until the resurgence of Elamite in the time of Antiochus IV (175–163 B.C.), and which continued until only 140 B.C. Her archaeological evidence is that in Achaemenian Susa the *apadana* was on one tell, Tell II in the north, and the court and its officials on another, in the south; yet in Esther they are together on the same tell, a situation which did exist in Antiochus III's time (223–187 B.C.). Persuasive at first glance, Stiehl's arguments are far from convincing. First, if the author of Esther did use a Jewish midrashic source, as seems probable, then he could easily have gotten his old, genuine Elamite names from it. Second, as Bardtke[99] has so clearly established, the local coloring and topographical details concerning the king's palace are ultimately nondescript and, in any case, could have come from the midrashic materials themselves rather than from the writer's personal, firsthand knowledge. If Esther was composed from various written sources, its "final" author need not have been a Jew of the Eastern diaspora or even have ever gone to Persia; he could have been a Palestinian Jew who never left Palestine. In any case, we cannot say who wrote Esther or where it was written, although the Persian setting and local coloring as well as the absence of all Greek influences do suggest a Jew in Persia for the narrative nucleus.

While 400 to 114 B.C. seem to be the extreme limits for the first and final[100] editions of Esther, it is most likely that Esther reached its final form in either the late Persian or early Hellenistic Period; but in any case, long before Daniel reached its final form. The principal reason for this is the more sympathetic attitude in Esther toward a "Gentile" king. To be sure, the stories in Dan i–vi reflect a somewhat sympathetic attitude toward Gentile kings,[101] but the visions of Daniel (vii–xii) clearly reflect the negative atti-

---

be an old Iranian theophoric name, antedating Xerxes' time; Pharšandatha in ix 7 to be a theophoric name; and the ten sons of Haman to be names of Elamite *daevas,* or demons (for brief introduction to Elamite religion, see HPE, pp. 24–29); see, however, pp. XLII–XLIV above on the difficulties involved in identifying personal names from the MT.

[99] Page 249, n. 20.

[100] It is generally recognized that Daniel reached its "final" form ca. 165 B.C.; see Eissfeldt, *The Old Testament: An Introduction,* pp. 512–29.

[101] The Gentile kings in Dan i–vi reluctantly recognize the power of Yahweh and grant certain privileges and concessions to Jews.

tudes and situation of the early Maccabean Period when Judas Maccabeus (167–161 B.C.) had to contend against the Seleucian king Antiochus IV, Epiphanes (175–163) for religious freedom.[102] Nor could one characterize the relations of his brothers Jonathan (161–143) and Simon (143–135) with Gentile kings as cordial or sympathetic. Yet in the final form of Esther the Gentile king is not unsympathetically treated: Xerxes had been misled by Haman, a trusted adviser (iii 8–11); Xerxes ultimately supported the Jewish people (viii 7–8), and rightfully prospered with the advice and help of his prime minister Mordecai (x 1–2). Such a view is quite possible for a Jewish writer in the Persian Period (539–332), but less appropriate in the Hellenistic Period (331–168), and highly unlikely in the Maccabean Period (167–135). Both Mordecai and Daniel (see Dan i–vi) are willing servants of Gentile kings, an intolerable situation for "good" Jews in the Maccabean Period. The author of the final version of Daniel was no doubt unhappy with Daniel's relationship to the Gentile kings in i–vi, but there was little he could do since those older stories had become fixed through tradition.

All of which does not mean, of course, that the Book of Esther, put in its final form before the Maccabean Period (167–135), was not especially meaningful to Jews in the dark days of the Abomination of Desolation. Certainly many Palestinian Jews in the time of Judas, Jonathan, and Simon could easily have identified with the ethnic and nationalistic pride—and fears—as incarnated in Esther and Mordecai. Nor is this to say that in Esther the king and Vashti were merely veiled figures or ciphers for Jewish enemies in Maccabean times, as some scholars have suggested;[103] rather, the Maccabean readers of Esther took the story of Esther at face value, hoping that as history had repeated itself by raising up new enemies against the Jewish people in the form of the Seleucids, so history would also raise up another Mordecai or Esther.

[102] See IDB, I, s.v. "Abomination that makes desolate."

[103] Thus, Ahasuerus has been interpreted as really representing Ptolemy III, Euergetes (Hugo Willrich, *Judaica: Forschungen zur hellenistisch-judischen Geschichte und Litteratur, Göttingen,* 1900); Alexander Balas (Paul Haupt, "Purim," *Beiträge zur Assyriologie* 6, 1906); Antiochus IV, Epiphanes (A. E. Morris, ET 42 [1930–31], 124–28); John Hyrcanus (Pfeiffer, *Introduction to the Old Testament,* pp. 740–42); and Herod the Great (Isidore Lévy, "La répudiation de Vashti," *Actes du XXIᵉ Congrès International des Oriental-istes, 1948* [1949], *XXIᵉ* 149 f.).

THE GREEK TRANSLATION OF ESTHER

Even a cursory comparison of the Greek and Hebrew texts of Esther shows that the Greek differs in four important ways, having (1) a number of additions, (2) many omissions, (3) some basic inconsistencies with and contradictions to the MT, and (4) several explicitly stated religious concerns. (A detailed treatment of the Greek text of Esther, as well as the Additions, will be presented by the present writer in the final volume of the AB Apocrypha.)

The Septuagint

The translation itself is a "literary" translation which rarely has a labored or awkward effect to remind the reader forcibly that it is a translation; Hebraisms are not totally lacking, however, for example, *ēmeran ex ēmeras* for *mywm lywm* in iii 7, *pesōn pesē* for *npwl tpwl* in vi 13, *kata chōran kai chōran* for *mdynh wmdynh* in viii 9, *kata genean kai genean* for *dwr wdwr* in ix 28. Content to paraphrase the Hebrew, the translator was not particularly concerned with preserving the Hebrew word order; nor did he mechanically translate a Hebrew word with the same Greek word; for example, *dbr* is rendered as *rēmata* in i 17, *ta lechthenta* in i 18, *logous* in iv 9, *rēma* in v 14; and *byt* is rendered *oikiais* in i 22, *ta idia* in v 10, *osa uperchen Aman* in viii 1, *epi pantōn tōn Aman* in viii 2, and *ta uparchonta* in viii 7.

The translator, obviously a man quite at home with the Greek language, translated verse by verse the content but not the exact wording of the Hebrew text before him. That his Hebrew text was substantially like our MT is highly probable, but in the absence of evidence from Qumran impossible to prove. His translation is free in detail within each verse but otherwise follows the text closely, verse by verse; that is, within each verse the sense is preserved or paraphrased even if the exact wording or idiom is not, thus, *ti Esthēr sumbēsetai,* "what shall happen to Esther," for *'t-šlwm 'str wmh y'śh bh,* "about Esther's well-being and progress," in ii 11; *eprōtobathrei,* "seated him in front of," for *wyśm 't-ks'w m'l,* "and set his seat above," in iii 1; *to akribes,* "the particulars," for *mh-zh w'l mh-zh,* "what this was and why it was," in iv 5;

and *ostis etolmēsen,* "who has dared," for *'šr-ml'w lbw,* "who fills his heart," in vii 5. The best indication of just how loose and free in detail the translation is may be seen from the fact that there is scarcely a verse in which the scribe who attempted to bring the LXX into agreement with the MT via the *Hexapla* (see Appendix II, COMMENT on F 11) did not add a word or phrase.

The A-text

In spite of certain "additions" (see NOTES *passim*), the A-text of Esther is considerably shorter than the Septuagint (or B-text), its brevity being due to its frequent "omissions" and "abbreviations." The A-text very frequently "omits" personal names, numbers, dates, and repetitious elements. Characteristic examples of its "abbreviations" of the LXX material may be found in i 19, ii 12–14, v 3, 11, 12, vi 2, and ix 16.

In the preceding paragraph the words "additions," "omissions," and "abbreviations" have been put in quotes because the present writer does not really believe that those variants in the A-text are actually additions, omissions, and abbreviations. Although virtually all modern scholars follow Paul A. de Lagarde[104] and Frederic Field[105] in regarding the A-text of Esther as the Lucianic revision of the Septuagint,[106] this view is certainly incorrect. As the present writer has shown in some detail elsewhere,[107] the A-text of Esther is not a revision of the Septuagint but a separate translation of the Hebrew. The principal reasons for this view are the following considerations: (1) the presence of passages that are translated quite differently in the A-text and the LXX but seem to presuppose the same Hebrew *Vorlage,* or original; (2) the *very* low incidence of verbatim agreement between the A-text and the LXX; (3) the presence of Hebraisms and infelicities of phrase in the A-text; and (4) the abundance of synonyms in the A-text,

---

[104] *Librorum Veteris Testamenti Canonicorum pars prior,* Göttingen: Hoyer, 1883.

[105] *Origenis Hexaplorum quae supersunt* (Oxford, 1875), pp. 793 ff.

[106] For helpful introductory statements on the problems surrounding this recension by the fourth-century Christian martyr Lucian, see Swete, *An Introduction to the Old Testament,* rev. by Ottley, I, pp. 80–85, and Roberts, OTTV, pp. 141–43.

[107] "A Greek Witness to a Different Hebrew Text of Esther," ZAW 79 (1967), 351–58.

some of which agree with Josephus or the MT. More significantly, it is the view of the present writer that the Hebrew text used by the translator of the A-text was radically different at points from both the MT and the one presupposed by the LXX, and that many of the so-called additions, omissions, and abbreviations of the A-text reflect a different Hebrew *Vorlage* rather than editorial treatment by the Greek translator.

If this theory is correct, then it follows that the A-text is of even less help than the LXX in reconstructing the MT. Nonetheless, especially interesting or relevant alternate readings of the A-text are to be found in the notes to the translation; a critical apparatus incorporating all of the variant materials of the A-text would be impractical here, if not impossible.

Only if one does not consider the Greek material can one agree with Bardtke (p. 267) that the textual problems of Esther are not as difficult as the literary and cultic problems, and that the MT is essentially identical with the Hebrew as it left the hands of its Jewish author. D. P. Schötz,[108] who gives an excellent and detailed discussion of Esther's textual history, rightly regards the problems of lower criticism in Esther as the most complicated in the Bible. Whether the presence of three such different Hebrew texts of Esther as found in the MT and as presupposed by the LXX and the A-text is the cause or the result of Esther's questionable canonical status is difficult to say, but the latter possibility is the more likely.

THE ORIGIN OF THE GREEK ADDITIONS

That Mordecai's dream and its interpretation (Additions A and F), the king's first and second letters (Additions B and E), the prayers of Mordecai and Esther (Addition C), and Esther's highly dramatic appearance before the king (Addition D) are properly called additions is scarcely debatable. Both the internal and external evidence indicate that these passages were originally conceived and composed in Greek rather than translated from a Semitic text. As the Hebrew presently exists in BH³, it is a consistent and intelligible whole; the Additions, on the other hand, contradict the MT at a number of points (see NOTES *passim.*). Modern scholars

[108] "Das hebräische Buch Esther," BZ 21 (1933), 255–76.

agree that the two letters of Artaxerxes (Additions B and E) are too florid and rhetorical in character to be anything but Greek in origin, and although the remaining four Additions are sufficiently simple in style as to be translations from the Hebrew, there is no certain evidence that they were. Neither the Talmud, Targums, nor the Syriac translation of Esther has these particular additions, and the Aramaic translation of the Additions dates from the Middle Ages. Finally, Jerome himself wrote following his translation of x 3 that he had deliberately removed these passages from their "proper" context in the Septuagint and put them at the end of his Latin translation of Esther because they were not in the Hebrew text current in his day.

OTHER VERSIONS OF ESTHER

For Esther, as for other books of the Bible,[109] the Sahidic, or Coptic, and the Ethiopic versions are translations of the Septuagint, not of the Hebrew. The Old Latin Version is also based on the Septuagint, but it does have a number of readings that agree with the A-text; usually these are additions, but sometimes they are substitutions. The Syriac and Vulgate, however, are based on the Hebrew text; both are quite faithful to it, although the Vulgate is not always as close to the MT as one would expect, especially given Jerome's claim to having translated it quite literally.[110] Unfortunately, only for the Greek and Vulgate are there what we might properly call "critical editions."[111] Esther's two Aramaic translations, or *targûmîm,* dating from no earlier than the eighth century A.D., render the Hebrew faithfully but also include much *haggadic* material which tells us little about Esther but much about Talmudic and post-Talmudic Judaism. All of the above being the case, readings from other versions will be cited in this commentary only if they are reasonable or possibly preferred alternatives to the MT, or if they are of theological or critical interest.

109 See Roberts, OTTV, pp. 227–35.

110 "What is found in the Hebrew I have expressed with complete fidelity," wrote Jerome immediately after Esther x 3. Given the diversity of the Hebrew texts of Isaiah and of other biblical books at Qumran, it is highly improbable, of course, that Jerome's Hebrew text would have been identical with our present MT.

111 See Bibliography, Versions of Esther.

BIBLIOGRAPHY

COMMENTARIES

Aalders, G. C. *Het boek Esther opnieuw uit den grondtekst vertaald en verklaard,* 2d ed. (Korte verklarung der Heilige Schrift, XI). Kampen: J. H. Hok, 1950.

Anderson, B. W. *The Book of Esther. Introduction and Exegesis* (IB, III, pp. 821–74). New York and Nashville: Abingdon Press, 1954. *Cited as* Anderson.

Bardtke, Hans. *Das Buch Esther* (Kommentar zum Alten Testament). Gütersloh: Mohn, 1963. *Cited as* Bardtke.

Barucq, Andre. *Judith, Esther,* 2d ed. (La Sainte Bible—Bible de Jérusalem). Paris: Cerf, 1959. *Cited as* Barucq.

Bertheau, Ernst, and rev. by Victor Ryssel. *Die Bücher Esra, Nehemia und Ester,* 2d ed. (Kurzgefasstes exegetisches Handbuch zum Alten Testament). Leipzig: Hirzel, 1887. *Cited as* Ryssel.

Bückers, Hermann. *Die Bücher Esdras, Nehemias, Tobias, Judith und Esther* (Herders Bibel-kommentar, IV). Freiburg: Herder, 1953.

Fritzsche, Otto. *Zusätzen zum Buch Esther* (Kurzgefasstes exegetisches Handbuch zu den Apokryphen des Alten Testaments, eds. O. Fritzsche and C. Grimm, I). Leipzig: Hirzel, 1851.

Girbau, B. M. *Esther* (La Biblia). Montserrat: Montserrat, 1960.

Goldman, Solomon. *The Five Megilloth,* 2d ed. (The Soncino Books of the Bible). London: The Soncino Press, 1952.

Gregg, J. A. F. *The Additions to Esther,* (The Apocrypha and Pseudepigrapha of the Old Testament, ed. R. H. Charles, I). Oxford University Press, 1913.

Haller, Max. *Die Fünf Megilloth* (Handbuch zum Alten Testament). Tübingen: Mohr, 1940. *Cited as* Haller.

Haupt, Paul. "Critical Notes on Esther," AJSLL 24 (1907–8), 97–186. Reprinted as "The Book of Esther: Critical Edition of the Hebrew Text with Notes," in *Old Testament and Semitic Studies in Memory of William Rainey Harper,* eds. R. F. Harper, Francis Brown, and G. F. Moore, I. The University of Chicago Press, 1911. *Article cited as* Haupt.

Keil, C. F. *Biblischer Commentar über die nachexilischen Geschichts-bücher: Chronik, Esra, Nehemia und Esther* (Biblischer Commentar über das Alte Testament). Leipzig, 1870. *Cited as* Keil.

Knight, G. F. *Esther, Song of Songs, Lamentations* (Torch Bible Commentaries). London: Student Christian Movement Press, 1955.

Öttli, Samuel. *Das Buch Ruth und das Buch Esther* (Kurzgefasstes Kommentar zu den heiligen Schriften Alten und Neuen Testaments). Nördlingen, 1889.

Paton, L. B. *A Critical and Exegetical Commentary on the Book of Esther* (International Critical Commentary). New York: Scribner, 1908. *Cited as* Paton.

Ringgren, K. V. H., and A. Weiser. *Das Hohe Lied, Klagelieder, Das Buch Esther* (Das Alte Testament Deutsch, XVI). Göttingen: Vandenhoeck and Ruprecht, 1958. *Cited as* Ringgren.

Ryssel, Victor. *Zusätzen zum Buch Esther* (Die Apokryphen und Pseudepigraphen des Alten Testament, ed. E. F. Kautzsch). Tübingen, 1900.

Schildenberger, Johannes B. *Das Buch Esther* (Die Heilige Schrift des Alten Testaments). Bonn: Peter Hanstein Verlag, 1941. *Cited as* Schildenberger.

Scholz, Anton. *Commentar über das Buch "Esther" mit seinen Zusätzen und über "Susanna."* Würzburg-Wien: Verlag Leo Woerl, 1892.

Siegfried, D. C. *Esra, Nehemia und Esther* (Handkommentar zum Alten Testament, ed. W. Nowack). Göttingen: Vandenhoeck and Ruprecht, 1901. *Cited as* Siegfried.

Soubigou, L. *Esther traduit et commente,* 2d ed. (La Sainte Bible—Bible de Jérusalem). Paris: Cerf, 1952.

Steuernagel, Carl. *Das Buch Ester,* 4th ed. (Die Heilige Schrift des Alten Testamentes, eds. E. F. Kautzsch and A. Bertholet). Tübingen: Mohr, 1923.

Streane, A. W. *The Book of Esther* (The Cambridge Bible for Schools and Colleges). Cambridge University Press, 1907. *Cited as* Streane.

Stummer, Friedrich. *Das Buch Ester* (Echter-Bibel). Würzburg: Echter Verlag, 1956.

Wildeboer, Gerrit. *Das Buch Esther* (Kurzer Hand-Commentar zum Alten Testament). Tübingen: Mohr, 1898. *Cited as* Wildeboer.

OTHER BOOKS

Ben-Chorin, S. Chalom. *Kritik des Estherbuches. Eine theologische Streitschrift.* Jerusalem, 1938.

Bentzen, Aage. *Introduction to the Old Testament,* I, 6th ed. Copenhagen: G. E. C. Gad, 1961.

Bickerman, E. J. *Four Strange Books of the Bible: Jonah, Daniel, Koheleth, Esther.* New York: Schocken, 1967.

———— *From Ezra to the Last of the Maccabees: Foundations of Post-Biblical Judaism.* New York: Schocken, 1962.

Bright, John. *A History of Israel.* Philadelphia: Westminster Press, 1959.

Brown, F., S. R. Driver, and C. A. Briggs (abbr. BDB). *A Hebrew and English Lexicon of the Old Testament.* Boston: Houghton, Mifflin 1906; Oxford University Press, 1907, repr. 1953, 1955.

Cameron, G. G. *The Persepolis Treasury Tablets.* University of Chicago Press, 1948.

Dieulafoy, M. A. *L'Acropole de Suse,* 4 vols. Paris: Hachette, 1893.

Dommershausen, Werner. *Die Esterrolle: Stil und Ziel einer alttestamentlichen Schrift,* Stuttgarten Biblische Monographien, eds. J. Hospecker and W. Pesch, VI. Stuttgart: Katholisches Bibelwerk, 1968. *Cited as* Dommershausen.

Dreissen, Josef. *Ruth, Esther, Judith in Heilsgeschichte.* Paderborn, 1953.

Driver, S. R. *An Introduction to the Literature of the Old Testament,* rev. ed. New York: Scribner, 1913.

Ehrlich, A. B. *Randglossen zur hebräischen Bibel textkritisches, sprachliches, und sachliches,* VII. Leipzig: Hinrichs, 1914. *Cited as* Ehrlich.

Eissfeldt, Otto. *The Old Testament: An Introduction, Including the Apocrypha and Pseudepigrapha, and Also the Works of Similar Type from Qumran,* tr. from the 3d Ger. ed. by Peter R. Ackroyd. New York: Harper & Row, 1965.

Freedman, Harry, and Maurice Simon, eds. *Esther in Midrash Rabbah.* London: Soncino Press, 1939.

Gaster, T. H. *Purim and Hanukkah in Custom and Tradition.* New York: Schumann, 1950.

Ghirshman, Roman. *The Arts of Ancient Iran from Its Origins to the Time of Alexander the Great,* tr. by Stuart Gilbert and James

Emmons, in The Arts of Mankind, eds. André Malraux and Georges Salles. New York: Golden Press, 1964.

——— Cinq Campagnes de fouilles à Suse, 1946–51. 1952.

Gunkel, Hermann. Esther. Tübingen: Mohr, 1916. Cited as Gunkel.

Hoschander, Jacob. The Book of Esther in the Light of History. Philadelphia: Dropsie College, 1923. Cited as Hoschander.

Jahn, Gustav. Das Buch Esther nach der Septuaginta hergestellt, übersetzt und kritisch erklärt. Leiden, 1901.

Joüon, Paul. Grammaire de l'hébreu Biblique (abbr. GHB), 2d ed. Rome: Biblical Institute Press, 1947.

Kahle, P. E. The Cairo Geniza, 2d ed. Oxford: Blackwell, 1959.

Katzenellenbogen, Ilja. Das Buch Esther in der Aggada. Würzburg, Phil. Diss., 1933.

Kautzsch, E. F., ed. Gesenius' Hebrew Grammar, the 2d Eng. ed. rev. by A. E. Cowley (abbr. GKC). From the 28th Ger. rev. ed., Leipzig, 1909. Oxford University Press, 1910, repr. 1946 and after.

Kittel, Rudolph, ed. Biblia Hebraica, 3d ed. (abbr. BH³). Stuttgart: Privilegierte Württembergische Bibelanstalt, 1937 and after.

Mazar, Benjamin, ed. Views of the Biblical World (abbr. VBW). Jerusalem and Ramat Gan, Israel: International Publishing Co., 1961. Reprinted as Illustrated World of the Bible Library. New York, Toronto, London: McGraw-Hill, 1961.

Myers, J. M. The World of the Restoration, in Backgrounds to the Bible Series, ed. B. Vawter. Englewood Cliffs, N.J.: Prentice-Hall, 1968.

Oesterley, W. O. E., and T. H. Robinson. An Introduction to the Books of the Old Testament. New York: Macmillan, 1934.

Olmstead, A. T. The History of the Persian Empire (abbr. HPE). University of Chicago Press, 1948.

Pfeiffer, R. H. Introduction to the Old Testament, rev. ed. New York: Harper, 1948.

Pritchard, J. B., ed. Ancient Near Eastern Texts Relating to the Old Testament (abbr. ANET), 2d ed. Princeton University Press, 1955.

Roberts, B. J. The Old Testament Text and Versions: The Hebrew Text in Transmission and the History of the Ancient Versions (abbr. OTTV). University of Wales Press, 1951.

Swete, H. B. An Introduction to the Old Testament in Greek, 2d ed., rev. by R. L. Ottley. Cambridge University Press, 1914.

Vaux, Roland de. Ancient Israel: Its Life and Institutions, tr. from the French by John McHugh. New York: McGraw-Hill, 1961.

ARTICLES

Albright, W. F., "Some Recent Archaeological Publications," BASOR 67 (1937), 37.

Altheim, Franz, and Ruth Stiehl, "Esther, Judith, und Daniel," in *Die aramäische Sprache unter den Achaemeniden* (Frankfurt am Main: V. Kostermann, 1963), I, pp. 195–213.

Anderson, B. W., "The Place of the Book of Esther in the Christian Bible," *Journal of Religion* 30 (1950), 32–43.

Bardtke, Hans, "Neuere Arbeiten um Estherbuch. Eine kritische Würdigung," *Ex Oriente Lux* 19 (1965–66), 519–49.

Bea, Augustin, "De origine vocis *pûr*," *Biblica* 21 (1940), 198–99.

Bévenot, Hugues, "Die Proskynesis und die Gebete im Estherbuch," *Jahrbuch für Liturgiewissenschaft* 11 (1931), 132–39.

Bickerman, E. J., "Notes on the Greek Book of Esther," PAAJR 20 (1950), 101–33.

———— "The Colophon of the Greek Book of Esther," JBL 63 (1944), 339–62.

Botterweck, G. J., "Die Gattung des Buches Esther in Spektrum neuerer Publikationen," *Bibel und Leben* 5 (1964), 274–92.

Brownlee, W. H., "Le Livre grec d'Esther et la royauté divine. Corrections orthodoxes au livre d'Esther," RB 73 (1966), 161–85.

Cazelles, Henri, "Note sur la composition du rouleau d'Esther," in *Lex tua veritas: Festschrift für Hubert Junker,* eds. H. Gross and F. Mussner (Trier: Paulinus Verlag, 1961), pp. 17–29.

Christian, Viktor, "Zur Herkunft des Purim-Festes," in *Alttestamentliche Studien für Fredrick Nötscher Festschrift,* eds. Hermann Junker and C. J. Botterweck (Bonn, 1950), pp. 33–37.

Cosquin, Emmanuel, "Le prologue-cadre des Mille et une Nuits. Les legendes perses et le livre d'Esther," RB 18 (1909), 7–49, 161–97.

Crenshaw, J. L., "Method in Determining Wisdom Influence upon 'Historical Literature,'" JBL 88 (1969), 129–42.

Daube, David, "The Last Chapter of Esther," JQR 37 (1946–47), 139–47.

Driver, G. R., "Problems and Solutions," VT 4 (1954), 225–45.

Duchesne-Guillemin, Jacques, "Les noms des eunuques d'Assuérus," *Muséon* 66 (1953), 105–8.

Ehrlich, Ernst, "Der Traum des Mardochai," *Zeitschrift für Religions und Geistesgeschichte* 7 (1955), 69–74.

Finkel, Joshua, "The Author of the Genesis Apocryphon Knew the Book of Esther," in *Essays on the Dead Sea Scrolls in Memory of E. L. Sukenik* (in Heb.) (Jerusalem: Hakhal ha-sefer, 1961), pp. 163–82.

Gan, Moshe, "The Book of Esther in the Light of the Story of Joseph in Egypt" (in Heb.), *Tarbiz* 31 (1961–62), 144–49.

Gaster, T. H., "Esther 1:22," JBL 69 (1950), 381.

Gehman, H. S., "Notes on the Persian Words in Esther," JBL 43 (1924), 321–28. *Cited as* Gehman.

Gerleman, Gillis, "Studien zu Esther-Stoff-Struktur-Stil-Sinn," *Biblische Studien* 48 (1966), 1–48.

Haupt, Paul, "Purim," *Beiträge zur Assyriologie* 6 (1906).

Jacob, Benno, "Das Buch Esther bei dem LXX," ZAW 10 (1890), 241–98.

Jensen, Peter, "Elamitische Eigennamen. Ein Beitrag zur Erklärung der elamitischen Inschriften," WZKM 6 (1892), 47–70, 209–26.

Klíma, Otakar, "Iranische Miszellen," ArOr 6 (1956), 603–16.

Lévy, Isidore, "La répudiation de Vashti," *Actes du XXIᵉ Congrès International des Orientalistes, 1948* (Paris: Imprimerie Nationale, 1949), pp. 114 ff.

Lewy, Julius, "Old Assyrian *puru'um* and *pūrum*," RHA 5 (1939), 117–24.

———— "The Feast of the 14th Day of Adar," HUCA 14 (1939), 127–51.

McKane, William, "A Note on Esther IX and I Samuel XV," JTS 12 (1961), 260–61.

Marcus, Ralph, "Dositheus, Priest and Levite," JBL 64 (1945), 269–71.

Mayer, Rudolf, "Iranisher Beitrag zu Problemen des Daniel-und-Esther-Buches," in *Lex tua veritas: Festschrift für Hubert Junker*, eds. H. Gross and F. Mussner (Trier: Paulinus Verlag, 1961), pp. 127–35.

Meissner, Bruno, "Zur Entstehungsgeschichte des Purimfestes," ZDMG 50 (1896), 296–301.

Metzger, Mendel, "The John Rylands Megillah and Some Other Illustrated Megilloth of the XVth to XVIIth Centuries," BJRL 45 (1962–63), 148–84.

Moore, Carey, "A Greek Witness to a Different Hebrew Text of Esther," ZAW 79 (1967), 351–58.

Moreau, J., "Un nouveau témoin du texte latin du livre d'Esther," *La Nouvelle Clio* 3 (1951), 398.

Morris, A. E., "The Purpose of the Book of Esther," ET 42 (1930–31), 124–28.

Motzo, B. R., "Il testo di Ester in Guiseppi," *Studi e Materiali di Storia delle Religioni* 4 (1928), 84–105.

———— "La storia del testo di Ester," *Ricerche Religiose* 3 (1927), 205–8.

Oppenheim, A. Leo, "On Royal Gardens in Mesopotamia," JNES 24 (1965), 328–33.

Paton, L. B., "A Text-Critical Apparatus to the Book of Esther," in *Old Testament and Semitic Studies in Memory of William Rainey Harper*, eds. R. F. Harper, Francis Brown, and G. F. Moore, 2 vols. (University of Chicago Press, 1911), II, pp. 1–52.

Rosenthal, L. A., "Die Josephsgeschichte mit den Büchern Ester und Daniel vergleichen," ZAW 15 (1895), 278–84; 16 (1896), 182; 17 (1897), 126–28.

Rudolph, Wilhelm, "Textkritisches zum Estherbuch," VT 4 (1954), 89–90.

Schneider, B., "Esther Revised according to the Maccabeus," *Liber Annus* 13 (1962–63), 190–218.

Schötz, Dionysius, "Das hebräische Buch Esther," BZ 21 (1933), 255–76.

Stiehl, Ruth, "Das Buch Esther," WZKM 53 (1956), 4–22.

Striedl, Hans, "Untersuchung zur Syntax und Stilistik des hebräischen Buches Esther," ZAW 55 (1937), 73–108. *Cited as* Striedl.

Talmon, Shemaryahu, "Wisdom in the Book of Esther," VT 13 (1963), 419–55.

Torrey, C. C., "The Older Book of Esther," HTR 37 (1944), 1–40.

Ungnad, Arthur, "Keilinschriftliche Beiträge zum Buch Ezra und Esther," ZAW 58 (1940–41), 240–43; 59 (1942–43), 219.

Yahuda, A. S., "The Meaning of the Name Esther," *Journal of the Royal Asiatic Society* (1946), pp. 174–78.

Zimmern, Heinrich, "Zur Frage noch dem Ursprunge des Purimfestes," ZAW 11 (1891), 157–69.

VERSIONS OF ESTHER

Brooke, A. E., Norman McLean, and H. St. John Thackeray, eds. *Esther, Judith, Tobit*. The Old Testament in Greek, III, Pt. I. Cambridge University Press, 1940.

Esteves Pereira, F. M., ed. *Le livre d'Esther, version éthiopienne*. Patrologia Orientalis, ed. R. Graffin, IX. Paris, 1913.

Hanhart, Robert. *Esther*. Septuaginta. Vetus Testamentum Graecum auctoritate Societatis Gottingensis editum, ed. J. Ziegler, III. Göttingen, 1966.

Kenyon, F. G., ed. *Ezekiel, Daniel, and Esther*. The Chester Beatty Biblical Papyri [of the Greek Bible], fasc. VII. London: Emery Walker, 1937.

Libre Hester et Job. Biblia Sacra iuxta Latinam Vulgalam versionem, ed. Ordinis Sancti Benedicti. Rome: Trypsis Polyglottis Vaticanis, 1951.

Thompson, H. F., ed. *A Coptic Palimpsest in British Museum containing Joshua, Judges, Ruth, Judith, and Esther in the Sahidic Dialect*. Oxford University Press, 1911.

ESTHER

1. QUEEN VASHTI IS DEPOSED
(i 1–22)

I [1] It was[a] in the days of Xerxes[b] (the Xerxes who used to reign from India [c]to Ethiopia[c] over a hundred and twenty-seven provinces), [2] at that time when King Xerxes sat on his royal throne in the acropolis[d] of Susa, [3] he gave a banquet in the third year of his reign for all his officials and courtiers: [e]the officers of[e] the army of Persia and Media, the nobles, and the rulers of the provinces who were present, [4] and displayed the great wealth of his empire and the glorious splendor of his majesty for many days (for half a year).

[5] Now when all that was over, the king gave [f]a week-long[f] party for all the men[g] staying in the acropolis of Susa, for both the important and the unimportant alike, in the courtyard of the king's pavilion. [6] The courtyard was decorated with white and violet cotton curtains, which were fastened by linen and purple cords to silver rings and marble columns; and couches of gold and silver were on a mosaic pavement of porphyry, marble, mother-of-pearl, and colored stones. [7] And the drinks were served in gold goblets, with no two alike; and there was plenty of royal

[a] Greek adds "after these things," referring to Mordecai's dream (A 1–11) and his informing on the conspirators (A 12–17).
[b] MT *'ḥšwrwš;* AT *Assuēros;* Vulg. *Asuerus;* LXX and Josephus have "Artaxerxes"; see NOTE.
[c–c] LXX omits; but some Greek manuscripts, AT, Josephus, and OL do have it.
[d] Instead of "acropolis" (*habbîrâ*), LXX has *tē polei* "the city"; but OL's *thebari* attests to the onetime existence of a Greek manuscript which transliterated instead of translated the Hebrew.
[e–e] MT omits *wśry* "the officers of"; see NOTE.
[f–f] Literally "for seven days"; LXX "for six days."
[g] MT "the people."

wine, as befitted a king. 8 The drinking, however, was not[h] according to the law: no one was constraining; for the king had ordered all the palace waiters to serve each guest as he wished. 9 Queen Vashti, too, gave a party for the women in the royal house of King Xerxes.

10 On the seventh day, when the king was feeling high from the wine, he ordered Mehuman[i], Biztha, Harbona, Bigtha, Abagtha, Zethar, and Carcas, the seven eunuchs who personally served King Xerxes, 11 to bring Queen Vashti, wearing the royal turban, before the king, so that he might show off her beauty to the guests[j] and the officials; for she was very beautiful.

12 Queen Vashti, however, refused to come at the king's order conveyed by the eunuchs. The king became very angry at this, and he was quite incensed. 13 The king [k]immediately[k] conferred with the experts, who knew the laws[l] (for that was the king's practice in the presence of all those who knew law and government; 14 and those next to him were [m]Charshena, Shethar, Admatha, Tarshish, Meres, Marsena, and Memukan,[m] the seven princes of Persia and Media who could personally converse with the king and who sat first in the kingdom) 15 as to what should be done, from a legal point of view, to Queen Vashti for not obeying King Xerxes' order brought by the eunuchs.

16 Memukan[n] then observed in the presence of the king and the princes, "It is not only the king whom Queen Vashti has wronged but also all the officials and people in all the provinces of King Xerxes. 17 When all the women hear the rumor about the queen, they will look down on their husbands, ([o]when it is said[o], 'King Xerxes ordered Queen Vashti to be brought before him, and she would not come!')[p] 18 So, this same day those ladies of the Persians and Medes who have heard about

[h] So LXX; see NOTE.
[i] LXX "Aman," an obvious error since Haman had wife and sons.
[j] MT "the peoples."
[k-k] Literally "and."
[l] Reading dtym, instead of 'tym "times"; see NOTE.
[m-m] LXX lists only three names; AT, none.
[n] Reading with Qrê, mmwkn, which agrees with vs. 14, instead of mwmkn.
[o-o] Literally "they (masculine plural) shall say." Since "they" here refers to the ubiquitous "they" of rumor, it is best translated impersonally.
[p] AT omits verse; LXX omits "King Xerxes ordered . . . would not come!"

the queen's conduct ^qshall show themselves obstinate^q to all the king's officials; and there will be contempt and anger to spare!

19 If it please the king, let him issue a royal edict, and let it be recorded among the laws of the Persians and Medes so that it cannot be revoked, that Vashti shall never again appear before King Xerxes; and let the king confer her royal post on a woman who is better than she. 20 Then, when the king's decree, which he has proclaimed, is heard throughout his kingdom (extensive as it is), all women, regardless of their status, shall show proper respect to their husbands."

21 This suggestion pleased the king and the princes. So the king followed Memukan's advice; 22 and he sent dispatches to all the royal provinces, to each province in its own script,^r and to each people in its own language, to the effect that every man should be master in his own home and say ^swhatever suited him.^s

^{q-q} Reading *tamreynâ*, instead of *tō'marnâ;* see NOTE.
^r AT omits verse; LXX omits "in its own script."
^{s-s} Reading *kl šwh 'mw*, instead of *klšwn 'mw;* see NOTE.

NOTES

i 1. *It was* (*wyhy*). Literally "and it came to pass." *Wyhy* is the first word in historical books such as Joshua, Judges, I and II Samuel, where it continues the narrative of the preceding book; but it also occurs at the very beginning of Ezekiel and Jonah, where no such claim to historical continuity can be made. Here it is best understood as a conventional opening formula which sets the stage for the reader in much the same way as does the phrase "once upon a time" in our children's stories. With some justification, Striedl, p. 73, regards it as part of the author's attempts to archaize, thereby increasing the authenticity of his account of Purim.

Xerxes (*'ḥšwrwš*). The author of Esther apparently knew of several Persian kings by the name of *'aḥašwērôš*, "the chief of rulers" (Gehman, p. 322) and wished to establish clearly which one was meant (cf. Ezra iv 6; Dan ix 1; Tob xiv 15). Regardless of who Ahashwerosh may have been in the above references, since the nineteenth century it has been clear from both the linguistic and archaeological evidence (see Ryssel; Paton, pp. 51–54) that *'ḥšwrwš* is Xerxes I (485–465 B.C.), son of Darius and Atossa, the Persian king whose defeats at the hands of the Greeks at Thermopylae (480 B.C.), Salamis (480), and Plataea (479) have been immortalized by Herodotus in his *History of the Persian Wars* VII–IX; see Introduction, pp. XXXV–XL. See, however, Hoschander (especially pp. 30–41, 77–79, 118–38), who follows the lead of the LXX and Josephus in translating *'ḥšwrwš* as "Artaxerxes," and argues that the literary and archaeological evidence indicate that *'ḥšwrwš* was Artaxerxes II (404–358 B.C.). It is almost gratuitous to say that while the author of Esther clearly wants his readers to understand that *'ḥšwrwš* is Xerxes the Great, that fact does not mean that the historical Xerxes was actually involved in the events narrated in Esther; see Introduction, pp. XLIV ff.

from India (hōddû) to Ethiopia (kûš). "India" refers to the northwestern part of the Indus River, which Darius had conquered (see Herodotus III. 94–106; HPE, pp. 144–45). Three *kûš* are mentioned in the Old Testament (see BDB, pp. 468–49); the one here is Ethiopia (see HPE, pp. 234–36). On a foundation tablet from his palace at Persepolis, Xerxes claims to rule over an empire extending from India to Ethiopia: "I am Xerxes, the great king, the only king (lit.: king of kings), the king of (all) countries (which speak) all kinds of languages, the king of this (entire) big and far (-reaching) earth—the son of king Darius, the Achaemenian, a Persian, son of a Persian, an Aryan (*ar-ri-i*) of Aryan descent.

"Thus speaks king Xerxes: These are the countries—in addition to Persia—over which I am king under the 'shadow' of Ahuramazda, over which I hold sway, which are bringing their tribute to me—whatever is commanded them by me, that they do and they abide by my law(s) —: Media, Elam, Arachosia, Urartu (Pers. version: Armenia), Drangiana, Parthia, (H)aria, Bactria, Sogdia, Chorasmia, Babylonia, Assyria, Sattagydia, Sardis, Egypt (*Mi-ṣir*), the Ionians who live on the salty sea and (those) who live beyond . . . the salty sea, Maka, Arabia, Gandara, *India*, Cappadocia, Da'an, the Amyrgian Cimmerians . . . (wearing) pointed caps, the Skudra, the Akupish, Libya, Banneshu (Carians) (and) *Kush*" [ANET, pp. 316–17; italics added]. Herodotus essentially confirms these claims of Xerxes; see III. 97, VII. 9, 65, 69 f.

a hundred and twenty-seven provinces. Mᵉdînôt are provinces (see also Neh i 3, vii 6; Ezra ii 1), not satrapies; the Persian empire never had more than thirty-one satrapies (concerning satrapal organization, see HPE, p. 59). Without the support of any version, Haller would delete "seven" to bring it into conformity with Dan vi 2 and ix 1, which state that Darius the Mede had a hundred and twenty provinces. Despite scholarly speculations, no satisfactory explanation exists for the particular number of provinces given here. For map of the Persian empire in the Achaemenian Period, see pp. XXXVI–XXXVII.

2. *at that time*. So also ii 21. Literally "in those days"; the phrase is resumptive, necessary because of the long parenthetical expression in vs. 1.

sat. The infinitive *kešebet* here has the force of a preterite and does not express the continuing action. Taking their clue from *ethronisthē* of the LXX, which suggests the idea of enthronement (see Benno Jacob, ZAW 10 [1890], 281), many scholars of the past and present see the word as meaning "when he sat *securely*," thereby alluding to the fact that Xerxes had to put down uprisings in Egypt in the early years of his reign (see Herodotus VII. 1, 7; HPE, pp. 234–36), and in Babylon (so Bardtke, p. 278, n. 3; see also HPE, pp. 236–37). Keil viewed the entire phrase as an effort to conjure up visions of Persian majesty, such as when Xerxes watched the Battle of Thermopylae while sitting resplendent upon his throne (see Herodotus VII. 102). For a picture of a Persian monarch sitting on his throne, see Plate 2.

his royal throne (*kissē' malkûtô*). Literally "seat of his kingdom," an expression of later Hebrew (cf. I Chron xxii 10, xxviii 5; II Chron vii 18); instead of *malkût*, older books have *mamlākâ*, as in I Kings ix 5. Of the eighty-seven occurrences of *malkût* in the MT, twenty-four are in Esther, twenty-eight in I and II Chronicles, fourteen in Daniel, six in Ezra, and the remaining fifteen are scattered throughout the Old Testament.

acropolis of Susa. See i 5, ii 3, *et passim*. *Bîrâ* is a late loan word (cf. Assyr. *bîrtu*, "fortress"; Pers. *bāru*), and literally means "a palace, a fortress"; see Neh i 1; Dan viii 2. In Esther, however, it represents the royal part of the capital which is separated from the city, hence, "acropolis," not "palace" (KJ) or "capital" (RSV). Susa, two hundred miles northeast of Babylon and the ancient capital of Elam, was a Persian capital, along with Ecbatana, Babylon, and Persepolis. It was excavated by the Frenchman M. A. Dieulafoy in 1884–86 (see Bibliography), when Near Eastern archaeology was still in an embryonic stage. Another Frenchman, Roman Ghirshman, worked the site again in 1946–51 (see Bibliography) and was able to clarify some previously cloudy issues. Excavations of the site have not disproved the statements, admittedly vague, made about Susa in Esther; see further A. Leo Oppenheim, JNES 24 (1965), 328–33; cf., however, NOTE on ii 3. For an aerial photograph of Susa, see Plate 8. For background on the city's location, climate, and earlier architectural features, see HPE, pp. 163–71.

3. *the officers of the army*. "The officers of" is missing in the MT, and *ḥyl*, "army," is syntactically unrelated to the rest of the clause in the Hebrew. Keil added a *lamed* ("namely"); Bardtke regards *ḥyl* as appositional; Ehrlich saw "officials and courtiers" as a gloss for *ḥyl*, to which Otakar Klíma agreed but added that *ḥyl* here means "nobility"

rather than "army" (ArOr 6 [1956], 614–15). The reading adopted by our translation sees *kai tois loipois*, "and the rest of," of the LXX as the translation of *wš'r*, which could very well be a corruption of *wśry*, "officers," a view held by many scholars. It is unlikely that the author of Esther could have meant the entire army, that is, 2,000 spearmen, 2,000 horsemen, and 10,000 foot soldiers (see Herodotus VII. 40–41 and HPE, pp. 237–47, for a description of the appearance and armor of the various contingents) although, according to Ctesias, the court physician to Artaxerxes Mnemon (405–359 B.C.), no less than 15,000 feasted at the table of the Persian kings (Fragment 37, see Streane, p. 3). And if the figure can be believed, Assurnasirpal had a ten-day celebration for 69,574 guests (see Bardtke, p. 279, nn. 19, 20; also Ernst Vogt, *Biblica* 38 [1957], 374).

Persia and Media. This is the usual sequence in Esther (cf. i 14, 18, 19, but see x 2); however, Dan v 28, vi 9, 13, 16, and viii 20 have "Media and Persia" inasmuch as the Medes were dominant then. For an artistic representation of Medes and Persians, see Plate 5.

nobles (happart^emîm). Derived from Old Pers. *fratama* (G. G. Cameron, JNES 17 [1958], 162, 166, n. 17). For photographs of stone reliefs of Median and Persian nobles, see reliefs on Apadana at Persepolis in VBW, IV, pp. 182–83.

4. *and displayed (b^ehar'ōtô)*. Despite the exegetical problems raised by this idea, the infinitive here denotes continuation, not purpose (so the Vulg. *ut ostenderet*). For descriptions of the fabulous wealth of the Persian kings, see Herodotus I. 126, III. 96, VIII. 27, 95 f., and IX. 8.

half a year. Literally "one hundred and eighty days." Since this figure seems excessive, many scholars have argued that the display of wealth was shown to *successive* groups of guests during that period rather than to all throughout the one hundred and eighty days; see, however, Jud i 16, where a victory celebration goes on for one hundred and twenty days. Bardtke argues (p. 275) that the entire phrase is a stylistic technique typical of the writer of Esther, that is, going from the general to the specific; however, the phrase "many days" is omitted by the Greek, and thus may be a later gloss in Hebrew.

Susa is so intolerably hot that no one would want to spend more than one hundred and eighty days there. According to Strabo XV 3. 10–11, the heat at noon was so intense that snakes and lizards trying to crawl across the roads were burned to death, and barley grains became "popcorn." To observe that Strabo was exaggerating is, of course, to miss the point: in the summer Susa is unbearably hot.

5. *Now when all that was over.* Literally "when these days were fulfilled." To the phrase "these days" the LXX adds "of the marriage"

(*tou gamou*), which represents a corruption of *tou potou*, "of the drinking"; the AT adds "of his deliverance."

the important and the unimportant alike. The LXX omits; literally "from the great to the small," the phrase probably refers here to rank (so II Chron xv 13; I Sam xxx 19).

pavilion. vii 7, 8. The *bîtan* was a summer house, "a small luxury structure, an independent architectural unit for the use of the king or the heir apparent . . . an open structure, probably a colonnaded open hall" (Oppenheim, JNES 24 [1965], 330–31).

6. A difficult and corrupt verse, which in the Hebrew is syntactically unrelated to the preceding material (see, however, Striedl, p. 86, who argues that the verse is not so much a corruption as a creation, i.e., that the author wanted to create an impression rather than offer a description). Our translation follows the lead of the LXX, which supplies the verb "decorated" and sees it in apposition to the "courtyard" of vs. 5. That a verse which describes furnishings and architectural features was corrupted should occasion no surprise, for many of the words involved are of a technical or uncertain meaning (see Paton, pp. 138–40, 144–46). Nor does the Greek offer any real help, apart from showing how doublets develop from a misunderstanding of the Hebrew. For example, the Heb. *wdr wshrt* "mother-of-pearl and colored stones" is read by the Greek as *wrdy shrt* "and roses in a circle"; the AT has "woven with flowers," which is a doublet with "caught up with linen cords," *'hwz bhbslt* having been misread for *'hwz bhbly bws.* According to Dommershausen (p. 146), the author used foreign words and *hapax legomena* to increase the exotic effect. For examples of the various Persian columns at Persepolis, see Roman Ghirshman, *The Arts of Iran,* p. 215.

7. *the drinks.* *Hašqôt* is the infinitive construct of *šāqâ,* thus "to give drink." Eating certainly played a part in the festivities, but the major emphasis was on drinking. For testimonies to the Persians' lavishness and drinking prowess, see Herodotus I. 133, IX. 80; Xenophon *Cyropaedia* VIII. 8, 10; and Strabo XV. 3, 19; also HPE, pp. 182–83. The Persians took understandable pride in their wine goblets; see Xenophon *Cyropaedia* VIII. 8, 18. For photograph of an Achaemenian drinking goblet, see Plate 6.

as befitted a king. Cf. ii 18. Translation uncertain; literally "according to the hand of the king," which the LXX translated as "which the king himself drinks"; see I Kings x 13; Neh ii 8.

8. A troublesome verse for versions and commentators alike. The Hebrew itself seems contradictory: on the one hand, the drinking *was* "according to law (*kdt*)" of the king, that is, whenever the king drank, everyone drank (cf. Herodotus I. 33; Xenophon *Cyropaedia* VIII. 8,

10; Josephus *Antiquities* XI. 188); on the other hand, "no one was compelling (*'ên 'ōnēs*)," that is, one could drink as much, or as little, as he wanted. Many commentators interpret *dāt* to mean here a special ruling for this particular feast. The reading adopted here follows the LXX, with its inclusion of the negative "not," and after Haupt (p. 106), understands the verb *'ns* to mean "constrain," that is, either "to urge *to* action" or to "refrain *from* action." Not without merit, however, is the suggestion of John Gray (*The Legacy of Canaan*, 2d ed., VTS, V [Leiden: Brill, 1956], p. 226) that *kdt* is a cognate of the Aram. *kaddā* "a large vessel" or "flagon"; thus *whštyh kdt 'yn 'ns* could be translated "the drinking was by flagons without restraint."

each guest. Literally "man and man." The repetition of a single word to express totality ("all") emphatically or a distributive sense ("each, every") is quite characteristic of Esther, for example, i 22, ii 11, iii 4, 14, viii 9; see GKC § 123c.

9. *Vashti* (*waštî*). For variant spellings in the versions see p. XLII. Efforts to identify Vashti linguistically with Xerxes' strong-willed wife, Queen Amestris (see Herodotus IX. 108–13), have been unconvincing. (Amestris' father Otanes was, along with Darius, one of the seven princes who overthrew "the False Smerdis," the Magian who had usurped the throne in 522 B.C.; see Herodotus III. 61–84.) Haupt and others see *waštî* as a corruption of the Avestan *vahishta*, "the best," while Gehman (p. 322) regards Vashti as the feminine passive participle of Avestan *uas*, meaning "the beloved, the desired one." The name itself, then, may well be Persian; but from where the author of Esther got the name, whether from a particular tradition or from some list of Persian names, is impossible to say at present. Actually, the identity of Vashti is of crucial importance only to those modern scholars, such as Johannes Schildenberger, who have a strong apologetic interest in the *strictly* historical accurateness of Esther.

10. *was feeling high.* Literally "the heart was good" (see Judg xvi 25; I Sam xxv 36; I Kings viii 66; Prov xv 15). For "the heart" as the center of thinking and sensation, see IDB, II, s.v. "Heart."

Mehuman . . . Carcas. Indispensable as part of the harem (for life in the Assyrian harem, see E. F. Weidner's article in AfO 17 [1956], 264 f.), the eunuch also played an important role in the imperial administration, being active sometimes even in the struggles for succession to the throne.

Despite the work of twentieth-century scholars such as Haupt, Paton, and, more recently, Gehman (pp. 323–24) and J. Duchesne-Guillemin (*Muséon* 66 [1953], 105–8), we are not much closer to knowing the eunuchs' actual names and their meanings than were the scholars of the nineteenth century. For a graphic illustration of the confusion and corruption of these names in the ancient versions, see the Introduction, pp. XLII f. Haller, however, certainly has exceeded the evidence by insisting that the names were invented by the author of Esther. The name *Carcas,* for example, occurs in Tablet xxii of G. G. Cameron's *Persepolis Treasury Tablets.* Moreover, the presence of probable Persian elements as well as the total absence of any Greek elements in these names makes Persian, or Iranian, origins entirely possible. The lack of any evidence for Greek influence in these names is certainly significant for the dating of Esther; for as D. N. Freedman has observed to the writer, "If these names were mere creations without historic verisimilitude, then the case for a Hellenistic date would be advanced thereby. In other words, if this were a second-century composition, one might naturally expect there to be anachronism and plain errors just of this kind." All of which does not mean, of course, that if the names should prove to be Persian or Iranian in origin, then the seven eunuchs were necessarily historical personages: it would only prove the author's knowledge of or access to Persian names. The view of Dommershausen (p. 146) that personal names as well as numbers in Esther always have a symbolic significance is quite suspect. The AT omits the personal names in this verse just as it does in ii 14, 15, iv 5, and ix 7–9.

11. *wearing the royal turban.* Literally "with the turban of the kingdom." Made of blue and white cloth, it probably contained a tiara; see ii 17.

12. *refused to come.* Although Vashti is no more disobedient here than Esther is later on in refusing *to stay away* at the king's command (see iv 11), they provoke a very different response: Vashti raises the king's anger while Esther stirs his mercy.

became very angry . . . was quite incensed. See iii 5, v 9, vii 7, 10; once again parallelism, a stylistic feature so characteristic of Esther.

13. *the experts* (literally "wise men"), *who knew the laws.* Cf. Herodotus III. 31, where Cambyses consults learned men about the wisdom of his marrying his own sister. The MT reads "wise men who knew the times," thereby suggesting the court astrologers (see Gen xli 33, 39; Dan ii 27, v 15; Isa xliv 25, xlvii 10–15; Jer l 35, li 57; I Chron xii 32; also Herodotus I. 107, VII. 19, where magi are consulted by Astyages and Xerxes, respectively); but such men could hardly be regarded as "knowers of the law and government." (Striedl [p. 90], however, sees *dāt* and *dîn,* "law and government," used here not so much for their accuracy in describing the specialties of the wise men as for stylistic considerations, that is, the author's preference for alliteration.) The reading adopted here follows Haller and others who read *dātîm,* "laws," instead of *'ittîm,* "times."

14. What was said about the problem of personal names in the NOTE

on vs. 10 is just as applicable here, that is, there is no certainty about either their form or meaning. For details, the interested reader should consult Haupt (pp. 110–11), Paton (pp. 68–69), and Gehman (pp. 324–25). For these names as they appear in the versions, see Introduction, p. XLIII.

the seven princes. Cf. Ezra vii 14, which mentions that Artaxerxes also had seven advisers. The seven princes figure prominently in Herodotus where, their conspiracy against the False Smerdis successful (see NOTE on vs. 9 above), they enjoyed special privileges at the court (Herodotus III. 84; cf. Xenophon *Anabasis* I. 4, 6, and Josephus *Antiquities* XI. 31; see also HPE, pp. 92–93, 107–10). Ordinarily, the Persian king was physically inaccessible to the people, but these advisers were so trusted and intimately associated with him that they could "personally converse with him" (literally "saw the face of the king").

who sat first in the kingdom. That is, they were the chief ranking officials of the kingdom.

15. *what should be done.* Literally "what to do with." The infinitive with *lamed* is frequent in Esther (i 17, iv 2, vi 6, vii 8, viii 8), and, characteristic of later biblical books, is treated more freely; see Striedl, p. 75.

from a legal point of view (*kᵉdāt*). Literally "according to law" (cf. HPE, p. 119); this word has occasioned many suggestions. It can be read with the preceding verse, that is, "who sat first in the kingdom according to law" (so Haupt, Haller); it can be omitted, representing dittography with the preceding consonants in *bmlkwt* of vs. 14 (Wilhelm Rudolph, VT 4 [1954], 89); or considered emphatic (Ryssel and others); but, most likely, it is resumptive, being necessary after the long parenthetical expression of vss. 13b–14.

16. *not only the king.* Although this phrase is in the emphatic position in the Hebrew, Mehuman nevertheless shrewdly plays down the element of the king's personal grudge against the queen by suggesting that any action taken by him will be in the best interests of all his subjects.

17. *all the women . . . the queen.* Literally "when the matter of the queen shall go out."

18. *those ladies.* Literally "the princesses," i.e., including wives of the men assembled at the banquet.

shall show themselves obstinate. A most difficult verse, since *tō'marnâ*, "they shall say," has no direct object. The reading here follows Haller, who reads *tamreynâ*, Hiphil of *mārâ*.

19. *If it please the king.* Literally "if it be good unto the king"; a deferential, almost obsequious formula found frequently in Esther (iii 9, v 4, 8, vii 3, viii 5, ix 13), and elsewhere (Neh ii 5, 7; I Chron xiii 2).

cannot be revoked. Cf. viii 8, ix 27. Outside of the Old Testament (see Dan vi 8, 9, 12, 15), there is no evidence for this irrevocability of the Persian law (cf. Herodotus IX. 109; Plutarch *Artaxerxes.* 27). Certainly such a law seems inflexible and crippling to good government and, hence, improbable. In any case, as II Targum and other commentators have pointed out, Mehuman wanted to be sure that the decree could not be reversed later on, for he hardly would want to face the wrath of a reinstated Vashti.

Vashti. The omission of the title "queen" here, in contrast to vss. 9, 11, 12, 15, 16, 17, 18, is probably deliberate.

on a woman who is better than she. Mehuman does not necessarily limit the candidates to the already existing harem: that would not have been so exciting a prospect for the king. *Tob* can refer to either physical beauty or moral goodness, including "obedience." A shrewd adviser would certainly have preferred to use the admittedly vague "better," allowing the king to read into it whatever meaning he chose.

20. *decree (pithgām).* An Aramaic form going back to Pers. *paitigāma,* "word, communication"; see Gehman, pp. 325–26.

(extensive as it is) (kî rabbâ hî'). The Greek omits, which *may* indicate a later gloss. The antecedent of *hî'* could be the decree (Ehrlich), or the success of the order (Ryssel); but most scholars rightly see it as referring to the "kingdom," which would require the feminine pronoun.

regardless of their status. Literally "from great unto small," which can refer to social status (so the Greek), age, or size; the translation adopted here intends to include all three.

all women . . . shall show. Literally "all women . . . they shall give"; the use of the third person masculine plural, instead of the more correct feminine plural, is either an error or an expression of the author's attempts at archaizing (so Striedl, p. 76).

22. *sent dispatches.* See iii 13, viii 5. Under the Persian empire there was an excellent postal system (see Herodotus VIII. 98; Xenophon *Cyropaedia* VIII. 6, 17 f.; HPE, pp. 299–301); see also NOTE on iii 13.

in its own script . . . own language. A number of languages and scripts existed in the vast Persian empire; for photographs of royal decrees by Xerxes in Persian, Elamite, and Babylonian, see VBW, IV, p. 189.

whatever suited him. The MT has *klšwn 'mw* "according to the language of his people." This difficult phrase, omitted by the Greek, has occasioned considerable debate. Older translations and commentators, perhaps taking their clue from Neh xiii 23 f., understood it to mean that a man should speak his mother tongue to his foreign wife. S. Talmon (VT 13 [1963], 451) understands it to mean the male's right "to have the last word." C. C. Torrey, taking his clue from Aramaic where *mdbr* means "ruling" rather than "speaking," understands it to mean "and ruler over every tongue of his family" (HTR 37 [1944], 35). The reading followed here in our text is the one proposed long ago by Hitvig and adopted by many commentators, namely, *kāl šōweh 'immô*, "whatever suited him." *Šwh* is also found in iii 8, v 13, vii 4.

COMMENT

Like the masterful artist who conveys a clear impression with a few deft strokes of his brush, the author of Esther quickly sketches the setting for his story in his very first sentence. In it he answers the questions of *who* (vs. 1), *where* (vs. 2), *what* and *when* (vs. 3), and hints at three interests which will subsequently color his narrative, namely, the historic quality of the events he is describing (see NOTES on vss. 1, 2, 3); the pomp and power of the court (vss. 3–4); and, by implication, the king's character (vss. 3–4). The rest of the chapter, concerned primarily with the deposing of Queen Vashti, draws these three emphases in greater detail.

The MT does not say why this lavish banquet (vss. 3–4) was held. The LXX suggests it was to celebrate the king's marriage (vs. 5), while the AT has "to celebrate his deliverance." Many commentators, both past and present, find their clue in the phrase "in the third year of his reign," i.e., just about the time that Xerxes, having subjugated Egypt, assembled at Susa the influential people of his realm to make arrangements for his invasion of Greece (see Herodotus VII. 8). Possibly the purpose behind Xerxes' display of his wealth (vss. 3–5) was to give his influential guests confidence in his strength and resources to defeat the Greeks, rather than to give expression to his great pride. In any case, as Paton (p. 129) has correctly observed, "These speculations in regard to the reason for the feast are of interest only if one is convinced of the strictly historical character of the book." (For splendid photographs of the architecture, sculpture, and other arts of the Achaemenian days, see Roman Ghirshman, *The Arts of Ancient Iran*, pp. 129–277.)

The fateful party mentioned in vs. 5 is not to be confused with the preceding banquet of a hundred and eighty days (vs. 3). The Greek rightly preserves here a basic distinction between the two by calling the one held first a *dochē,* "banquet," and the second a *potos,* "drinking bout."

Women could be present at Persian meals (see Herodotus V. 18, IX. 110; Plutarch *Artaxerxes* V), but Queen Vashti chose to have a separate party for the women. We should understand the segregation of the sexes here in the narrative as a literary device of the author, whereby he sets the stage for the intoxicated king's request at his stag party (vs. 10).

The king's behavior in this instance (vss. 10–13) suggests one who was neither cold sober nor dead drunk; rather he was "feeling good"; and presumably so were his guests, a fact which may explain the rather absurd letter of which his advisers approve, a letter in which Queen Vashti is not even mentioned (vs. 22)!

The MT gives no reason for Vashti's refusal to answer the king's summons (vs. 12), thus opening the doors for speculation. Since she was specifically commanded to come with the royal turban (vs. 11), the Megilla, I and II Targums, and other ancient commentaries inferred that Vashti was commanded to wear *only* that, and was, in effect, commanded to appear stark naked; and so she refused. Modern interpreters all agree, however, that the king was in effect insisting that she appear fully attired, with her lovely turban. Since Josephus (*Antiquities* XI. 191) says that strangers were not allowed to look at the beauty of Persian wives, many commentators have seen Vashti's defiance as a modest and totally justifiable refusal to appear, even fully clad, before a group of drunken men. A few Christian scholars have gone so far as to say that by her refusal Vashti showed herself to be the only admirable person in the book, a view which may say more about the scholars than Vashti. Certainly Ehrlich misses the point in saying that the king was furious because Vashti had given no reason for refusing to come before him: from a literary point of view, Vashti *had* to be deposed, else how could the Jewish Esther have ascended the throne and saved her people? Then too, the Vashti incident is a splendid literary device to better acquaint the reader with Xerxes. (The whole incident is vaguely reminiscent of the account in Herodotus [I. 8–13] of how the Lydian king Candaules contrived to have his servant Gyges see his wife naked, so proud was Candaules of her beauty. For H. Ringgren's view that this story in Herodotus is related to an original Persian New Year Festival, see SEÅ 20 [1955], 21.

That the king should have been infuriated at his queen's defiance is just as understandable as his subsequent removal of her as queen; but that he should have brought into full play the communications system of the entire Persian empire for such a purpose is ridiculous. Then again, drunken men sometimes are ridiculous. There is much merit to T. H. Gaster's observation that we have in ch. i a "deliciously humorous tale. . . . What can the poor husbands do to save face and protect their authority but to have the king issue a formal decree, under full protocol" (JBL 69 [1950], 381). As D. N. Freedman has observed to the writer, "There is some irony in the fact that this decree by which the king establishes the supremacy of the male in his own household initiates a story whereby the king having got rid of one recalcitrant wife ends up with one who controls him completely." Then, too, in vss. 13–22 the author provides the reader with a knowledge of the extensive communications system as well as the irrevocability of royal edicts, all of which will figure prominently later on in the king's decrees as drawn up by Haman (iii 11–15) and Mordecai (viii 8–14). But above it all looms the fascinating figure of Xerxes, the mighty king, mastered by wine, defied by his queen, and ill-advised by his friends. Xerxes stands desperately in need of a good consort.

2. ESTHER IS CHOSEN QUEEN
(ii 1–18)

II ¹ Some time later, when King Xerxes' anger had subsided, he remembered*ᵃ* Vashti, and what she had done and what had been decreed against her. ² So the king's pages said, "Let beautiful young virgins be selected for the king, ³ and let the king appoint commissioners in all the provinces of his kingdom to gather together every beautiful young virgin to the acropolis of Susa, to the harem under the authority of Hegai*ᵇ*, the king's eunuch who is in charge of the women; and let him give them their beauty treatment. ⁴ Then, let the girl who most pleases the king be queen in place of Vashti." This advice appealed to the king, so he followed it.

⁵ Now there was in the acropolis of Susa a Jew whose name was Mordecai the son of Jair, son of Shimei, son of Kish, a Benjaminite; ⁶ he*ᶜ* had been carried away from Jerusalem with the exiles who had been deported with Jeconiah king of Judah, whom Nebuchadnezzar king of Babylon had taken into exile. ⁷ And he had reared his cousin*ᵈ* Hadassah (Esther, that is) since she had neither father nor mother. The girl was shapely and had a beautiful face. After her father and mother had died, *ᵉ*Mordecai adopted her*ᵉ*.

⁸ Later on, when the king's edict was promulgated and when many young girls were brought to the acropolis of Susa and placed in Hegai's custody, Esther was also taken to the palace and was entrusted to Hegai, who had charge of the women.

ᵃ LXX adds "no longer"; see NOTE.
ᵇ *Hg'* here, but *hgy* in vss. 8 and 15; see NOTE.
ᶜ MT "who"; see NOTE.
ᵈ OL and Vulg. "niece." LXX adds "daughter of Ameinadab," this name appearing also in ii 15 and ix 29 of LXX where MT has *'byḥyl*.
ᵉ⁻ᵉ LXX "he took her as a wife"; see NOTE.

9 The girl pleased him and gained his support so that he promptly gave her her beauty treatment and her delicacies, and he provided her with the seven special maids from the palace and transferred her and her maids to the best quarters of the harem. 10 *f*Esther had not said anything about her origins because Mordecai had forbidden her to do so; 11 and every day Mordecai used to walk about in front of the court of the harem so as to find out about Esther's well-being and progress.

12 Now when the turn came for each girl to go in to King Xerxes, after having been treated according to the regimen for women for twelve months (for this was the prescribed length for their treatment: six months' treatment with oil of myrrh, and six months with perfumes and other cosmetics for women), 13 when the girl was to go in to the king, she was given whatever she wanted to take with her when she left the harem for the king's apartment. 14 She went in in the evening; and the next morning she returned to the second harem to the custody of Shaashgaz*g*, the king's eunuch who had charge of the concubines. She never again went to the king unless the king desired her especially, and she was summoned by name.

15 Now, when the turn came for Esther, the daughter of Abihail the uncle of Mordecai *h*(who had adopted her as his own daughter)*h*, to go to the king, she asked for nothing beyond that which Hegai, the king's eunuch in charge of the women, had advised. Esther had charmed all who saw her; 16 so when Esther was taken to King Xerxes, to his royal apartment, that is, *i*in the tenth month, which is Tebeth*i*, in the seventh year of his reign, 17 the king loved Esther more than all his other wives; and more than all *j*the other girls*j* she won his favor and devotion so that he placed the royal turban on her head and made her queen in place of Vashti. 18 Then the king gave a great banquet for all his officials and courtiers (it was a banquet in

f AT omits vss. 10–13.
g LXX *gai* (as in vs. 8); LXXᴺ *sasgaios*. For name in versions, see Introduction, p. XLII.
h–h LXX omits; possibly a later gloss in Hebrew from vs. 7.
i–i LXX "in the twelfth month, which is Adar."
j–j MT "the virgins."

honor of Esther) and proclaimed a holiday for the provinces and distributed gifts as worthy of a king.

NOTES

ii 1. *Some time later.* Literally "after these things." An imprecise way of dating events, the phrase could mean anything from two hours to two years, the latter date being the *terminus ad quem* for those who accept the historical character of the story, since Xerxes departed for Greece two years after he had assembled the mighty of the realm at Susa to lay plans for the invasion of Greece (Herodotus VII. 8).

had subsided. Cf. vii 10. Like the flood in Gen viii 1 where the verb *škk* is also used, the king's overpowering and destructive anger finally subsided.

remembered Vashti. That is, the king remembered her *with affection.* The preceding phrase "when King Xerxes' anger had subsided" suggests that the king may have had some "morning after" regrets about his conduct toward Vashti (so Josephus *Antiquities* XI. 195, I and II Targums, and many modern commentators). But the Greek translator, failing to see the three phrases "he remembered Vashti," "and what she had done," "and what had been decreed against her" as parallel to one another, understood the last two phrases as explanations of the first phrase; hence he concluded that the king "remembered Vashti *no longer."*

2. *pages.* Literally "the young men who ministered to him"; cf. vi 3, 5. Not his friends (so Josephus and the OL), but his personal attendants who regularly waited upon him and who were best able to see, and most likely to suffer by, the king's discontent. For a relief dating from the time of Darius, Xerxes' father, showing a beardless youth holding perfume in one hand and a towel in the other, see VBW, IV, p. 192.

let . . . be selected. Literally "let them seek." The use of the third person plural form of the verb in an impersonal sense is very frequent in Aramaic, so the LXX's "let there be sought out" is quite correct here. The pages' proposal is made more interesting for the reader by their use of direct address (cf. also iii 11, v 5, vi 3–5, vii 8–9). But even here the formalities of court etiquette are preserved, for the pages use the formal third person rather than the second person when speaking to the king. Only Haman in iii 8 and Esther in vii 3 presume to address the king in the second person singular.

beautiful young virgins. Literally "young women, virgins, agreeable of appearance"; cf. Deut xxii 23; Judg xxi 12 for "young virgins."

3. *commissioners.* P^{e}qîdîm also appears in the Joseph Cycle (Gen xli 34), a story which exerted a strong influence on the writer of Esther (see Introduction, p. LII).

every beautiful young virgin. Literally "each girl, virgin, fair of appearance"; cf. GKC, § 117*d*.

the harem. Literally "the house of the women"; cf. ii 9, 11, 13, 14. The harem was within the acropolis, but that is about all we can say with certainty about its location. Many modern commentaries have followed Dieulafoy, the excavator of Susa in 1884–86, who located the harem in the northwestern corner of the palace (*Revue des Études Juives* [1888], pp. 255–56), but it is best to regard Dieulafoy's identification of various sites within the Susan acropolis with considerable suspicion for two very good reasons. First, as Hoschander (p. 73) has rightly pointed out, the palace in which Xerxes resided had been destroyed by fire and was rebuilt by Artaxerxes II, a fact which in itself is not damning provided that the excavator is in complete control of the pottery and stratigraphy of his site. But, and this is the second major reason, Dieulafoy's excavations were conducted during the embryonic stages of scientific Near Eastern archaeology, that is, long before W. F. Albright and Kathleen Kenyon had made their great contributions respectively to pottery chronology and stratigraphy.

Hegai. The name is somewhat reminiscent of Xerxes' eunuch *'egias* (see Herodotus IX. 33). For variants in the versions, see Introduction, p. XLII.

and let him give. Literally "and to give." For the use of the infinitive absolute in later biblical books to continue the tense-value of the preceding verb, see Joüon, GHB, § 123*x*.

their beauty treatment. Literally "their massage." For details on the treatment, see NOTES on vs. 12.

4. *let the girl . . . be queen.* Not "let the girl . . . reign" as Paton and others have translated it: Esther was called queen, but she did not rule; even after being queen for five years (see iii 7), Esther still occupied a weak and precarious position—in her own eyes at least—for she was most uncertain about her fate and her powers over the king (see iv 11).

who most pleases the king. Literally "who is good in the king's eyes"; cf. vs. 19. Presumably he would have been pleased by more than one candidate, but it was the one who pleased him *the most* who would become queen.

This advice appealed to. Literally "the word was good in the eyes of." The dangers of a mechanical, one-for-one translation of the Hebrew are seen in this verse. The Hebrew idiom "be good in the eyes of" appears twice in this verse and must certainly be translated differently in each

case. In this case, the proposal seemed "sound" rather than "pleasant."
The king recognized the sensible political advice behind this suggestion:
every king must have a queen. That his harem would be enlarged and
rejuvenated was a very pleasant, but incidental, by-product of a political
and social necessity.

5. In the MT "a Jewish man" is in the emphatic position, no doubt
because vss. 5–7, which introduce the hero and heroine to the reader,
interrupt abruptly the story of the king's search for a queen (so Dommershausen, p. 41; but see Striedl, p. 99). Whether Mordecai lived in
the acropolis or just visited there is not known; in contrast to A 2,
which had Mordecai living there and serving in the court of the king,
the MT says simply that he "sat at the King's Gate" (see NOTE on vs.
19).

Mordecai. A good Babylonian name, *mord^akay* is the hebraized form of
mardukâ whose theophorous element is Marduk. Although the MT
form is corrupt (see Introduction, p. L), it is less corrupt than Marduk's
name as preserved in Jer 1 2, *m^erodāk*. That a religious Jew should
have had such an unhebraic, not to say idolatrous, name has been of
some concern to scholars. D. C. Siegfried insisted that the name is
Aramaic and means "pure myrrh"; others, like Haupt, have seen in the
name clear vestiges of a Babylonian New Year Festival (see Introduction,
pp. XLVII f.). Streane believes that the originally theophorous meaning
may have "been forgotten," that is, "just as the name Martin, for example,
St. Martin of Tours, is completely devoid of associations with its
etymological source, Mars" (p. 12). In support of this last position, it
should be noted that a certain Mordecai was one of the first of the
faithful exiles returning with Zerubbabel (cf. Ezra ii 2; Neh vii 7).
Probably most correct, however, is D. N. Freedman's suggestion to the
writer that Mordecai was his "Gentile" name over against his synagogue
name which, like Zerubbabel's, has not survived. In the Diaspora,
Jewish kings as well as less important personages such as Daniel and
his friends (see Dan i 6–7) had both Babylonian and Hebrew names.
Concerning Mordecai's possible historicity, see Introduction, p. L.

the son of Jair. Unlike his son, Mordecai's father had a good Hebrew
name; cf. Num xxxii 41; Deut iii 14; Josh xiii 30; Judg x 3.

son of Shimei, son of Kish, a Benjaminite. Following the lead of
Josephus and the Targums, most commentators rightly see these names
as those of distant, well-known ancestors of Mordecai, rather than of
his grandfather and great-grandfather. Thus Shimei represents the one
who cursed David in II Sam xvi 5, and Kish refers to the father of Saul
(I Sam ix 1–2). This genealogy argues somewhat for the historicity of
Mordecai. Had he been a totally fictitious character, the author of
Esther could easily have made him a direct descendant of Saul, thus

setting up a perfect parallel with Haman, who was a descendant of Agag (see NOTE on iii 1).

6. *he* (literally "who") *had been deported with . . . king of Judah.* On both grammatical and exegetical grounds (see NOTE on vs. 5), the relative pronoun *'ašer* modifies Mordecai, not Kish, and immediately raises a problem in chronology (see COMMENT).

Jeconiah (*yᵉkonyâ*). For three variant spellings of the name, see Jer xxii 24, xxiv 1, xxvii 20. Known also as Jehoiachin, Jeconiah was carried off by Nebuchadnezzar in the deportation of 597 B.C. (II Kings xxiv 6–17). Actually, he was the last king of Judah, because Zedekiah, who succeeded him, was only a regent, and the royal line of David was counted through Jehoiachin, not Zedekiah.

Nebuchadnezzar (*nᵉbûkadne'ṣṣar*). The first two *r*'s of the Babylonian form *nabu-kudurriuṣur* experienced a phonetic shift in Hebrew here (see also II Chron xxxvi 6; Dan i 1; Jer xxvii 6; Ezra ii 1; II Kings xxiv 1; Neh vii 6) in that the *r* is either dissimulated to *n* because of the final *r,* or assimilated to *n* because of the initial *n,* or both. But see Jer xxi 2, where the *r* is preserved.

7. *had reared.* The participle used here means "a foster father" in Num xi 12; Isa xlix 23.

Hadassah. Although P. Jensen (WZKM 6 [1892], 209) saw the word as related to *hadāš-ša-tum,* a synonym of *kallatu,* "a bride," most scholars follow the Targums which interpret it to mean "myrtle" (see Isa xli 19, lv 13; Zech i 8, 10, 11): "because," says II Targum, "as the myrtle spreads fragrance in the world, so did she spread good works. And for this cause she was called in the Hebrew language Hadassah because the righteous are likened to myrtle." The name is missing from all the versions except the Vulgate. Bardtke is correct in insisting that efforts to equate Hadassah with Atossa, daughter of Cyrus and wife of Darius (Herodotus III. 133), have been useless.

There is, of course, no great difficulty in believing that a Jewish girl could be part of a Persian king's harem. When it came to foreign wives, kings could be quite broad-minded; for example, the Assyrian king Sennacherib had in his harem a Palestinian wife, the famous Zakutu-Naqiya.

Esther. Like the prophet Daniel in Dan i 7, Esther had two names, one Hebraic and one non-Hebraic, the latter being derived from either the Pers. *stâra,* "star," or Ishtar, the Babylonian goddess of Love (so Jensen, WZKM 6 [1892], 70); see also Introduction, p. LI. Esther may have been the royal name given her at the time of her coronation (so Anderson); Bardtke (p. 300) sees Hadassah as belonging to the Mordecai tradition cycle, and Esther to another tradition.

adopted her. Literally "took her to himself for a daughter." The

LXX and *Megilla* 13*a* both have "he took her to himself for a wife."
The problem here clearly lies with the Greek, not with the Hebrew,
for the latter makes perfectly good sense. Since Esther was taken to the
king's harem (ii 8), she was obviously regarded by all as a virgin (see
vs. 2). Haupt (p. 116) offered the ingenious suggestion that the LXX's
translation "for a wife" represents the misreading of *lbt*, "for a
daughter," as *lbyt*, which in the Talmud can mean either "for a house"
or "for a wife."

8. *Later on*. Literally "and it came to pass" (cf. NOTE on i 1); resumes
the thought of vs. 4.

king's edict was promulgated. Literally "king's command and edict
were reported."

many young girls. No number is given, but there could have been
many, for example, Josephus says four hundred virgins were brought.
According to Plutarch, the Persian king Artaxerxes had "three hundred
and sixty concubines, all women of the highest beauty" (*Artaxerxes*
XXVII. 5).

palace. Literally "the house of the king." Here the phrase does not
mean "the king's private apartment" (ii 13), but rather the entire
palace complex (iv 14). In the present verse, the clause "when many
young girls were brought to the acropolis of Susa, and placed in
Hegai's custody" is a precise parallel with "Esther also was taken to
the palace and was entrusted to Hegai, who had charge of the women."
Since "palace" is parallel here with "acropolis," it must be understood as
"palace complex" or "palace" rather than as "the king's private apartment."

Esther was also taken. In sharp contrast to C 25–30 of the Additions
(see Appendix I), the MT gives no indication that Esther went to Susa
under any coercion, or even reluctantly. Nor does the verb used here
(*lqḥ*) suggest anything unpleasant, since it was also used by the author
in vs. 15 to describe Mordecai's adoption of Esther.

9. *gained his support* (*wattiśśāʾ ḥesed lᵉpānāyw*). The verb used here
is *nśʾ*, "to carry, to gain," not *mṣʾ*, "to find." *Nśʾ* and *mṣʾ* are not exact
synonyms in Esther; the former is more active while the latter more
passive in character, for example, when Esther speaks to the king
face to face (vii 3, viii 5), she uses the flattering phrase "find favor,"
thereby stressing her dependence upon the king's good will. But when
the writer of Esther describes Esther's effect upon others (ii 15, 17,
v 2), he says she "gained favor," i.e., she herself had done something to
deserve it. Also in D 8 of the Additions, *God* changed the attitude of
the king (see also Gen xxxix 21; Dan i 9); but in the MT it is Esther
herself who earned the favor of Hegai, the king, and of all who saw
her.

he promptly gave her. Literally "he hastened to give to her." The twelve-month regimen itself (vs. 12) could not be shortened, but its initiation could be hastened or delayed. The shrewd eyes of Hegai, who knew better than anyone else the king's taste in women, saw in Esther the likely successor to Vashti. Thus to satisfy the king, and perhaps to gain the potential queen's good will, Hegai promptly began her twelve-month program.

and her delicacies. Cf. ii 18, ix 19, 22; Neh viii 10, 12; Dan i 5, 10. Literally "her portions." Unlike Daniel and Judith, Esther did not refuse—at least not in the MT—these delicacies, many of which were presumably non-kosher. That Esther was able to conceal her Jewishness, that is, her adherence to the Jewish religion, clearly indicates that she did not observe all the Jewish dietary laws, the claims of II Targum and C 28 of the Additions notwithstanding.

"Massage" and "delicacies" precede the infinitive "to give," making an Aramaism; cf. GKC, § 142 *f*, n. 2.

the seven special maids. Cf. D 2. Prefixing the definite article to the Hebrew noun (literally "the delicate ones") and its adjective suggests that these seven girls were something special, possibly attendants deliberately reserved by Hegai for the most likely successor to Vashti. For a cylinder-seal scene of a Persian lady being waited on, see VBW, IV, p. 186.

10. *her origins.* Literally "her people and her descent." Noting that these two Hebrew words do not appear together elsewhere in the MT, Hoschander (p. 108) argued that *mwldth,* "and her descent," was originally *wdth,* "and her religion"—a tempting theory, but totally without support from the versions. The phrase "her people and her descent" occurs in reverse order in vs. 20, thus forming a chiasm, or crisscross pattern, which serves as an *inclusio* to bind together the subject matter of vss. 10–20. Another clear instance of chiastic structure serving as an *inclusio* is where "if I have found favor with the king and if it please the king" in v 8 is rendered as "if it please the king and if I have found favor before him" in viii 5. Here the chiasm frames the narrative of Esther's crisis. For other instances of chiastic construction, see Dommershausen *passim.*

Mordecai. In the emphatic position, thus reaffirming the continued subordination of Esther to Mordecai.

11. *to find out about.* Literally "to know." In the absence of any details in the MT, many commentators have offered their speculations as to how Mordecai got his information about Esther in the harem. Some have argued that Mordecai must have been a eunuch, otherwise how could he have had access to her? The word *lāda'at,* "to know," however, does not necessarily imply that Mordecai *saw* her. Other

Gate of King Xerxes at Persepolis.

Darius and his son Xerxes giving audience before two fire altars (6th-5th century B.C.).

Symbol of the Persian god Ahura-mazda, from the east door of the Tripylon at Persepolis (6th-5th century B.C.).

Stone relief showing a Chorasmian with his horse, from the east stairway of the Apadana at Persepolis.

Stone relief of Persian and Medean guards, from the stairway of the Tripylon at Persepolis.

Gold drinking cup in the form of a winged lion (5th century B.C. Achaemenian).

Gold ring, with antelope, found at Persepolis.

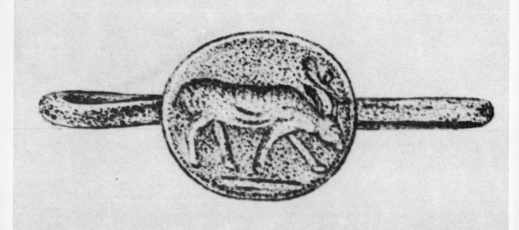

Aerial view of Susa.

Aerial view of Persepolis.

Plan of Persepolis (*opposite*).

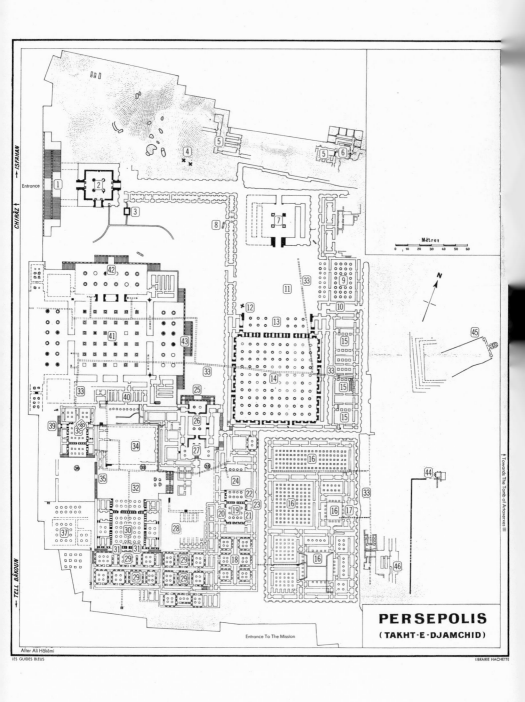

CHIRĀZ → ISFHAN

← TELL BĀKOUN

Entrance

Towards The Tomb of Artaxerxes III

Mètres
0 10 20 30 40 50 60

N

Entrance To The Mission

After Ali Hâkêmi

PERSEPOLIS
(TAKHT-E-DJAMCHID)

LES GUIDES BLEUS   LIBRAIRIE HACHETTE

Illustrated *Megillah* scroll of the book of Esther, from Prague ca. 1700.

scholars have suggested that Mordecai may have used a eunuch here as an intermediary, just as he did in iv 2–16. Better yet, as Ryssel has noted (p. 402), if one considers the care, perseverance, and cleverness that some men apply to realizing their goals, then there is no problem: Mordecai did see Esther. But the best interpretation of all is that the writer left out the details as not essential to his main purpose, which was to affirm the fact that Mordecai kept in contact with Esther.

and progress. Literally "and what was done with her," that is, her twelve-month beauty program (see vs. 12).

12. *turn.* "Turn" is not to be understood here in the sense of Herodotus III. 69, where the wives of the False Smerdis took turns sleeping with the king; rather the LXX has correctly preserved the meaning of the Hebrew word *tōr* by using Greek word *kairos,* which means "the critical moment," "the opportune time." After all, unless the king was highly pleased with her, she might never again come to him (cf. vs. 14).

after having been treated. Literally "at the end of its being to her." Ehrlich (p. 113) may be correct in calling the phrase "unhebraic," but he is not justified in deleting it from his Hebrew text.

according to the regimen (*kdt*). Spelled out in the parenthetical expression as being six months of massage with oil of myrrh and six months with balsam and other unspecified cosmetics.

13. *when.* Literally "and in this." Not "in this way" (so RSV), but as correctly translated by the LXX as "and then," where it *resumes* the narrative which was interrupted by the long explanatory remark in vs. 12.

whatever she wanted. Literally "the all which she should say." "Whatever" is in the emphatic position in the MT, thereby underscoring the fact that she got *anything* she wanted, be it clothes or jewelry. Whether she had to return this the next morning or could keep it as a *mōhar,* "wedding gift," is not known.

for the king's apartment. Literally "for the king's house." Since she went to his sleeping quarters, "palace" would be too comprehensive a word here; cf. NOTE on "palace" in vs. 8.

14. *second harem* (*bêt hannāšîm šēnî*). Here, as in so many other places in Esther, there are a host of difficulties concerning numbers. Grammatically unrelated to the rest of the verse, *šēnî* was omitted by Haupt, but the Hebrew had a word which was read as *haššēnî*(*t*), "the second," by the LXX. Ryssel and others have proposed reading *šēnît,* "a second time," but that makes little sense. The reading adopted here understands the "second harem" to mean either a second group of women, that is, the concubines, or a separate wing in the harem complex. This interpretation is all the more plausible since the "second" harem was under

someone else's supervision, namely, Shaashgaz. There is little hope of archaeology solving this problem (see NOTE on "harem" in vs. 3).

unless . . . summoned by name. A difficult and frustrating situation for the king's concubines, and even for Queen Esther (see iv 11); Xerxes' brides, however, were still quite fortunate in comparison to those of King Shekriya in *A Thousand and One Nights:* they were executed immediately after the wedding night!

15. *the daughter of Abihail.* Cf. ix 29. A popular name in the Old Testament for both sexes (cf. Num iii 35; I Chron ii 29, v 14; II Chron xi 18), Abihail is corrupted to Ameinadab in the extant Septuagint manuscript, but the reading *Abiel* in the OL clearly attests to the existence at one time of a Greek transliteration quite similar to the Hebrew. (This assertion is based on the universally accepted view that the OL is a translation of the Septuagint, while the Vulgate is based on the Hebrew; see Introduction, p. LXIV.) Totally without support is Haupt's assertion that both names are fictitious, invented by the writer of Esther to give the impression that Esther's father was well known.

Hegai. Since all the ancient versions but the Vulgate were based on the Septuagint rather than the Hebrew (cf. above), it is totally predictable that Hegai, which the LXX omits here, is mentioned only in the Vulgate, and not in the OL or Ethiopic.

beyond that which Hegai . . . had advised. Apparently some of the candidates used this occasion to gratify their own personal whims in jewelry and clothes; Esther, however, was wise enough to dress according to the king's taste rather than her own. Trusting Hegai's knowledge of the king's preference in feminine attire, Esther not only made herself more appealing to the king, but she also showed herself to be humble and cooperative, two qualities conspicuously lacking in Vashti. Older commentators saw in her actions an expression of either her great modesty or her confidence in her own unadorned natural beauty.

16. *to his royal apartment.* Literally "to the house of the kingdom." Synonymous with "king's apartment" in vs. 13, the phrase is apparently used to avoid repetition with "the king" (so Ryssel).

in the tenth month, which is Tebeth. A *hapax legomenon, ṭēbēt* is December–January, and is derived from the Babylonian word, meaning "sinking in" or "muddy" (BDB, p. 372).

seventh year. The MT does not say why it took four years after the deposing of Vashti to find her successor. Those who maintain the historicity of Esther often cite the fact that Xerxes would have been away in Greece for two of those four years.

17. *all the other girls.* Literally "all the virgins," that is, all his new wives, the recent candidates for the title of queen.

favor (*ḥn*) *and devotion* (*wḥsd*). It is possible that we have hendiadys here and should translate this as "his devoted favor."

18. (*it was a banquet in honor of Esther*). Literally "Esther's banquet." Grammatically unrelated to the rest of the clause in Hebrew, the phrase "Esther's banquet" is probably corrupt. The LXX has instead "and celebrated the marriage of Esther."

proclaimed (literally "he made") *a holiday. Hᵃnāḥâ*, which occurs only here and seems to be patterned after the causative infinitive in Aramaic (see Joüon GHB, § 88*Lb*), literally means "a causing to rest." Not surprisingly, almost every translator interprets it differently: "holiday" (Vulgate); "remission of taxes" (I Targum and RSV); "amnesty" (Greek). Perhaps it is relevant that when the False Smerdis ascended the throne, he granted his subjects freedom from taxation *and* military service for a period of three years (Herodotus III. 67).

gifts. Literally "portions"; the meaning here is unclear; cf. Amos v 11; Jer xl 5; and Gen xliii 34; also Xenophon *Cyropaedia* VIII. 2, and *Anabasis* I. 9, 22.

COMMENT

If Xerxes had any "morning after" regrets about his treatment of Vashti (see NOTE on vs. 1), the irrevocability of his edict (see i 19) effectively prevented him from reinstating her. The suggestion of his pages (vss. 2–4) that he launch a large-scale search for a new queen must have struck him as both necessary and appealing. Certainly the story of this search was quite appealing to the writer of Esther; for unlike the AT, which tells the story in an obvious hurry to get it over with (see textual note *ᶠ*), the author of Esther dwells fondly on the details of the selection process (vss. 12–14).

Virtually every modern commentator has alluded to the legendary elements of Xerxes' search and its final results, and especially its similarities to *A Thousand and One Nights*. In that well-known tale King Shekriya enjoyed a different bride every night, only to have her executed the next morning; it was Scheherazade who finally captured his imagination and heart, thereby winning life and queenship for herself, and the post of vizier for her father (cf. Est viii 2, 15). Whether or not *A Thousand and One Nights* has a historical basis, historical parallels for such a quest as we have in Esther *are* found in Byzantium and China (see Bardtke, pp. 295–96), not to mention I Kings i 1–4, where a similar search was made to find a girl suitable for the aging King David. But it is almost gratuitous to say that no number of historical parallels can establish the historicity of this particular phase of the Esther story. Ringgren is probably closer to the truth when he asserts that the writer of Esther is writing legends here and nothing more (p. 383).

Fortunately for Esther, a beautiful face and figure were the only qualifications for the virginal candidates (vs. 2); she would have been ruled out from the start had Xerxes followed the practice cited by Herodotus (I. 135, III. 84, VII. 61), namely, that Achaemenian kings could marry women only from one of seven noble Persian families.

The story of the king's search is interrupted by vss. 5–6, which briefly introduce the hero and the heroine, both of whom have non-Hebraic as well as idolatrous names (see NOTES and Introduction, pp. L f.). Mordecai's genealogical origins (vs. 5) are of no little concern to the author, for he wishes to establish that Mordecai is a descendant of Kish, whose son, Saul, conducted an inconclusive campaign to exterminate all the Amalekites (see I Sam xv). Haman, the villain of the story, is of course a descendant of the Amalekites (see NOTE on iii 1), and therein lay the basis for the antipathy between the two. But apart from establishing Esther as Mordecai's cousin, the author is not concerned with her genealogical lines; rather it is the lines of her face and figure (vs. 7) that are most important.

Mordecai's presence in Susa is explained, in part, by noting that he had first gone to Babylon with King Jeconiah in the deportation of 597 B.C. (see NOTE on vs. 6), but that raises a serious problem in chronology. If Mordecai had been only one year old in 597 B.C., he would have been about 115 years old in the third year of Xerxes (i 3), and about 119 years old when Esther became queen (cf. vs. 6). Lest it be argued that some men do retain their physical and intellectual vigor to quite an advanced age, for example, Moses (see Deut xxxiv 7), it should be countered that if Esther was even forty years younger than her cousin Mordecai (ii 7), she still would have been in her sixties when she captivated the king and outstripped all her competitors. Older commentators, seeing the chronological problems, argued that the relative pronoun at the beginning of vs. 6 referred to Kish rather than to Mordecai, or that the phrase "he had been carried away" really meant "the ancestors of Mordecai had been carried away" as in Gen xlvi 27, where Joseph's sons are said to have come to Egypt *with* Jacob. Commentators of the twentieth century, however, tend to view the whole matter as either a chronological blunder or, more politely, a "telescoping of history" as Anderson (p. 841) calls it, such as is found in Ezra iv 6; Dan i 21, v 30, vi 1; or Tob xiv 15. Haller, taking his clue from the Septuagint, where the phrase "with the exiles who had been deported with Jeconiah king of Judah" is missing, deletes it from his Hebrew text; but this does not really solve the problem. The AT solves the problem nicely for its readers by omitting the entire verse.

That Esther was chosen queen was not just a matter of good luck. Unlike some beautiful women, she did not rely exclusively on her good looks. Esther did not just "find favor"; she earned it (see NOTE on vs. 9). She won the respect and affection of *all* who came in contact with her (vs. 15), a fact which will receive additional comment later. Whether Hegai, who was in charge of the women, gave Esther preferential treatment (vs. 9) out of genuine affection and respect or out of self-interest is impossible to say. He may not have been above feathering his own nest by ingratiating himself with the probable future queen. In any case, when Esther's turn came to go in to the king, she did not use the occasion to gratify her own personal whims in jewelry and clothes; rather she dressed according to the advice of Hegai (vs. 15), who knew better than anyone else the king's taste in women.

Esther wanted to become queen (see NOTE on "Esther also was taken" in vs. 8). Apart from her own not inconsiderable efforts, she realized that goal because of the support and counsel of others. Mordecai helped, Hegai helped, but the really crucial question is whether or not God helped her. Certainly the author of Esther nowhere explicitly says so; but Mordecai's final argument persuading Esther to intercede for her people certainly implies as much: "It's possible that you came to the throne for just such a time as this" (iv 14; see also NOTE). Although God is not explicitly mentioned there (see, however, NOTE on "from another quarter" in iv 14), faith in the Providence of God seems to be implied. (For the role of God in Esther, see Introduction, pp. XXXII–XXXIV.) There can be no doubt, of course, that for the author of the Greek Additions

Esther's marriage was all part of the Divine Plan; see especially F 1 ("this is God's doing" and F 3).

One final point must be made. If a man can be judged by the friends he keeps, he can also be judged by the enemies he has; and, significantly, *everyone* had a good impression of Esther (vs. 15). For her to have accomplished this must have involved some "compromises" in the area of religion: a Judith or a Daniel could never have won the good will of all. In order for Esther to have concealed her ethnic and religious identity (see vs. 10) in the harem, she must have eaten (see NOTE on vs. 9), dressed, and lived like a Persian rather than an observant Jewess. Even the Jewish author of a Midrash felt compelled to justify Esther's conduct here: "Mordecai thought to himself: how is it possible that this righteous maiden should be married to a non-Israelite? It must be because some great calamity is going to befall Israel who will be delivered through her" (quoted by Solomon Goldman in *The Five Megilloth,* p. 204); see also C 25–30. The Esther of the MT was neither a Judith nor a Daniel (cf. Dan i 8–15), Jews who had to display their Judaism regardless of the consequences.

Esther had been commanded by Mordecai to conceal her Jewishness (ii 10); but why she concealed it so successfully is uncertain. Possibly she was afraid of lessening her chances of becoming queen; but, more likely, the plot and literary effect demanded that her Jewish identity remain unknown, at least to Haman. Wildeboer's observation, however, that "Esther is certainly worldliwise, but not honorable" (p. 181), is rather unfair and fails to take into consideration the complexities of life in the Golah. In this life the same individual may be called "fanatic" or "saint," "wise" or "compromiser" by different people; in any case, the description is not fact but a value judgment.

3. MORDECAI FOILS A PLOT AGAINST THE KING
(ii 19–23)

II 19 [a]Now when various[b] virgins were being gathered together and Mordecai [c]was sitting at the King's Gate[c] 20 (Esther had not revealed her ethnic origins because Mordecai had so instructed her[d]; for Esther still obeyed Mordecai just as she had [e]when she was being raised[e] by him), 21 at that time when Mordecai was sitting at the King's Gate, Bigtan and Teresh, two of the king's eunuchs who guarded the threshold, were angry with the king, and so they planned to assassinate King Xerxes. 22 The plot, however, became known to Mordecai, who disclosed it to Queen Esther who, in turn, informed the king in Mordecai's name. 23 When the plot was investigated and its existence confirmed, then [f]the two conspirators[f] were hanged on the gallows; and the whole affair was recorded in the daily record in the king's presence.

[a] AT omits vss. 19–23.
[b] Reading *šnwt*, instead of *šnyt*, "a second time"; see NOTE.
[c-c] LXX "served in the king's court"; see NOTE.
[d] LXX adds "to fear God and to do his commandments"; see NOTE.
[e-e] Reading *beʾāmnāh*, instead of *beʾomnâ*; see NOTE.
[f-f] MT "the two of them."

NOTES

ii 19. *various virgins*. Verse 19 is one of the most difficult verses in all of Esther, primarily because of the word *šēnît*, "a second time." Paton's detailed summaries (pp. 186–87) of the interpretations of dozens of scholars proves conclusively only one thing: there are almost as many different explanations for *šēnît* as there are commentators on it, a clear indication that not enough evidence is available to make a certain judgment. Significantly, the LXX omits the matter of the virgins entirely, and says simply "and Mordecai was serving in the court [MT 'was sitting at the gate'] of the king." The passage could, of course, refer to a second contingent of girls who arrived too late, that is, after Esther had already been given the crown (so Bardtke and others). More likely, as Grotius long ago suggested, we have here *retrogressio*, that is, the author uses here the phrase "when virgins were being gathered" in the sense of "at that time" (cf. vs. 21), that is, in those days when various virgins were being assembled, referring to that very collection of which Esther herself had been a part. The reading adopted here, *šōnôt*, "various," for *šēnît*, "a second time" (as the Dead Sea scrolls clearly illustrate, to confuse *y* and *w* is very easy) follows the emendation of Ehrlich, and understands vss. 19–20 to be a parallel statement to vss. 8–10. Ringgren's observation (p. 385) that we have here an incomplete joining of the Esther and Mordecai motifs is not without merit; certainly vss. 19–20 seem to be a doublet of vss. 8–10.

at the King's Gate. According to Xenophon *Cyropaedia* VIII. 1, 6 and Herodotus III. 120, officials had to stay at the gate of the royal palace. See Xerxes' elaborate gateway with sphinxes at Persepolis on Plate 1.

Starting here and continuing thereafter (ii 21, iii 2, v 9, vi 10, 12) where the Hebrew has "at the King's Gate," the LXX has "in the king's court." This contradiction, which also occurs in A 2 and 12, undoubtedly originated in the Greek, where an early copyist read *aulē*, "court," instead of *pulē*, "gate."

20. Verse 20 is a parenthetical aside which helps to explain why Mordecai continues to sit at the gate after Esther has been made queen, that is, she has concealed the fact that she is related to him.

Mordecai had so instructed her. Although the MT undeniably means that Esther obeyed Mordecai by concealing her ethnic (and, in effect, her religious) identity, the LXX piously, and characteristically (see Introduction, pp. xxxii–xxxiii), amplifies the meaning by adding "to fear God and to do his commandments" and "she did not change her way of life."

when she was being raised by him. Literally "during her upbringing with him"; the proposed reading of *beʾāmnāh* instead of *beʾomnâ* (after G. R. Driver, VT 4 [1954], 235) is also in accord with the LXX, Vulgate, and I and II Targums. The continuing obedience of Esther to Mordecai is crucial to the plot; cf. iv 8–17.

21. *at that time.* Literally "in those days." Of no value whatsoever for dating purposes, the phrase simply resumes the narrative interrupted by vs. 20.

Bigtan and Teresh. Cf. vi 2; for these names as they appear in the versions, see Introduction, p. xlii. While *bigtān* here and *bigtānāʾ* of vi 2 are undoubtedly the same person, he should not be identified with *bigtā'* of i 10, as Streane has done. Bardtke may be exceeding the evidence here in claiming that the names serve only to increase "the historical believability" of the narrative (p. 312), but he is quite correct in pointing out that it is an open question as to where most of the Persian names in Esther come from. See, however, Introduction, p. LIX.

who guarded the threshold. Cf. II Kings xxv 18; Jer lii 24. Possibly these are the men who guarded the king's private apartment (Herodotus III. 77, 118).

to assassinate. Literally "to send the hand against"; cf. iii 6; Gen xxxvii 22; I Sam xxiv 7, 11.

22. *The plot.* Literally "the word" or "thing," which the LXX rightly translates as "plot" (*epiboulē*).

who disclosed it to Queen Esther. The MT does not indicate how Mordecai got the word of the plot to Esther. Older discussions on whether or not Mordecai was a eunuch are quite irrelevant here: the Hebrew does not say he *saw* or spoke directly with her in the harem but only that "he made it known" or "disclosed" (*ywgd*) it to her.

23. *on the gallows.* Literally "on the wood." Cf. Josh x 26. The translation is not completely certain. To be sure, Xerxes did impale offenders on stakes (see Herodotus III. 125, 159, also IV. 43), but the height of "the wood"—at least the one built by Haman for Mordecai (seventy-five feet high in v 14 and vii 9)—argues against "the wood" as "impaling stake." See IDB, II, s.v. "Hanging."

the daily record. Cf. I Kings xv 7. Literally "book of the Things of the Days." That Persian kings kept such annals has long been known, for example, Artaxerxes in Ezra iv 15. In some such book Xerxes recorded the names of the men who served him well in order to reward them (Herodotus VII. 100, VIII. 85, 90).

in the king's presence. Literally "before the king." Actually, whether the phrase means "in the king's presence" (Ryssel), "kept in the king's apartment" (Paton), or "at the king's direction" (Anderson) is almost beside the point. The humiliation of Haman in vi 1–12, which is a high point of the plot, requires that Mordecai's efforts go unrewarded at the time.

COMMENT

In contrast to A 1, the MT does not fix the point at which Mordecai learned of the plot against the king (see NOTE on "at that time" in vs. 21). By giving no reason for the anger of Bigtan and Teresh, the MT allows translators and commentators to speculate on why they hated the king. The LXX adds "because Mordecai had been promoted," which makes good sense in the LXX since Mordecai was a member of the court (so A 2 and 12); but it is contrary to the MT since Mordecai was not promoted until later (vi 3, viii 1–2, 15). Prior to his promotion, Mordecai sat "at the gate" (ii 19, 21, iii 2, v 13) rather than served "in the court" (see NOTE on vs. 19). The speculations of other writers make more sense than the LXX, but they remain just that—speculations. Actually, the reason for the guards' anger is immaterial. Courts have ever been rife with courtiers and guards who have hated their king; in fact, Xerxes himself was finally assassinated in just such a conspiracy (cf. *Diodorus Siculus* XI. 69; Ctesias *Persica* 29; HPE, p. 289).

Nor does the MT say how Mordecai learned of the plot. Ancient sources suggest he may have overheard the conspirators while serving in the court (so A 12), thanks to his mastery of seventy languages (I Targum), or to a holy spirit (II Targum), or to a Jewish slave named Barnabazos, the servant of Teresh, one of the conspirators (Josephus *Antiquities* XI. 207). For the author of the Hebrew text, however, apparently the question was just not important.

How could Xerxes have been so forgetful, so unappreciative as to have allowed Mordecai to go without reward? Scholars have offered a variety of explanations, including the suggestion that Xerxes *did* order a reward but his wish was lost somewhere through bureaucratic red tape. The simple fact is, however, that if Mordecai had been rewarded at this time, then the sudden fall of Haman and Mordecai's rapid promotion would have been far less dramatic; thus the demands of the plot required that Mordecai go unrewarded—for a while.

4. HAMAN PLANS THE DESTRUCTION
OF ALL THE JEWS
(iii 1–15)

III 1 ᵃSome time later onᵃ King Xerxes promoted Haman, the son of Hammedatha, the Agagite, advancing him and making him the prime minister.

2 So all the king's servants at the King's Gate used to bow down and prostrate themselves before Haman; for that is what the king had commanded to be done to him.

Mordecai, however, would never bow down and prostrate himself. 3 So the king's servants at the King's Gate said to Mordecai, "Why do you disobey the king's command?" 4 Finally, ᵇwhen they had spokenᵇ to him day after day and he had not listened to them, then they informed Haman in order to see whether Mordecai's conduct would be tolerated. (For he had confided to them that he was a Jew.) 5 When Haman had seen for himself that Mordecai did not bow down nor prostrate himself before him, he was furious. 6 However, he hated to kill just Mordecai (for they had told him who Mordecai's people were); and so Haman sought to wipe out all the Jews throughout the whole kingdom of Xerxes, along withᶜ Mordecai.

7 In the first month, which is the month of Nisan, of the twelfth year of King Xerxes, the *pur* (that is, the lot) was cast in Haman's presence to determine the day and the month; ᵈand the lot indicated the thirteenthᵉ day of the twelfth monthᵈ,

---

ᵃ⁻ᵃ Literally "after these things"; AT and OL add "and it came to pass," which presupposes *wyhy* in Hebrew.

ᵇ⁻ᵇ Following *keʾāmrām* of *Qrê*, instead of *beʾāmrām*, "while they were speaking."

ᶜ Reading *ʾim*, "with," rather than *ʾam*, "people"; see NOTE.

ᵈ⁻ᵈ So LXX; lacking in MT by haplography.

ᵉ So AT; here LXX has "fourteenth," but elsewhere "the thirteenth" (see iii 13, viii 12, ix 1 of LXX).

which is the month of Adar. [8] Then Haman said to King Xerxes, "There is a certain people scattered, yet unassimilated, among the peoples throughout the provinces of your kingdom whose statutes are different from every other people's. They do not observe even the king's statutes! Therefore, it is not appropriate for the king to tolerate them. [9] If it please the king, let it be recorded that they are to be destroyed; and I shall pay ten thousand silver talents to the proper officials to deposit in the king's treasury." [10] So the king took his signet ring from off his hand and gave it to Haman, son of Hammedatha, the Agagite, the enemy of the Jews.

[11] "Well, it's your money," said the king to Haman, "do what you like with the people."

[12] Then the king's secretaries were summoned on the thirteenth day of the first month; and the edict was written exactly as Haman had dictated to the king's satraps, the governors of every province, and the officials of every people (it was written to each province in its own script and to each people in its own language) in the name of King Xerxes, and was sealed with the royal signet ring. [13] Dispatches were sent out by couriers to all the king's provinces, *to wipe out, slaughter, and annihilate* all the Jews—men and boys, women and children—in a single day, on the thirteenth day of the twelfth month, which is the month of Adar, and to plunder their possessions.*g* [14] The contents of the document were to be promulgated in each province, to be published to all peoples, namely, to be ready for that day. [15] At the king's command the couriers went out quickly, and the edict was published in the acropolis of Susa. Then the king and Haman sat down to drink, but the city of Susa was thrown into confusion.

f–f LXX *aphanisai*, "to efface"; see NOTE.
g Between vss. 13 and 14 the LXX has Addition B: "The First Letter of King Artaxerxes."

NOTES

iii 1. This verse sets up a sharp contrast between the unrewarded merit of Mordecai and Haman's unmerited rewards.

Some time later on. Like the opening phrase in ii 1, this is a vague indication of a later date which may have been any time from the seventh (ii 16) to the twelfth year of the king (iii 7).

Haman. The etymology of Haman's name and country as well as that of his father are shrouded by our ignorance. According to the MT, Haman was a descendant of the Amalekites (see NOTE on "Agagite" below); E 10 of the AT also asserts that he was not a Persian. Various proposals have been offered for Haman's name, including Omanes, a Persian name in classical writers (G. H. Rawlinson), and Humman or Humban, that of an Elamite deity (Jensen, WZKM 6 [1892], 10); see also R. Stiehl, WZKM 53 (1956), 11. See Introduction, p. XLII.

Hammedatha. Proposals abound, but no certainty exists concerning the origin and meaning of this name. In times past many scholars have argued for *mâh dāta,* Persian for "given by the moon" (F. Spiegel, see BDB, p. 241), or *Madatēs* (as in Xenophon *Cyropaedia* V. 3, 41; Curtius V. 3, 12). Jensen saw in the name the Elamite god Humman, while Gehman (p. 326) suggests *hama dātur,* Persian for "the equal giver." See also Introduction, p. XLII.

Agagite (*h'ggy*). For spelling among the versions, see Introduction, p. XLII. *Hǎᵃgāgî* could be the Persian name of an unknown family or place (so Ringgren and others), a *nomen dignitatis* like "pharaoh" (Keil), *gagean* or "northern barbaric" (Haupt), or an allegorical nickname (Jan Jozef Simons, *The Geographical and Topographical Texts of the Old Testament* [Leiden: Brill, 1959], II, p. 485). Regardless of its original meaning, now it clearly represents a *nomen gentilicium,* meaning a descendant of Agag, king of the Amalekites. This is the view of Josephus (who rendered it *amalekiten*), the Talmud, and the Targums, as well as of most commentators, who rightly view Haman as a descendant of the Amalekites, a people who frustrated Israel in Exod xvii 8–16, whose downfall was predicted by Balaam (Num xxiv 7), and whose King Agag was slaughtered with many (I Sam xv 8) but not all (I Chron iv 42 f.) of the Amalekites. For the curse on the Amalekites, see Deut xxv 17–19.

The LXX's rendering of *hǎᵃgāgî* with *bougaion* is especially puzzling. Although one cannot categorically rule out such possibilities as a name

containing the word *baga*, or God (Hoschander), or Bagoas, a favorite
of Alexander the Great (Curtius VI. 5, 23), the use of "Macedonian"
instead of *bougaion* in ix 24 and E 10 suggests that it is a term of re-
proach (so Haupt), which was "modernized" for the Greek-reading Jew
who knew the reputation of the Macedonians. Of considerable relevance
here is the reminder of F. Altheim and R. Stiehl (*Die aramäische
Sprache*, I, p. 212) that symbolic or allegorical names loomed large in
Jewish apocalyptic literature such as found at Qumran, for example, the
use of the phrase "the House of Absalom" in 1QpHab to designate
contemporary enemies of Qumran. Thus, while the MT used "Agagite"
as a name suggesting the implacable archenemy of the Israelite days,
so Greek editors used meaningful contemporary terms for their Greek-
reading Jews, for example, Macedonian. (Gogite of the AT may be
related to Gog in Ezek xxxviii–xxxix.) But when all the evidence
is considered, the judgment of Keil made over a hundred years ago still
stands: we know of Haman and his father and their origins nothing
more than what little is in the MT, and attempts to clarify the names are
uncertain.

making him the prime minister. Literally "placed his seat above all
others that were with him." Cf. x 3; Gen xli 39–45.

2. *that is what the king had commanded.* Since Persians regularly
bowed down to high-ranking officials (cf. Herodotus I. 134) as well as
to the king, Streane and others have argued here that the king *had* to
command respect for Haman because of some reluctance on the part of
his subjects to do so. Actually, the literary demands of the plot provide
adequate reason for the king's command: it emphasizes the seriousness
of Mordecai's defiant attitude toward Haman.

would never bow down. Why did Mordecai act in this very rash way?
His defense in vs. 4 was that he was a Jew, an admission which does not
really solve the problem for the reader (see NOTE on vs. 4) since Jews
regularly bowed down to kings (I Sam xxiv 9[8]; II Sam xiv 4; I Kings
i 16) as well as to other superiors (Gen xxiii 7, xxvii 29, xxxiii 3). Fur-
thermore, after Mordecai succeeded Haman as prime minister (viii 2,
x 3), he himself would certainly have had to prostrate himself before
the king (cf. Herodotus III. 86, VIII. 118; see, however, VII. 136,
where a delegation of Spartans refused to bow before King Xerxes
because it was not a Greek custom). In the LXX, Mordecai's refusal
to do obeisance to Haman is explained by his unwillingness to give to a
mortal that homage due only to God (so C 7), and explained in the
Targums and Midrashes by the presence of an idol worn on Haman's
chest, both explanations obviously being just speculations. Ehrlich is
certainly on surer ground when he sees Mordecai's actions, in the MT
at least, as an expression of Jewish national spirit and pride rather

than adherence to Exod xx 5, that is, Mordecai simply would not bow down to a descendant of Agag of the Amalekites (see NOTE on "Agagite" in vs. 1), that cursed people who had opposed the Israelites (Exod xvii 8–16) and had been almost wiped out by King Saul in the *ḥērem*, "ban" (I Sam xv; see, however, I Sam xxx 13). For discussion of *ḥērem*, see IDB, I, s.v. "Devoted."

3. *Why?* Were the servants genuinely concerned for Mordecai's safety and chiding him in a friendly way, were they merely curious, or were they resentful of his "superior" attitude toward Haman? The MT does not say.

4. *Finally*. Literally "and it came to pass."

would be tolerated. Literally "would be continued" (cf. Prov xii 7; Isa lxvi 22; Dan xi 17b). The LXX has instead "that Mordecai was disobeying the words of the king." Did the king's servants wish to use Mordecai's conduct as a test of whether Jews could be exempted from some Persian laws? Or did they simply disapprove of such arrogant disobedience on the part of a foreigner (so Streane)?

he had confided. Cf. ii 22. Literally "made known."

that he was a Jew. See NOTE on "would never bow down" in vs. 2. Mordecai's explanation for his conduct here is not quite clear, in part because of the ambiguity of the word "Jew." Does Jew here refer to Mordecai's "racial" or ethnic extraction (so Haupt) or to his religious affiliation (so Hoschander, p. 156)? To be sure, these are two distinct concepts, but throughout the Old Testament they are often inseparably and inextricably bound up with one another in a mutually supportive relationship. Just as Saul's *ḥērem* against the Amalekites (I Sam xv) contains both ethnic and religious elements, so here, too, both elements may have been involved.

6. *he hated*. Literally "he despised in his eyes"; cf. i 17. According to Dommershausen (p. 62), this verse is a veiled allusion to the Holy War Concept.

to wipe out (*lᵉhašmîd*). A most popular word in Esther, occurring twenty-five times in ten short chapters.

all the Jews. Although Saul had been unsuccessful in killing *all* his enemies (I Sam xv), he, Haman, would succeed.

with Mordecai. Reading with Gunkel and others '*im*, "with," rather than '*am*, "people," the latter being syntactically unrelated to the rest of the clause as well as semantically less appropriate than the proposed reading.

7. Many scholars believe that vs. 7 is intrusive, breaking as it does the narrative flow of vss. 6 and 8 (but see Bardtke, pp. 243–44). The verse undoubtedly was added by a later editor for whom the liturgical

and cultic aspects of the story were of primary importance. For further
discussion of Purim, see NOTE on ix 26 and Introduction, p. XLIX.

Nisan. Patterned after the Bab. *nisannu, nîsān* is the post-Exilic
equivalent of the pre-Exilic *'ābîb,* the first month of the Jewish year.
The beginning of the New Year was an especially appropriate time for
Haman to resort to divination because, according to the Babylonian re-
ligion, at that time the gods also come together to fix the fate of men.
For parallels on the casting of lots on the Babylonian New Year, see
P. Haupt, "Purim" in *Beiträge zur Assyriologie* 6 (1906).

in the twelfth year. That is, in the fifth year of Esther's being queen.

the pur *was cast.* Literally "he cast *pur.*" The subject of the verb
is not specified, and so many scholars have understood it to be Haman;
but the phrase "in Haman's presence" militates against that. Probably
an astrologer or magian would have cast the lot for Haman (see
Herodotus III. 128; Xenophon *Cyropaedia* I. 6, 46, IV. 5, 55); and thus
the verb should be translated impersonally, that is, "the *pur* was cast."
It is impossible to tell whether Haman was determining the propitious
day for presenting his petition to the king (so Paton) or the best day for
his pogrom (so iv 7 of the AT, and most commentators).

Consistent with the author's practice elsewhere of explaining foreign
words and practices (see Introduction, p. LVI) he rightly uses here the
well-known Hebrew word *gôrāl,* "lot" (Isa xxxiv 17; Neh x 35; I Chron
xxvi 14; Ps xxii 19; Jonah i 7; Prov xviii 18) to explain the foreign word
pûr.

to determine the day and the month. Literally "from day to day,
and from month to month." It is, of course, impossible to say exactly
what procedure was used in casting the lot; but logic, which admittedly
does not always correspond with historical fact, would suggest that the
propitious day and month would have been picked on one day, at one
sitting (hence the translation adopted here) rather than that each day
for eleven months Haman had the lot cast to determine whether that
particular day was the propitious one.

Adar. Derived from *addaru,* "be darkened," the twelfth month of the
Babylonian calendar (March–April); cf. iii 13, viii 12, ix 1, 15; Ezra vi
15.

8. *There is. Yešnô,* which appears also in Deut xxix 14; I Sam xiv
39, xxiii 23, may be incorrectly pointed in the MT; cf. GKC § 100*o,*
and Joüon, GHB, § 82*l.*

certain. Literally "one"; cf. Gen i 9; I Sam i 1; II Kings iv 1.
'ehād is variously translated: "single" (Paton); "insignificant" as in II
Sam xviii 10 and I Kings xiii 11 (H. J. Flowers, ET 66 [1954–55], 273);
"only one" (Wildeboer). By slyly omitting the name of the people involved, Haman himself has unwittingly set the stage further for Esther's
unexpected opposition and her victory over him.

scattered, yet unassimilated. The LXX is clearly incorrect here in regarding these two participles as needlessly repetitious synonyms which may be rendered with the one word "distributed." The first participle refers to the Jews' being scattered throughout the hundred and twenty-seven provinces of the empire, while the second participle refers to their self-imposed separateness, or exclusiveness, a practice which helped them to preserve their religious and ethnic identity. (That the Jews were so very much scattered throughout the empire at this time may suggest a late date in the Persian Period for such a description; see Introduction, pp. LVII ff.)

whose statutes (dātêhem) are different. Like other minorities in the Persian empire, in matters of speech, diet, dress, calendar—in so many major and minor ways—the Jewish customs, or statutes, *were* different. That fact, however, given the variety and tolerance of the Persian empire, would not have been damning in and of itself. Intending to malign and slander the Jews, Haman had, thus far, accurately described them (cf. C 1–7; Deut iv 5–8).

do not observe even the king's statutes. In the MT, the phrase "the king's decrees" is in the emphatic position. For a similar charge against the Jews, see Ezra iv 12–16.

not appropriate (LXX "not expedient") *for the king.* Cf. v 13, vii 4.

9. I shall pay. Literally "and I shall weigh out into the hands of."

ten thousand silver talents. In the MT this phrase is in the emphatic position, and justly so, for the amount represents a fabulous sum. Commentators have sometimes tried to express the value of Haman's offer in terms of their own country's currency, for example, 75,000,000 Deutsche Marks (Wildeboer); £3,600,000 (Paton), and $18,000,000 (Anderson). But as any tourist who has struggled with foreign currencies knows almost intuitively, trying to express the intricacies of ancient monies in terms of modern purchasing power is virtually impossible. Ten thousand silver talents cannot possibly represent $18,000,000 in 1908 (so Paton) *and* in 1954 (so Anderson). The only meaningful comparison is that made with roughly contemporaneous coinage; for example, Paton, using Herodotus III. 95, where the total revenue of the Persian empire is given in terms of 14,560 Euboeic talents, has estimated Haman's offer to represent almost two-thirds of the annual income of the Persian empire; and according to Strabo, the booty which Alexander the Great brought to the treasury at Susa was 49,000 talents of gold and silver, which would be at least five times the value of Haman's offer (so Ringgren, p. 128, n. 1). In short, the amount offered by Haman was a fabulous sum—indisputable evidence of the extent of his great hatred for Mordecai, if not also evidence of his own great wealth (see v ii, viii 1). Whether this enormous amount was to come from Haman's well-filled pockets or represented the value of the booty involved is debated by scholars. In either case, an offer of such a large amount of money may suggest that while the Jews may have been politically insignificant at that time, they were of some economic and financial prominence (so Bardtke, p. 320). See IDB, IV, s.v. "Weights and Measures," the paragraphs on "talents," especially pp. 830–31.

proper officials. Literally "doers of the work"; cf. ix 3. Probably referring to the revenue officers of the royal treasury (cf. I Sam viii 16; I Kings xi 28; Ps cvii 23; Dan viii 27; I Chron xxix 6) rather than to those who would carry out the massacre.

treasury. Cf. iv 7. *G⁰nazîm* is a loan word from Persian, see BDB, p. 170.

10. *signet ring.* Used for sealing the official documents of the king (see viii 8, 10; Gen xli 42), it gave Haman, in effect, full authority for phrasing the decree and thus unlimited power over the Jews. See Plate 7 for a gold signet ring from Persepolis.

enemy of the Jews. Cf. viii 1, ix 10, 24.

11. *Well, it's your money.* Literally "the silver is given to you," that is, "if you want to spend it that way, it's all right with me." Most scholars, following the LXX ("Keep the money!"), understand the king to be returning the money; after all, they argue, it would have been below the king's dignity to have accepted money for acting in the public's best interests. Moreover, they can point to the fact that Xerxes once turned down an even larger sum of money when Pythius, the Lydian, offered Xerxes for his war effort "two thousand talents of silver, and of gold four million Daric staters, lacking seven thousand." The grateful Xerxes not only declined the offer—he donated the seven thousand staters so that the generous Pythius might have exactly four million (Herodotus VII. 27–29). It seems more likely, however, that the king accepted the money, possibly bargaining with Haman in a way somewhat reminiscent of Abraham's bargaining with Ephron for the field in Machpelah, in Gen xxiii 7–18. For although Ephron said to Abraham "I give you the field, and I give you the cave that is in it, in the presence of the sons of my people I give it to you; bury your dead," he nonetheless ended up accepting from Abraham four hundred shekels of silver. (The Greek translation of Esther iii 11, "Keep the money!" sounds very much like an initial stage in typical Near Eastern bargaining.) It should also be remembered that what the Westerner so opprobriously calls "bribery" is known in the Near East as the quite ancient and honorable system of *bakshish* (so Max Vogelstein, "Bakshish for Bagoas?" JQR 33 [1942–43], 89–92). Besides, Mordecai expressly states that the money would go into the king's treasury in iv 7; and Esther's word "sold" in vii 4 certainly suggests the same.

do what you like with the people. Literally "and the people with it as is good in your eyes." More than one commentator has rightly expressed great doubt that a Persian king would so blithely hand over an entire nation within his empire for destruction.

12. *secretaries.* Literally "the writers"; they were simply the stenographers and copyists (Herodotus VII. 100, VIII. 90), not the professional class of learned scribes (cf. Jer xxxvi 26, 32). For further information on scribes, see A. Leo Oppenheim, "Note on the Scribes in Mesopotamia," in *Studies in Honor of Benno Landsberger on his Seventy-fifth Birthday, April 21, 1965,* Assyriological Studies, No. 16 (University of Chicago Press, 1965), 253–56; *Reallexikon des Assyriologie* 1 (1932), 456; and Joachim Begrich, ZAW 58 (1940–41), 1–29.

satraps. *'aḥašdarpᵉnîm*, "satraps," is the hebraized form of the Pers. *khshatrapanan.* *Paḥôt*, "governors," which is a loan word from the Akk. *paḥâti*, ruled over provinces and cities; for example, Nehemiah was a *peḥāh* (Neh v 14). The *śārîm* were the native chiefs.

13. *were sent.* For this use of the niphal absolute infinitive, see GKC, § 142*gg*, and Joüon, GHB, § 123*xy*.

couriers. Literally "runners"; cf. viii 10, 14, where their horses are specifically mentioned. These are undoubtedly the famous *aggaroi* (see Herodotus V. 14, VIII. 98), who, like the Pony Express riders of our frontier days, were stationed along the major roads at regular intervals and could thus carry messages great distances in a very short time.

wipe out (*ḥašmîd*), *slaughter, and annihilate.* Since it seems unnatural to us for the king to have used three synonymous terms here, and since Esther uses these same three words in vii 4, where under the circumstances such repetitious terms of horror would be quite natural in her excited state, some scholars contend that two of the verbs here represent a gloss taken from vii 4; but the use of three synonyms probably represents the legal device of being as specific and precise as possible in order to avoid confusion and uncertainty. For Dommershausen (p. 52), however, the three verbs symbolize the thoroughness of the destruction. (Significantly, the LXX omits the last two verbs here in vs. 13, but not in vii 4.)

men and boys, women and children. Literally "from boy to man, children and women." Lest the phrase "all the Jews" be loosely interpreted by either the merciful or the "weak-willed," the edict, in typical legal fashion, catalogues with chilling inclusiveness all the categories involved.

the thirteenth. An "unlucky number" according to Dommershausen (p. 66).

to plunder their possessions. Cf. Judg v 30. When the tables were

turned, the Jews were allowed to plunder their enemy's goods (so viii 11),
but did not (so ix 10, 15, 16; see, however, NOTE on ix 10).

14. *The contents.* Literally "the copy of" (cf. iv 8, viii 13; Ezra iv
11, 23, v 6, vii 11). *Patšegen* is a loan word from the Persian through
Aramaic (Gehman, p. 326).

15. *quickly.* Literally "hurrying themselves"; cf. viii 14; II Chron
xxvi 20.

sat down to drink. A most striking piece of literary contrast. In
Hoschander's view (p. 181), however, it illustrates a practice mentioned
by Herodotus I. 133, which asserts that the Persians drank over a
decision made while sober and, conversely, when sober reconsidered
any decision made while drinking.

the city of Susa. That is, in contrast to the acropolis. Scholars differ
as to whether "the city" here means the Jewish inhabitants alone
(Ehrlich) or the Gentiles as well (Bardtke, Anderson, and others).

COMMENT

In chapter iii the author skillfully introduces the villain (see
NOTE on vs. 1), who sets a seemingly inescapable trap for the
Jews. Although the MT does not clearly state why Mordecai refused to bow down to Haman (see NOTES on vss. 2 and 4),
one must infer from the MT, where Haman is identified as a
descendant of Agag of the Amalekites (see NOTE on "Agagite"
in vs. 1), that Mordecai simply refused to bow down to a descendant
of such a hated and vanquished enemy. Just as Shimei, a descendant
of Kish, refused to bow down before the mortal enemy of his
father's house (I Sam xvi 4–14), so now Mordecai, a later descendant of Kish, refuses to bow down before Haman, a descendant
of Agag. Mordecai's reason may seem to the reader to be inadequate for his rash stand, but ethnic and religious prejudices are
often absurd to those who do not share them. Certainly the antipathy that Mordecai had for Haman was reciprocated; as soon
as Haman learned that Mordecai was a Jew, he immediately
initiated his personal vendetta against the entire people (vs. 6).

Haman's accusation of the Jews (vs. 8) was diabolically clever
in its construction, proceeding as it did from the truth (see NOTE
on "scattered, yet unassimilated") to half-truth (see NOTE on
"statutes are different") to an outright lie ("They do not observe
even the king's statutes"). Such an indictment invited reaction, not

investigation or confirmation. One can almost hear the king respond-
ing to these three specifications as they were made: "That's not
so good"; "That's worse"; and finally, "That's intolerable!" This
weak and pliable king, dominated and manipulated by his prime
minister here and by Esther later (see v 3, vii 2–6, viii 3), is a
far cry from the historical Xerxes as characterized by Herodotus
VII–IX. The wily Haman neither named the accused people specifically nor did he mention Mordecai's personal effrontery toward
him. By stressing what was in the "best interests" of the kingdom
(see vs. 8), Haman succeeded in getting his personal revenge
against Mordecai without letting the king know all his motives.
Nor do we know them. For the king's part there was obviously
an economic motive (see vss. 9–11). Haller goes too far in assert-
ing that Haman's motive was purely personal revenge, and in no
way conditioned by religious or cultural considerations. Certainly
the terrible pogroms against the Jews in Russia and Nazi Germany
were motivated by a variety of conscious and unconscious reasons.
Men have never lacked the capacity to deceive even themselves and
to find "good" reasons for their evil deeds.

Sweeping though the destruction was to be (see vs. 13), it was
not without parallel. Even in antiquity, without benefit of the terrible efficiency of twentieth-century technology, such thoroughgoing
slaughter was possible. Bloodthirsty massacres were carried out
by the Persians against the Scythians (Herodotus I. 106) and
against the Magi at the accession of Darius I (III. 79). And as
Ringgren has pointed out (p. 129), Cicero accuses Mithradates
of Pontus of killing between 80,000 and 150,000 Romans in one
day in 90 B.C. (*Oratio de lege Manilia* III. 7). In our own
century, Hitler almost succeeded where Haman failed.

Ironically, the terrible fate of the Jews was sealed the day before they were to celebrate the Passover (vs. 13), the festival
commemorating their deliverance from Egypt (see Lev xxiii 5–8).
Why did Haman send the edict out eleven months in advance of
the proposed day of slaughter? Or, as Paton so drolly posed the
problem: "The massacres of St. Bartholomew would not have been
a great success if the Huguenots had been informed a year ahead"
(p. 209). To give the Jews ample time to change their religious
affiliations (so Hoschander, pp. 180–81) is a novel but absurd suggestion. This problem of the day, like so many other problems
in Esther, is grounded in literary rather than in historical con-

siderations, that is, the author needed time for his story's dé-
nouement. The author concludes the chapter with a striking piece
of dramatic contrast: the city was in a state of confusion, but
the king and Haman started to drink (vs. 15).

5. ESTHER AGREES TO GO UNSUMMONED
TO THE KING
(iv 1–17)

IV 1 When Mordecai learned of everything that had been done, Mordecai tore his clothes and put on sackcloth and ashes. Then he went out into the midst of the city and wailed *a*bitterly*a*; 2 and then he came as far as the King's Gate (for no one in sackcloth was allowed to enter the King's Gate). 3 And in every province *b*where the king's command was heard*b* there was loud mourning among the Jews, with fasting and weeping and wailing; most of them were lying in sackcloth and ashes.

4 When Esther's maids and eunuchs came*c* and told her, the queen was quite shocked; and she sent clothing for Mordecai to wear so that he could take off his sackcloth, but he would not accept it. 5 So Esther summoned Hatak, one of the royal eunuchs whom the king had appointed to wait on her, and ordered him to go to Mordecai to learn the full particulars. 6 So Hatak went out to Mordecai in the city square which was in front of the King's Gate. 7 Mordecai then informed him of everything that had happened to him, and also of the exact amount of money that Haman had promised to pay to the royal treasury for the extermination of the Jews. 8 Mordecai also gave him a*d* copy of the written decree which had been posted in Susa concerning their destruction so that he might show it to Esther and report to her, and that he might instruct her to go to the king to intercede and beg with him for her people.

9 So Hatak went and told Esther everything*e* Mordecai had

a-a LXX "An innocent people is condemned to death!"
b-b MT "place where the word of the king and his decree arrived"; LXX "where the letters were posted."
c Reading *wattābô'nâ* (cf. Jer ix 16), instead of *wattābô'ynâ*.
d MT "the."
e So LXX and Vulgate; "everything" lacking in MT; see NOTE.

said. 10 Then Esther talked to Hatak and gave him this message for Mordecai: 11 "All the king's courtiers, and even the people of the king's provinces, are well aware that there is one penalty for every man or woman who approaches the king inside the inner court without having been summoned: to be put to death, the one exception being that person to whom the king extends the gold scepter so that he may live. And I have not been summoned to come to the king for the past thirty days!"

12 When ʲHatak had conveyedʲ to Mordecai allᵍ Esther's words, 13 then Mordecai said to reply to Esther, "Don't think that ʰbecause you're in the king's house you'll be safer than the rest of the Jews!ʰ 14 For, if you persist in keeping silent at a time like this, ⁱrelief and deliverance will appear for the Jews from another quarterⁱ; but you and your family will perish. It's possible that you came to the throne for just such a time as this."

15 Thereupon, Esther said to reply to Mordecai, 16 "ʲGo and gather all the Jews now in Susa, and fast for me. Don't eat or drink for three days, either day or nightʲ; and I, with my maids, will fast as you do. In this condition I'll go to the king, even though it's against the law. And if I perish, I perish!" 17 Mordecai then left and carried out all Esther's instructions.ᵏ

ʲ⁻ʲ Reading with LXX and OL, *wayyagēd hᵃtāk* instead of *wayyagîdû;* see NOTE.
ᵍ So LXX; see NOTE on "everything" in vs. 9.
ʰ⁻ʰ Literally "to escape in the king's house more than all the Jews."
ⁱ⁻ⁱ AT "But God shall be their help and salvation"; see NOTE.
ʲ⁻ʲ AT "Propose a service and earnestly beg God."
ᵏ In the Greek, Addition C follows: "The Prayers of Mordecai and Esther."

NOTES

iv 1. *learned of everything.* Exactly how Mordecai had learned all about the transactions behind the formal edict, including the matter of the *bakshish* (see vs. 7), is not stated. Friends at the court (so Haupt), his opportunities at the King's Gate (cf. ii 21–22), the ubiquitous eunuchs of the Persian court (so Hoschander)—any one of these means is a logical possibility, but these speculations are of great importance only to those who subscribe to the story's complete historical accurateness.

sackcloth and ashes. What Mordecai did in this verse is quite clear;

what he intended and why he did it are not. For Mordecai tearing his clothes and putting on sackcloth may very well have been a deeply religious act (so Paton, Anderson, and others); on the other hand, it may just have been a conventional way of expressing grief and humiliation (see II Kings xviii 37; Job vii 5; Gen xxxvii 29), and need no more be interpreted as proof of deep religious faith than the presence of an officiating clergyman at an American funeral means the deceased was a "believer." Also, the sprinkling on of ashes was an expression of humiliation (II Sam xiii 19), contrition (Dan ix 3), or mourning (Job ii 8); see also Herodotus VIII. 99, IX. 24.

Were Mordecai's actions an expression of self-reproach for bringing all this misfortune on the people by not bowing down to Haman (so Wildeboer), or a natural expression of grief over the fate of his people (so the LXX), or a quick and certain way of getting the queen's attention (Haller, Ringgren, Anderson)? The last view may be a confusion of final result with original intent.

wailed bitterly. Literally "cried with a loud and bitter voice." Cf. Gen xxvii 34; another parallel with the Joseph Cycle, see Introduction, p. LII.

2. *the King's Gate.* Not an entrance to the city by that name but the palace door itself (see Oswald Loretz, "*š'r hmlk*—'Das Tor des Konigs' [Est 2, 19]," *Die Welt des Orients* 4, No. 2 [1967], 104–8). With the possible exception of Herodotus III. 17, there is no evidence outside of the Bible that this prohibition existed. Apparently the wearing of sackcloth made one ceremonially unclean.

3. Basing their argument on the fact that the OL has a reading very similar to this verse immediately after iii 15, Haller, Ringgren, and Ehrlich put iv 3 immediately after iii 15; but the verse is better left here because it well serves a literary purpose: it provides, without explicitly stating so, a pause during which Mordecai may be seen by the servants of the king (so Bardtke).

fasting . . . sackcloth and ashes. Fasting, weeping, and the wearing of sackcloth and ashes were essentially religious acts for many, if not most, Jews. And since prayer often accompanied fasting (see Jer xiv 12; Neh ix 1; Ezra viii 21, 23; I Sam vii 6; Joel ii 12; Jonah iii 8), there must have been those Jews who also prayed for Esther's success. Thus the omission of any mention of prayer or God, both here and in verses 14 and 16 (see NOTES), is certainly deliberate, and is consistent with the author's avoiding any explicit mention of distinctively religious ideas, concepts, and vocabulary; see Introduction, pp. XXXII–XXXIV.

most of them . . . and ashes. Literally "sackcloth, with ashes, was spread out (*yuṣṣa'*) to most of them." Cf. II Sam xxi 10; Isa lviii 5.

4. With vs. 4 the scene changes, but no clue is given in the MT as

to how much time has elapsed, whether two hours or two days. Although Esther's servants recognized Mordecai as one whose welfare was of possible interest to the queen (see ii 11, 22), they need not have known that Esther was Jewish.

quite shocked. The LXX adds "when she heard what had happened," i.e., that Mordecai was dressed in sackcloth. The Hithpalpal of *ḥîl* occurs in the OT only here; possibly it should be translated as "perplexed" since the Greek translation for it is *etarachthē*, the verb used to translate *nābôkâ* in iii 15 and *nibʻat* in vii 6.

would not accept it. The MT offers no reasons for Mordecai's refusal. Josephus' explanation was that "the sad occasion that had made him put it [the sackcloth] on had not yet ceased"; but Anderson is probably closer to the truth when, recalling Talmudic Judaism's stress on not making a public display of personal sorrow, he suggests that Mordecai's refusal emphasized that it was not just a matter of personal sorrow but of dire public calamity. Contrary to common scholarly opinion, the verb here, *qbl*, is not late, for it occurs in an Amarna letter; see BASOR 89 (1943), 31.

5. *Hatak.* The versions spell his name in various ways (see Introduction, p. XLII); in the Targums he is called Daniel. His name may mean "courier" (J. Scheftelowitz, *Arisches im Alten Testament* [Berlin, 1901], pp. 44–45), or "the good one" (Gehman, p. 327).

appointed to wait on her. Literally "whom he had caused to stand before her"; cf. I Chron xv 16, and Driver, VT 4 (1954), 235. In spite of the fact that Hatak was one of the king's own servants, Esther apparently regarded him as trustworthy.

full particulars. Literally "what this was, and why it was," which the LXX rightly translates as *to akribes,* "the accurate statement."

6. *city square.* Literally "the broad place"; a traditional place for mourning (cf. Amos v 16; Isa xv 3; Jer xlviii 38).

7. *amount (pārāšat).* Cf. x 2. The LXX and the OL add "ten thousand talents," which is a gloss from iii 9. The fabulous size of the *bakshish* (see NOTE on iii 11) indicates to Esther the seriousness of the situation: it was not just a matter of Haman's personal vendetta against some Jews. Now Haman's hatred had joined hands with the king's avarice.

8. There is a significant addition to this verse in the Greek versions, namely, "Remembering your humble station when you were supported by my hand because Haman, who is second to the king, has sentenced us to death. Call upon the Lord, and speak to the king concerning us, and save us from death."

9. *everything.* So the LXX. The MT probably erroneously omitted *kl,* "all"; apart from being trustworthy, the single most important quality in a servant like Hatak was that he reported all that was said, thereby

enabling his mistress to catch any meanings or nuances which he might have unconsciously missed.

10. *gave him this message.* Literally "she charged him unto Mordecai." The LXX has direct address ("Go to Mordecai and say") which is free but not incorrect, since she is sending back a message, not just a messenger.

11. Now, making use of the messenger to avoid needless repetition, the author turns to direct address, thereby increasing the scene's dramatic effect.

inner court. The place where the king could be seen (cf. v 1), in contrast to the outer court where he could not (cf. vi 4).

without having been summoned. Whether this was a safety precaution designed to protect the king's life, time, or privacy is uncertain; according to Josephus *Antiquities* XI. 205, this rule applied only to the royal family (literally *tōn idiōn,* "his own"). Herodotus, however, supports none of these views (cf. I. 99, III. 72, 77, 84, 118, 140). Josephus also adds the interesting note that "round his throne stood men with axes to punish any who approached the throne without being summoned."

scepter. *Šarbîṭ* here and in v 2, viii 4; an Aramaism for the Heb. *šēbeṭ.*

the past thirty days. Literally "this is thirty days." Esther implies here that she no longer enjoys the king's highest favor. (There is no basis for reading with Ehrlich, instead of "thirty days," "three days" in the vague sense of "a long time.")

The AT, OL, and Vulgate add "and how can I go to the king without being summoned?" Since it is unusual for the Vulgate and the OL to agree against the MT, in this case either the Vulgate represents a contamination by the OL or the clause was in Jerome's Hebrew text; the former possibility is the more likely.

Since the pogrom was still eleven months away, there would have been ample time for Esther to take the safer course and formally request an audience with the king in order to avoid the danger of coming to him unsummoned. That she did not do so has been variously explained. Possibly she would have had to make her appeal for an audience through the prime minister, and despaired of that (so Bardtke). Possibly, had she requested an audience with the king, he would have denied it in order to avoid facing her and admitting that he no longer loved her (so Hoschander, pp. 199–200; lest the idea that a mighty king should fear the emotional reactions of a mere woman seem too absurd, it should be noted that the great Xerxes did fear the wrath of his Queen Amestris, *vide* Herodotus IX. 109). But the most probable answer is also the most obvious: for Esther to risk her life makes for more interesting reading, as Addition D so clearly illustrates.

12. *Hatak had conveyed.* So the LXX and the OL (see textual note *f-f*, above). Hebrew has *wayyagîdû*, "they had told," which must be a scribal error as additional people would hardly have become involved in the communications at this point.

13. *think.* Literally "form an idea in yourself." Cf. II Sam xxi 5; Judg xx 5. The LXX has "say to yourself," which is also an acceptable translation of the Hebrew. The crucial question here is whether Mordecai was offering merely a factual statement (so Paton, Bardtke, and others) or a threatening one (so the OL, Hoschander, and others); cf. NOTE on "your family . . . will perish" vs. 14.

14. *a time like this.* Literally "in this time"; the LXX rightly uses here *kairos*, not *chronos;* cf. NOTE on ii 12.

relief. Literally "space"; cf. Gen xxxii 17; the LXX has *boëtheia*, "help, aide."

from another quarter. This particular phrase is one of the most crucial yet debatable phrases in all of Esther. Did Mordecai have in mind another individual, some nameless Nehemiah; or possibly political help from another quarter, such as that requested of Rome by Judas Maccabeus and later by Jonathan (I Macc viii 17–18 and xii 1)? While either view is a possibility, the AT, Josephus, and I and II Targums are certainly correct to see in the Hebrew a veiled allusion to God, just as "mercy" is a veiled allusion to God in I Macc xvi 3, and as "the kingdom of Heaven" in Matthew is a surrogate for the "kingdom of God." For the use of the word *māqôm*, "place," in connection with God's name in early Talmudic literature, see A. Spanier (MGWJ [1922], pp. 309–14). The fact that Esther asked the Jewish community to fast on her behalf (see NOTE on vs. 16) clearly indicates that divine help was being sought here, regardless of whether it took a "natural" or supernatural form. The writer of Esther is affirming a religious concept, faith in divine Providence (see also below, NOTE on "It's possible that . . .").

your family ("house of your father") *will perish.* Is this a simple statement of fact or a threat? If Mordecai was thinking in terms of divine deliverance, says Bardtke, then it is likely that he was also thinking here of divine punishment rather than mortal revenge by the Jews, the latter view being that of Josephus.

It's possible that (literally "who knows if") *you came to the throne* (literally "you came to the royalty"). Having "threatened" Esther, Mordecai then tried to encourage her by suggesting that something providential was involved in her becoming queen. For an extended discussion on the difficulties in this verse, see especially Haupt, pp. 137–38, and Paton, pp. 224–25.

16. *Go and gather* (*lk knws*). Esther had understood and taken command, as evidenced here by the use of the imperative. Whereas the AT expressly mentions God himself, Dommershausen (p. 74) sees in *knws* a "veiled allusion" to *bêt k^enesset*, "the synagogue."

now. Literally "who are found." Apparently a sizable number of Jews, since they were responsible later for killing three hundred men (ix 15).

fast for me. Jews in the Old Testament often resorted to fasting in periods of stress (Judg xx 26; I Kings xxi 9; Jer xxxvi 9; Jonah iii 5; II Chron xx 3); so also the Diaspora Community at Elephantine (Willi Staerk, *Alte und neue aramäische Papyri* [Kleine Text 94], 26 Altorientalische Texte zum Alte Testament, ed. Hugo Gressman, 2d ed. [Berlin and Leipzig, 1926], 451). Moreover, since prayer frequently accompanied fasting (see I Sam vii 6; II Sam xii 16, 22; I Kings xxi 27; Ezra viii 21, 23; Neh i 4, ix 1; Jer xiv 12; Jonah iii 3–8; Joel i 14, ii 12; and Dan ix 3), Esther was certainly asking, in effect, for the Jewish community to intercede with God on her behalf, even as the AT explicitly states (see textual note *j–j*, above). In keeping with the author's practice elsewhere, he studiously avoided clear references to things *obviously* religious, like the words "God," "prayer," "intervene"; see Introduction, pp. xxxii–xxxiv. (It is quite possible, of course, that a glossator has deleted all mention of God and prayer.) That Esther fasted so strictly made her, presumably, less attractive to the king but more acceptable to God. The fast also obviously has an aetiological character here, since a Purim fast would be established later (see ix 31).

either day or night. A very strict fast, observed even throughout the night; it was not, however, seventy-two hours long, for Esther appeared before the king (v 1) on the third day of the fast.

I, with my maids. The "waw of accompaniment"; see Joüon, GHB, § 151a.

In this condition (*wbkn*). Literally "and in thus"; cf. Eccles viii 10; "then" of the LXX is incorrect.

17. *left* (*wayya'^abōr*). Literally "he crossed," whether in the sense of Gen xviii 5, or literally: Mordecai crossed either the square (see vs. 6) or the Ab-Kharkha River separating Susa from the acropolis. Ancient Jewish commentators erroneously understood the verb to mean "transgress," since by fasting for three days Mordecai fasted on the fifteenth of Nisan, the feast of Passover (Exod xii 1–20).

Immediately after this verse the Greek has Addition C: "The Prayers of Mordecai and Esther."

COMMENT

In Act IV of the impending tragedy the God of the Jews is not
on stage, nor is his name even mentioned. He is, however, standing
in the wings, following the play and encouraging the actors, or
so at least the references to sackcloth and ashes (see NOTES
on vss. 1 and 3) and fasting (NOTES on vss. 15, 16) seem to
suggest. There can be little doubt that Mordecai's promise that
"relief and deliverance will appear for the Jews from another place"
is a veiled allusion to God (see NOTE on vs. 14). That same
phrase, as well as "It's possible that you came to the throne for
just such a time as this" (vs. 14), seems to affirm the author's
faith in God's providential care. (For a discussion of why the
author did not stress God's role in Esther, see Introduction, pp.
XXXII–XXXIII.) In the Greek versions God is seen hovering above the
stage, and he is explicitly mentioned in vs. 8.

Scholars have speculated on why Esther had not heard about
the edict. Had Mordecai acted so quickly that the word had not
yet even gotten around in the acropolis? Was Esther so isolated
in the harem that she had heard nothing? Or was she so indifferent to the problems of the outside world and of her people
that she did not care? The MT does not say. It is worth noting,
however, that time and time again the MT simply states a "fact"
or describes an act, without giving the motive or reason or details behind it. The reason for this is clear: the author wishes to
tell an interesting and fast-moving story, and in doing so, ignores
minor or explanatory details from time to time.

According to the MT, Esther's reluctance to intercede for her
people with the king was based on the "fact" (see NOTE on "without having been summoned" in vs. 11) that no one was allowed,
under penalty of death, to appear unsummoned in the king's inner
court. Either the author was misinformed about Persian customs in
this particular matter or, more likely, to increase the reader's suspense and appreciation of Esther's subsequent bravery, he deliberately exaggerated the dangers confronting her.

Bardtke's inference that Esther was selfish and unfeeling because
of what she *did not say* to Mordecai, namely, she offered no
alternatives to Mordecai for helping her people, not even so much

as a word of sympathy for them, is unfair since it is essentially "an argument from silence." Bardtke's inference is also unrealistic, failing, as it does, to take into consideration the natural human reluctance to undertake great risk without some strong assurance of success. Isaiah may have immediately leaped at the opportunity of serving the Lord and Israel (Isa vi 8), but Moses (Exod iii 11–iv 13), Barak (Judg iv 8), and Jeremiah (Jer i 6) certainly did not!

Whether out of fear of God's punishment or Jewish reprisals against her (see NOTE on "your family will perish" in vs. 14), Esther finally agreed to go to the king unsummoned, saying, "If I perish, I perish." Her words have been variously interpreted, ranging from very flattering views such as Bardtke's, where Esther is a selfless and courageous "freewill offering" (p. 335), to something much less than that: "a despairing expression of resignation to the inevitable . . . she goes as one would submit to an operation, because there is a chance of escaping death that way" (Paton, p. 226). Like all human beings, Esther was not without flaw; but certainly our heroine should be judged more by the brave act she performs than by the natural fears she had to fight against. The rash man acts without fear; the brave man, in spite of it.

6. ESTHER LAYS A TRAP FOR HAMAN
(v 1–8)

V ¹ᵃSo it was that on the third day Esther ᵇput on her royal robesᵇ and stopped in the inner court of the palace, opposite the royal apartment. The king was seated on his throne in the throne room, facing the building's entrance. ² Finally, when the king noticed Queen Esther standing in the court, she won his favor; and the king extended to Esther the gold scepter that he was holding. Then Esther came up and touched the tip of the scepter. ³ The king then said to her, "What do you want, Queen Esther? What is your petition? Even if it be half my kingdom, you may have it."

⁴ "If it please the king," said Esther, "let the king come with Hamanᶜ today to a dinner that I have prepared for him."

⁵ "Bring Haman right away," said the king, "so that we may do as Esther wants."

So the king and Haman came to the dinner that Esther had arranged. ⁶ While they were drinking, the king said, "What's your request? It shall be given you. What's your petition? ᵈEven if it be half the kingdomᵈ, it shall be done!"

⁷ So Esther answered, saying, ᵉ"All rightᵉ. ⁸ If I have found favor with the king and if it please the king to grant my request and to fulfill my petition, then let the king and Haman come tomorrowᶠ to a dinner which I shall give for them; and tomorrow I will do as the king has said."

ᵃ A Greek editor expanded vss. 1 and 2 into the sixteen dramatic verses of Addition D, the high point of the Greek Book of Esther.
ᵇ⁻ᵇ MT "put on royalty." See NOTE.
ᶜ AT and OL add "your friend," see NOTE
ᵈ⁻ᵈ LXX now omits; but AT and Josephus have it.
ᵉ⁻ᵉ MT "my request and my petition"; see NOTE.
ᶠ So LXX; see NOTE.

NOTES

v 1. *on the third day.* Esther's fast would thus have been some forty hours in duration; to try and establish the approximate time of day she made her request, as some scholars have done, is pointless.

put on her royal robes. Literally "put on royalty." Possibly an ellipsis, but our reading follows the Greek and the OL, which presuppose *lᵉbûš,* "clothing" (cf. vi 8, viii 15). Feminine strategy, as well as court etiquette, required that Esther not appear before the king in sackcloth.

stopped. Literally "stood"; cf. Josh x 13; Judg ix 35.

royal apartment (byt hmlk). See NOTE on ii 16.

throne room (byt hmlkwt). Although the physical setting in this verse is very carefully described, the exact meaning of the terms is far from clear, in part because the root *mlk,* with various vocalizations, occurs six times throughout. Most scholars regard *byt hmlkwt,* "house of the kingdom," as synonymous with *byt hmlk,* "palace," and point to i 9 to support their view. However, just as *byt hmlk* in ii 16 does not mean "the palace" (see NOTE ad loc.), so it is not at all unlikely that *byt hmlkwt* here in vs. 1 is distinct from *byt hmlk,* "palace," of vs. 1 and, thus, should be translated as "throne room," as the throne was located there; see, however, HPE, pp. 280–83, for Olmstead's description of the *apadana.* In any case, "facing the building's entrance" is correct; but it is uncertain whether the phrase refers to the king himself or the throne room's position in the building.

2. *Finally.* While rather inappropriate here, *wyhy* is, in all likelihood, the author's way of indicating the passage of time (cf. NOTE on i 1); it is far less likely to be a vestigial remnant of an "addition" between vss. 1 and 2, such as Addition D.

won his favor. Cf. NOTE on "who most pleases the king" in ii 4.

3. *What do you want . . . ?* Literally "What to you?"

half my kingdom. A polite oriental exaggeration which was not meant to be taken too literally; for a somewhat parallel situation, see Herodotus IX. 109–11, where after Xerxes in an extravagant mood offered his mistress Artaynte anything, she proceeded to take him at his word, asking him for the gaily colored mantle Amestris, his queen, had woven for him with her own hands. Xerxes tried to get out of it by offering her "cities instead, and gold in abundance, and an army for none but herself to command. . . . But as he could not move her, he gave her the mantle; and she, rejoicing greatly in the gift, went flaunting her finery." Concerning Xerxes' problems with his harem, see HPE, pp. 206–7; see also Herod's identical promise to Salome in Mark vi 23.

you may have it (*weyinnātēn lāk*). Literally "and it shall be given to you." Since *yinnātēn* is masculine in form, it refers to *mah*, "what," rather than to *baqqāšātēk*, "your petition," so also in v 6 and ix 12.

4. To the reader's surprise, Esther does not intercede for her people. Instead she invites the king and Haman, her enemy, to a dinner. Why? Possibly she perceived that this was not psychologically the "right moment" (so Streane); perhaps she lacked the courage at the last minute (Gunkel); or perhaps she regarded a drinking party as the more appropriate place to discuss her case (Hoschander, p. 202, following Herodotus I. 133). But most likely the reason for the postponement lies with the needs of the author: he needed time to work out Mordecai's victory over Haman in v 9 – vi 11. Moreover, the delay increases the reader's suspense.

let the king come with Haman today. In some medieval manuscripts *Ybw' Hmlk Whmn Hywm* is printed in such a way as to call attention to the fact that the first letter of each of these four Hebrew words, taken together, spells God's personal name, *YHWH*. But the sequence is certainly accidental, and not the author's way of including God's name in his book.

with Haman. For Esther to have invited Haman seems to be tempting fate. There are almost as many reasons offered for Esther's invitation to Haman as there are commentators: to lull Haman into a sense of false security, making his fall all the more dramatic (Ringgren); to make the king suspicious of Haman (Haller) or jealous (Ehrlich); to avoid being alone with the king (Bardtke); to avert suspicion on Haman's part (Hoschander), to force the king into making a judgment then and there, when she would be in a better position to interpret the situation, sense developments, and make adjustments in her plan as necessary (so D. N. Freedman). In any case, withal, one "fact" remains: regardless of whether Esther deliberately contrived the "seduction" scene or not (vii 8), Haman's actual downfall came while he was present at her party.

The AT and OL add here "your friend," a phrase which makes Haman the king's social equal and may have been intended by Esther to arouse the king's resentment against him. Apropos is the fact that the first dinner was in honor of the king alone, while the second was prepared for both of them (cf. v 8).

5. *Bring . . . right away.* Cf. Gen xviii 6; I Kings xxii 9.

that we may do as Esther wants. Literally "for the doing of the word of Esther."

6. *While they were drinking.* Literally "at the banquet of wine."

half the kingdom. The same exaggerated statement of favor is again made (see NOTE on vs. 3), only this time while they are drinking (cf. NOTE above). In any case, the king rightly understood the purpose behind Esther's invitation. Rather than feeling put upon, however, he obviously enjoyed his role dispensing favors.

The English translation attempts to produce the very loose and informal response of the king while he is drinking.

7. *All right.* Literally "my request and my petition." Since Biblical Hebrew had no word for "yes," the idea was expressed by repeating the preceding speaker's words (for this idiom see E. A. Speiser's *Genesis*, AB, vol. 1, NOTE on "Yes, you did" in Gen xviii 15).

As an alternative interpretation, one may translate the Hebrew literally as an anacoluthon: "My request and my petition are . . . ," arguing that Esther started to answer the king and then broke her sentence off in mid-air. By postponing her request till the next day the author has vided time for the resolution of the personal conflict between Mordecai and Haman (v 9 – vi 11) and increased the reader's suspense.

8. *tomorrow to a dinner . . . and tomorrow I will.* The first "tomorrow" (*māḥār*) is now missing from the MT by haplography, that is, as the LXX indicates, it immediately preceded the second *māḥār*, and an early Jewish scribe omitted it.

COMMENT

Having carefully prepared herself spiritually (iv 16) and physically (v 1) for her ordeal, Esther now stood radiant, but nonetheless unsummoned, in the inner court before the king. The magic of her beauty, which had captivated the king from the very beginning (ii 17), apparently saved her, although according to Addition D 8 *God* was responsible. In any case, the king, realizing that only a very urgent request could have compelled Esther to risk her life, immediately reassured her with an obvious hyperbole that her most extravagant wish would be granted (see NOTE on vs. 3).

The dramatic effect of the narrative is increased in vss. 4–8, where the author has Esther deliberately pass up two splendid opportunities to intercede for her people, after the king in each instance had committed himself to granting her almost any request. From the reader's point of view, refusing to state her real request may have been defensible the first time (vs. 4), but her second refusal (vs. 8) was tempting fate. Postponing her real request another time was a most questionable gamble; any number of things could go wrong in the interval between the two dinners: the king's benevolent mood could change, for example, or Haman

could learn of Esther's true feelings toward him or of her relationship to Mordecai. The author of Esther, however, recognized these
possibilities, and counted on his readers also recognizing them—
and agonizing over them. For as D. N. Freedman has observed,
"The third time is the charm in literary accounts. It is like the
acrobat or magician who deliberately fails twice in trying to perform
his most difficult feat, before succeeding on the third try. This
enhances the suspense and the expectation of the audience, as
well as winning for the performance the applause he deserves but
is not likely to get if the audience thinks that there is no danger
or limited need of skill to succeed."

7. HAMAN RESOLVES TO HANG MORDECAI
(v 9–14)

V ⁹ So that day Haman left joyful and exuberant. But when Haman noticed Mordecai at the King's Gate, and that he neither stood up nor trembled in his presence, Haman was infuriated with Mordecai. ¹⁰ Nevertheless, Haman restrained himself, went home, and assembled*a* his friends and his wife Zeresh; ¹¹ and Haman recounted to them the extent of his wealth, his large number of sons, every instance where the king had honored him, and how he had advanced him beyond the officials and courtiers. ¹² "Besides all that," said Haman, "Queen Esther invited only me to attend the dinner she gave for the king. And along with the king, I have been invited by her again tomorrow. ¹³ But all this fails to satisfy me whenever I see Mordecai the Jew sitting at the King's Gate." ¹⁴ So his wife Zeresh and all his friends advised him, "Have them make a gallows seventy-five feet high; and tomorrow morning speak to the king and have them hang Mordecai on it. Then, in good spirits accompany the king to the dinner." This advice appealed to Haman so he had the gallows erected.

a So the Greek; see NOTE.

NOTES

v 9. Here the author leaves Esther and the fate of the Jews to take up the story of Mordecai's personal struggle with Haman (v 9 – vi 13).
exuberant. Literally "good of heart"; cf. I Sam xxv 36.
10. *assembled.* So the Greek, which rightly regards the MT's "sent and brought" as hendiadys. The custom implied here is that of having slaves bring the guest to a banquet (cf. v 12, vi 14).
Zerest (zereš). LXX *zōsara.* See Introduction, p. XLII, for spellings in

the versions. Etymology uncertain; possibly a corruption of *grš*, or *Qiri(ri)sha*, the name of an Elamite goddess (Jensen, WZKM 6 [1892], 209–26) or "one with dishevelled hair" (Gehman, p. 327); see also Paton, p. 70. The view of Haller and Ringgren that "and his wife Zeresh" is a gloss supplied from v 14 is without support.

11. *his large number of sons*. Like the ancient Jews (cf. Ps cxxvii 4–5), the Persians regarded a large number of sons as one of life's greatest blessings (see Herodotus I. 136). Haman had ten (ix 6–10).

how he. That is, the king.

12. That Haman felt so highly honored is eloquent testimony to Esther's success in concealing her true feelings toward him, the persecutor of her people.

invited. Literally "cause to come," again referring to the custom of having slaves escort the guests to dinner.

13. *fails to satisfy me*. Literally "is not sufficient for me."

whenever. Literally "in every time."

14. *seventy-five feet high*. Literally "fifty cubits high." An obvious exaggeration, unless the gallows was erected "on some high structure" (so Hoschander, p. 205) or hill, so that all could see it. For a discussion of "cubit," see IDB, IV, s.v. "Weights and Measures," especially pp. 836–37.

Comment

Haman was elated as he came away from the queen's party, until he saw Mordecai. Small wonder he was infuriated (vs. 9)! Despite the king's edict consigning Mordecai and all his people to destruction, Mordecai gave no outward sign of recognition to the author of all his troubles, not by even a flicker of recognition acknowledging his presence (cf. Job xxix 7 ff.), let alone trembling before him. Mordecai simply remained seated at his accustomed place at the King's Gate (ii 19 *et passim*), in his regular clothes (iv 2), as if nothing had happened. Once again the author has heightened the reader's suspense by having the hero act in a manner which seems needlessly rash and almost certain to bring instant reprisal.

And now, in spite of all his material possessions (vss. 11–12), Haman is not content (vs. 13). For just as a small coin held too closely to the eye can block out the entirety of the sun, so Haman's preoccupation with revenge blocked out for him all his other blessings. The suggestion of his wife and friends, however, changes all that (vs. 14). Mordecai would be hanged the next day. This cheers Haman up considerably—but, thanks to the skill of the author, not the reader. Esther has not yet spoken to the king about the pogrom; the king still does not know Mordecai saved his life; and now a gallows has been set up for Mordecai. Never have things looked worse!

8. MORDECAI IS FINALLY REWARDED
(vi 1–13)

VI ¹ The king could not sleep that night so he gave orders to bring the record book, the daily record; and they were read ᵃto himᵃ. ² And it was found recorded there that Mordecai had given information about ᵇBigtan and Tereshᵇ, the two royal eunuchs who had guarded the threshold and who had plotted to assassinate King Xerxesᶜ. ³ Whereupon, the king asked, ᵈ"What great honorᵈ was conferred on Mordecai for this?"

Then replied the king's servants who were waiting on him, "Nothing has been done for him."

⁴ "Who is in the court?" asked the king.

(Now Haman had just entered the outer court of the king's apartment to ask the king about hanging Mordecai on the gallows he had prepared for him.) ⁵ So the king's servants told him, "Haman is waiting in the court."

"Let him enter!" said the king.

⁶ When Haman entered, the king said to him, "What should be done for the man whom the king especially wants to honor?"

Now, Haman reasoned to himself, "Whom would the king especially want to honor besides me!" ⁷ So Haman said to the king, "ᵉAll rightᵉ. ⁸ Have them bring a royal robe which the king has worn and a horse the king has ridden, one with a royal crown on its head. ⁹ Then have them hand the robe and the

ᵃ⁻ᵃ So LXX; MT "before the king."
ᵇ⁻ᵇ Since Greek omits, MT may well be a post-Septuagint gloss; see NOTE on ii 21.
ᶜ AT and OL add "Mordecai is a faithful man for protecting my life since he has kept me alive until now, and I sit on my throne, and I did nothing for him; I have not acted justly"; see NOTE on vs. 3.
ᵈ⁻ᵈ Hendiadys; MT "what honor and dignity."
ᵉ⁻ᵉ MT "the man whom the king especially wants to honor"; see NOTE.

horse over to one of the king's most noble princes and have him robe*f* the man whom the king especially wants to honor, and *g*have the prince*g* lead him on horseback through the city square, proclaiming before him, 'This is what is done for the man whom the king especially wants to honor!' "

10 "Hurry up" said the king to Haman, "and take the robe and the horse, and do exactly as you have advised to Mordecai the Jew who sits at the King's Gate. Do not omit a single detail that you have suggested!"

11 So Haman took the robe and the horse; and he robed Mordecai, and led Mordecai through the city square, proclaiming before him, "This is what is done for the man whom the king especially wants to honor." 12 Mordecai then returned to the King's Gate; and Haman hurried home, despondent and with his head covered. 13 When Haman had recounted to his wife Zeresh and all his friends everything that had just happened to him, then his advisers and his wife Zeresh advised him, "If this Mordecai before whom you have started to fall is Jewish, you won't succeed against him, but will undoubtedly fail*h*."

f Reading, with Greek, the third person singular verb forms hilbîšô, hirkîbāhû, and qārā', instead of the plural, hilbīšû, hirkîbûhû, and qārᵉ'û, which may, however, be impersonal.
g–g MT and all versions have "have him"; "the prince" is substituted here for the sake of clarity.
h All versions except the Vulgate add "For God is with him."

NOTES

vi 1. *king could not sleep.* Literally "the sleep of the king fled." The sleeplessness of kings is not an uncommon theme in literature (cf. Dan vi 18[19]; III Esdras iii 3; Shakespeare's *Henry IV, Part II*, III i 4–31), but the author of Esther leaves the cause of the insomnia to the reader's imagination. Driver's suggestion (VT 4 [1954], 239) that nādᵉdâ, "fled," should be read as containing the abbreviation for YHWH, "Lord," that is, *ḥ*, and thus should be read as a pōʿēl, namely, nōdāh *ḥ*, "YHWH made to flee," is ingenious but unconvincing.

Not surprisingly, however, all the ancient versions except the Vulg. (see Introduction, p. LXIV) state an explicit reason, namely, God prevented the king from sleeping.

record book. Literally "book of memorials"; cf. Mal III 16; Ezra iv 15. Although it is assumed here that "record book" is in apposition to "the daily record" (literally "Things of the Days"), it may, of course, be a portion of it; see NOTES on ii 23 and on "exact account" in x 2.

3. That Mordecai had gone unrewarded for saving the king's life was a reflection on the Persian king, for whom it was a point of honor to reward his benefactors (Herodotus III. 138, 140, V. 11, VIII. 85, IX. 107; Thucydides *Peloponnesian War* I. 138); see also textual note *c*.

servants who were waiting on him. Probably not the same as "the pages" of ii 2, since the latter would hardly have been so conversant with all that the king had done unless, of course, the king only wanted to know what the record book said about rewards for services rendered.

4. *king's apartment.* Literally "house of the king"; see NOTE on ii 13.

This verse well illustrates the author's love of alliteration, *lē'mōr lammelek litlôt* (see Striedl, pp. 90 ff.), as well as his gift for irony: here the early bird is gotten by the worm.

5. *waiting.* Cf. vii 7; also Exod ix 28; Eccles i 4. Literally "standing"; he *had* to wait; he might not have been standing. That only Haman was waiting there suggests how early he had come to the palace.

6. *especially wants* (*ḥāpēṣ*). In ii 14 this verb was used to describe the king's desire for a specific woman.

reasoned to himself. Literally "said in his heart."

besides me (*yôtēr mimmennî*). Found only here and Eccles ii 15, vii 11, and xii 12.

This verse is a splendid example of dramatic irony; cf. the irony here with that in II Sam xii 1–7 and II Sam xiv 1–17, where the question posed was by one who, unlike King Xerxes, was fully aware of its implications.

7. *All right. Literally* "The man whom the king especially wants to honor"; see NOTE on v 7. An alternative possibility is to translate the Hebrew literally and argue that Haman is so eager to express himself that he blurts out only part of his answer; then, realizing he has started poorly, he pauses and, in vs. 8, begins anew his suggestions for honoring "himself." But even then he is so sure of himself that he neglects to preface his advice with the conventional opening phrase "If it please the king."

8. Thinking that the rewards prescribed are for himself, Haman suggests the highest honors of the kingdom for the unnamed benefactor— a royal robe and horse which have actually been used by, not just owned by, the king himself (cf. Gen xli 38–44; I Sam xviii 4; I Kings i 33). Haman's desire for a robe of the king is reminiscent of Teribazus' request for Artaxerxes II's robe: "And when Teribazus replied, 'Put on

another for thyself, but give this one to me,' the king did so, saying,
'I give this to thee, Teribazus, but I forbid thee to wear it.' Teribazus
gave no heed to this command (being not a bad man but rather light-
headed and witless), and at once put on the king's coat and decked
himself with golden necklaces and women's ornaments of royal splendor
. . . but the king merely laughed and said, 'I permit you to wear the
trinkets as a woman, and the robe as a madman' " (Plutarch *Artaxerxes*
V).

robe. The LXX adds "linen" (Heb. *šēš*), while Josephus *Antiquities*
XI. 254, adds "a gold necklace" (Heb. *rᵉbîd hazzāhāb*). Both additions
are obviously made under the influence of Gen xli 42–43, where Joseph
is elevated by Pharaoh (cf. L. A. Rosenthal, ZAW 15 [1895], 278–84;
16 [1896], 182). That the writer of Esther was quite familiar with the
Joseph narrative has been more recently confirmed by Moshe Gan
(*Tarbiẓ* 31 [1961–62], 144–49); Gan fails, however, to prove his thesis
that the author of Esther drew his inspiration for the entire story from
the Joseph narrative.

on its head. That is, on the horse's head. For Persian horses with
crowns, see the reliefs of Xerxes' *apadana* at Persepolis, and on Plate 4.

9. *most noble princes* (*śārê happartᵉmîm*). See NOTE on "nobles" in
i 3.

lead him. Literally "caused him to ride."

city square. Not the square of the acropolis (cf. iv 6), but the square
of the city, where many more people would have witnessed the event.

10. *Mordecai the Jew.* Unless "the Jew" is a gloss here (it is legitimately
used in viii 7, ix 29, 31, and x 3), then it is part of Mordecai's title, to
distinguish him from others with the same theophorous name. The
king's use of the word "Jew" here raises several questions which
scholars have discussed in detail. How did the king learn that Mordecai
was a Jew? Would the king now exclude Mordecai from the pogrom?
Would the king be more favorably disposed toward the Jews now
that he knew Mordecai was Jewish? The author answers none of these
legitimate questions; rather, he simply tells his fascinating story, leaving
the speculations to his readers. But he does not leave the reader in any
doubt as to the irony of it all: the king's command exceeds even the
suggestions of Haman: the prime minister himself shall do the honors!

11. While the AT has an addition here which purports to give an
account of what happened between Haman and Mordecai ("And Haman
said to Mordecai 'Take off the sackcloth!' And Mordecai was troubled,
like one who is dying; and in distress he took off the sackcloth. But
then he put on the splendid garments, and he thought he beheld an
omen, and his heart was to the Lord; and he was speechless"), the MT

is more effective by leaving the entire encounter to the reader's imagination and telling only the sequel (vs. 12). With some justice, however, Anderson argues that the author of Esther omitted any dialogue between Mordecai and Haman because his "interest centers in plot rather than character" (p. 860).

12. Life continues on as before for Mordecai: he goes back to his regular place at the King's Gate, for he will not be elevated until the king learns about his relationship to Esther (viii 1). But for Haman life has now taken a most tragic turn: with his head covered as a sign of grief (cf. II Sam xv 30, xix 4; Jer xiv 3–4; Ezek xxiv 17; Curtius IV. 10, X. 5), he returns home to lick his wounds and seek solace with his wife and friends.

13. Zeresh is expressing here the views of the author, not her own. He knew better than any pagan woman the relevant biblical passages concerning the ultimate victory of the Jews over the Amalekites (see NOTE on "Agagite" in iii 1). For other examples of Gentiles predicting a Jewish victory, cf. Josh ii 9–14; Judith v 20–21; and III Macc iii 8–10, v 31.

friends. Literally "wise men"; LXX "friends." Probably a synonym for "friends" (so v 10, 14) rather than a second group of men to be distinguished from his friends. Nonetheless, Goldman (*The Five Megilloth*, p. 226) may be correct in seeing "wise men" used here in a deliberately ironical sense, that is, they were wise *after the fact* (v 14).

is Jewish. Literally "is from the seed of the Jews."

you . . . will undoubtedly fail. Literally "you . . . will certainly fall before him." Unlike the ancient versions (see textual note *ʰ*), the author of Esther tells his story without offering explicit theological explanations, letting the events speak for themselves.

COMMENT

Unable to sleep, the king had his record book read to him, thereby finally learning that Mordecai had saved his life. Unlike the ancient versions, the MT does not attribute the king's sleeplessness to God. This does not mean, however, that the author of the Hebrew Esther did not believe in the active hand of Providence here (see first paragraph of COMMENT on § 5, iv 1–17); for Mordecai's victory over Haman (vs. 11) results from a series of seemingly trivial circumstances, or coincidences—the sleeplessness of the king (vs. 1); the particular passage concerning Mordecai's service to the king being read, in spite of all the recorded material available (vs. 2); Haman's early appearance in the king's court (vs. 4); and Haman's assumption that the king is really asking for new ways to honor him (vs. 6). While the skeptic may well call this series of events "luck" ("good luck" for Mordecai, "bad" for Haman), the religious person is more likely to call it "Providence" or "the hand of God."

But if Providence sealed Haman's fate, Haman himself certainly gave it a helping hand. Verse 6 is a masterful piece of dramatic construction. The king's question to Haman creates instant dismay in the reader: how unfortunate that the king should consult Haman, of all people, on the way to reward Mordecai! Even before the full ramifications of that idea can sink in to the reader's mind, however, the author has Haman assume that he himself is the one to be honored. Thus, just as Haman had managed in iii 8 to conceal from the king the identity of "a certain people," so here the king unintentionally (see, however, Hoschander, pp. 200–11) keeps from Haman the identity of Mordecai as "the man whom the king especially wants to honor." Haman, therefore, unwittingly prescribes the highest honors for his enemy and brings the greatest humiliation upon himself (vss. 8–11).

Mordecai has been honored, but he is not safe; neither is Esther nor the Jews. But even as Zeresh and his friends sense in Haman's humiliation a foreshadowing of his further failure (vs. 13), so the reader sees it to augur well for Esther's success before the king and for the Jews' ultimate victory over their enemies.

9. HAMAN IS UNMASKED AND EXECUTED
(vi 14 – vii 10)

VI ¹⁴ While they were still talking with him, the king's eunuchs arrived; and they hurried to bring Haman to the banquet that Esther had prepared. **VII** ¹ When the king and Haman were there at Queen Esther's party ² on the second day, the king again asked Esther while they were drinking, "What do you want, Queen Esther? It shall be granted you! What's your petition? Even if half the kingdom, it shall be done *for you*."

³ Then Queen Esther answered, saying, "If I have obtained your favor, Your Majesty and if it please the king, let my life be granted to me as my request. And my people's as my petition! ⁴ For we've been sold, I and my people, for destruction! For slaughter and annihilation! If we had just been sold as slaves and servant girls, *I would have kept quiet*; *for our problem would not have been worth bothering the king*."

⁵ "Who is it?" *exclaimed King Xerxes to Queen Esther*. *"Where is he* and who has the nerve to do this?"

⁶ "An enemy! An adversary!" said Esther, "This wicked Haman here!"

Haman was dumbfounded before the king and queen; ⁷ but when the king *arose in anger from his wine and went out* into

---

ᵃ⁻ᵃ Reading with a number of LXX manuscripts and OL. See NOTE.

ᵇ⁻ᵇ LXX now has "I have heard"; but Ethiopic, a translation based on the LXX, has "I have kept silent."

ᶜ⁻ᶜ AT "But I did not want to announce it so that I would distress my lord"; see NOTE.

ᵈ⁻ᵈ So LXX; see NOTE.

ᵉ⁻ᵉ Greek errs in omitting this since Esther answers *two* questions (see NOTE on vs. 6).

ᶠ⁻ᶠ So LXX rightly translates the ellipsis of the MT: "he arose from his wine in anger."

the garden of the pavilion, Haman remained behind to beg Queen Esther for his life. For he saw that the king had decided to punish him. ⁸ As the king came back from the garden of the pavilion to the banquet hall, Haman was prostrate on the couch where Esther was; so the king exclaimed, "Would he actually violate the queen while I'm in the building?"

As soon as these words were spoken, they covered Haman's face. ⁹ Then observed Harbonah*g*, one of the eunuchs in attendance on the king, "Then, too, there is the gallows at Haman's house which he made for Mordecai who saved the king's life. Seventy-five feet high!"

"Hang him on that!" said the king.

¹⁰ *h* So Haman was hanged*h* on the same gallows that he had erected for Mordecai. Then the king's anger abated.

g MT ḥarbônâ (cf. ḥarbônā' of i 10). LXX *bougathan*.
h–h So LXX rightly renders Hebrew's impersonal usage, "and they hanged Haman."

NOTES

vi 14. *they hurried to bring.* Literally "they hastened to bring." This emphasizes Haman's importance, not any supposed tardiness on his part. There is little justification for some scholars' view that as the result of Haman's humiliating experience in vi 11, he either had completely forgotten about his appointment with the queen or was reluctant to keep it. On the contrary, Haman needed just such a party to bolster his deflated ego.

vii 1. *were there . . . party.* Literally "they came to drink with." Probably the author intended the infinitive *lištôt* to mean neither "to come for the sole purpose of drinking excessively" nor "to drink for the purpose of deliberating" (Hoschander, p. 219); rather he used it as a denominative from *mišteh*, "banquet," which is literally "drinking"; cf. I Kings xx 12; Job i 4 (so Paton). The hour of the party is not stated; presumably it would have been in the afternoon rather than in the evening since so much happened later that same day, namely, Haman was hanged (vs. 10), and Mordecai was personally received by the king (viii 1–2), all of which would have taken some time.

2. *while they were drinking.* Literally "at the banquet of wine."

for you. The AT adds here "Esther was uneasy about speaking because the enemy was right in front of her, but God gave her the courage for the challenge." Unlike the MT, the AT has God change the hearts of both the king (D 8) and Esther.

3. *your favor.* Despite the tensions within her, Esther manages to speak with dignity, using the prescribed courtly expressions, but also with feeling, using the more intimate second person form of address (cf. v 4, 8, where she uses the third). After all, she was addressing the king as his queen. The long, formal courtly expressions notwithstanding, Esther's requests themselves are quite abbreviated, that is, "my people's as my petition" is ellipsis for *"the deliverance* of my people as my petition." This abruptness no doubt reflects her nervousness and desperation.

The AT somewhat overplays Esther's outward calm by adding to vs. 5, "But when the queen saw that it seemed terrible to the king and that he hated the evil, she said, 'Don't be angry, my lord! It's enough that I have your support. Enjoy yourself, my king. Tomorrow I shall do as you have commanded.' But the king urged her to tell him who had behaved so arrogantly as to do this; and he promised with an oath to do for her whatever she should ask."

4. In this verse Esther justifies her requests in vs. 3. Unfortunately, her rationale is far from clear, probably because of corruption in the MT (see below).

we've been sold. An allusion to the monetary transaction between Haman and the king (see first NOTE on iii 9), although many scholars understand "sold" to be used here in the sense of "delivered over to" (as in Deut xxxii 30; Judg ii 14, iii 8, iv 2, 9, x 7).

If (weʾillû). Contraction of *we* and *'im lû,* and found only here and in Eccles vi 6; but frequent in Aramaic.

for our problem (literally "distress") . . . *the king.* Undoubtedly the most difficult clause to translate in all of Esther, primarily because the meanings of three of the six words in it are uncertain, namely, *haṣṣār,* "enemy," or "distress" (or *haṣṣālâ,* "deliverance"); *šōweh,* a participle with a variety of possible meanings; and finally, *benēzeq,* a hapax legomenon* in Hebrew. Paton (pp. 261–62) clearly presented and evaluated the various proposed readings up to his day; research since then has not led, unfortunately, to any better explanations. The LXX's "for the slander is not worthy of the king's court" represents a rendering of *'yn hḥṣr šwh bmzyq hmlk* (so Hoschander). The reading adopted here, which agrees in substance with the AT (see textual note *c–c*), understands Esther to say that if the Jews had been sold only into slavery, she would have kept quiet since she would not have bothered the king with their "petty" problems. For *haṣṣār* as "distress," see Isa v 30, xxvi 16; Pss iv 2, xxxii 7; Job vii 11, xv 24. Haupt's suggestion (p. 147) that *nēzeq* corresponds to the Ar. *naziqa,* "to be easily angered," and the noun *nazâqa*, "sudden anger, a fit of disappointment," is the most acceptable of all suggestions.

5. *exclaimed* (*wayyōʾmer*) *King Xerxes to Queen Esther.* MT has "then King Xerxes said, and he said to Queen Esther," which is a dittography. Ehrlich and Ringgren, however, read *wayyᵉmahēr*, "and he hurried," in place of the first *wayyōʾmer*, while Bardtke retained both verbs and translated them as "then spoke King Ahasuerus; and he said to Queen Esther," contending that the first *wayyōʾmer* increases the reader's suspense, raising the question in his mind "Did the king speak to Haman or Esther?" As it turned out, the king spoke to Esther, thereby giving Haman no opportunity to defend himself.

who has the nerve? Literally "who fills his heart" (cf. Eccles viii 11; Acts v 3); the verb form (*mᵉlāʾô*) is probably under the influence of Aramaic, cf. Joüon, GHB, § 78*j*. First the king's life was threatened (ii 21–23), and now the queen's; small wonder he was so excited. According to the AT (see NOTE on vs. 3 above), the more upset the king got, the more calm Esther became.

6. *"An enemy! An adversary!"* This is Esther's answer to the king's first question "Who is it?" in vs. 5; and "This wicked Haman!" is her answer to his second question in vs. 5. Instead of *hārāʿ*, "wicked," Ehrlich (p. 120) reads *hārēaʿ*, "the lover" (as in Jer iii 1; Hosea iii 1), and interprets the phrase as a piece of irony, that is, "My 'lover' here!", arguing that Esther designed it deliberately to make the king jealous of Haman. Although conceivably supported by the AT which adds "your friend," Ehrlich probably is still not correct; in part, because the regular word for "friend" in Esther is *ʾōhēb* (v 10, 14, vi 13), not *rēaʿ*.

was dumbfounded. More in the sense of "taken by surprise" (so Haupt, p. 150) than "was afraid"; see Dan viii 17; I Chron xxi 30.

7. *from his wine.* Literally "from the banquet of wine."

went out. Regardless of what the king's reason for leaving the room may have been, and commentators have offered many explanations (for a long list of possibilities, see Paton, p. 262), the king's absence sets the scene for the incident which seals Haman's fate (cf. vs. 8).

remained. Literally "he stood"; cf. II Kings xv 20.

to beg Queen Esther. D. N. Freedman has observed, "A curious point is to be found in Haman's decision to appeal to Esther rather than the king. It adds drama and irony because Haman seals his own doom thereby. But that he should appeal to a Jewess to save him, when he had condemned them all to death is ironic. It shows him to be stupid and perhaps vain."

that the king had decided to punish him. Literally "he saw that evil was determined against him from the king." The LXX has "for he saw himself to be in trouble."

8. *banquet hall.* Literally "to the house of the banquet of wine"; the LXX omits.

was prostrate (*nōpēl*). When the king left the room, Haman did not follow him to seek his pardon but stayed with the queen, realizing that unless she interceded for him, he was surely doomed. So Haman approached Esther's couch where she, in true Persian fashion, was reclining as she ate (cf. Herodotus IX. 80, 82; Xenophon *Cyropaedia* VIII. 8, 16), to beg for her intercession with the king. Many scholars argue that Haman, in a typical Near Eastern gesture of humility and contrition, either seized Esther's feet (so the AT) or even kissed them. If so, this would explain the king's claim that Haman was making improper advances (vs. 8). The king's response has been variously characterized by scholars—excessive, drunken, a cruel jest, unreasonable, and so on; but one must remember that in antiquity very strong feelings and strict regulations centered on the harem (cf. Plutarch *Artaxerxes* XXVII. 1, 2; see also Weidner's article on some harem regulations in AfO 17 [1956], 257–93). Had Haman knelt as much as a foot away from the queen's couch, the king's reaction could still have been justified.

As soon as . . . spoken. Literally "the word went out from the king's mouth." So serious was the king's accusation that his servants immediately treated Haman like a condemned man (see below).

they covered Haman's face. The LXX has "he was confounded in the face," which may mean that the LXX read *ḥāpērû*, "his face grew red" (so Felix Perles), or *ḥāwērû*, "his face became pale" (Rudolph, VT 4 [1954], 90). Arguing that the verb is not used transitively elsewhere (cf. Esther vi 12; Jer xiv 3–4; II Sam xv 30), D. N. Freedman sees a Niphal form here, with a double-duty *n* from the previous word (*hmn phy*) or haplography (*hmn nphy*). However, the MT's reading seems quite intelligible and correct, even though there is no evidence outside the Old Testament that the Persians covered the heads of the condemned; for evidence of such a practice among the Greeks and Romans, see Curtius VI. 8, 22 and Livy I. xxvi. 25, respectively. See also A. Condamin, RB (1898), pp. 253–61.

9. *Then, too* (*gam hinnēh*). In addition to suggesting an appropriate way to execute Haman, Harbonah's observation also had the effect of introducing a second accusation against him, namely, that he had knowingly tried to kill a benefactor of the king. If there had been any uncertainty in the king's mind concerning Haman's fate, this ended it. One need not, however, agree with Hoschander (p. 226) that without Harbonah's accusation Haman could not have been summarily executed

but, in accordance with Herodotus I. 137, would have been formally tried and given ample opportunity to defend himself; as it turned out, this was something he was not allowed to do. In any case, Harbonah's suggestion struck the king as perfect poetic justice. "He who digs a pit will fall into it" (Prov xxvi 27).

who saved the king's life. Literally "who spoke good concerning the king," referring to Mordecai's informing on the conspirators against the king in ii 22.

COMMENT

Haman's mood on the occasion of Esther's second party may have been quite different from that of the first one (v 8–9), but Esther's was not. She knew nothing of Mordecai's recent personal triumph (vi 11) or, at least, the author gives no such indication. So far as Esther was concerned, Haman was as powerful, confident, and to be feared as ever, all of which makes her task more dangerous and her courage more impressive to the reader.

She must have been considerably relieved to hear the king utter essentially the same sweeping promise (vs. 2) that he had made to her on two previous occasions (cf. v 3, 6). Once he heard her request, he could, of course, still refuse to grant it; but, having offered such emphatic assurances on three separate occasions, he could hardly deny that he had really made such a promise. Thus the king had painted himself into a corner.

Nonetheless, Esther needed all the reassurance she could get; as the AT indicates (see NOTE on "for you" in vs. 2), for her this encounter was still a matter of life and death. Once she revealed her ethnic and religious origins to the king, not to mention her opposition to the king's most powerful official, her future was most uncertain.

Esther's petition in vs. 3 was more than a request: she had made an admission—and a confession. In effect, she had admitted to being a Jewess; she had confessed her oneness with her people, testifying to the very close reciprocal relationship between the individual and the group in Judaism. Historically, Jews have always recognized what the Nazi holocaust proved so tragically to everyone in the twentieth century: whether he likes it or not, the Jew, so long as he remains a Jew, stands in a close relationship of interdependence with the Jewish community—for weal and woe. By identifying Haman she had unmasked the villain, but she had also unmasked herself.

The king, of course, vindicated Esther, and promptly sentenced Haman to death (vs. 10). Anderson has accurately expressed the views of many recent scholars when he writes of the main characters in this chapter: "The reader sees all three characters as they really are: Haman, actually an arrogant bully who turns into a whining coward when trapped; the king, capricious and impressionable, and weak despite his show of power; and Esther, victorious through the exercise of her feminine charms but *callous and indifferent* as the once proud heathen asks for mercy . . . *she looks on in cold silence*" ([italics added], p. 862). The present writer is in sharp disagreement with the italicized words, and "naïve" is the only word to describe Paton's suggestion that the author of Esther could have made Esther more attractive by representing her "as interceding for Haman *even if* [italics added] the king did not grant her request" (p. 264). Nor need Esther be given a "white-wash," as Bardtke (p. 359) has done by arguing that court etiquette prevented her from even trying to speak to the king under the circumstances, that is, in a case involving the violation of strict harem regulations. The simple truth is that at this point Haman was not defeated: he was a falling, not a fallen, enemy. He had lost a crucial battle, but he had not necessarily lost the war. Were Haman to survive this round, he might recover and score a knockout in the next. So long as an enemy as powerful and shrewd as Haman lived, he was a threat to Esther, Mordecai, and the Jewish community. To say here that Esther was merciless and unfeeling is to misinterpret the entire situation. Thus, while her heart might have prompted her to be merciful, logic and prudence restrained her.

10. THE KING BEGINS TO UNDO THE EVIL
OF HAMAN
(viii 1–17)

VIII ¹ That same day King Xerxes gave Queen Esther the entire estate of Haman, the enemy of the Jews; and when Mordecai was presented to the king (for Esther had disclosed to him their relationship), ² the king took off the signet ring which he had recovered from Haman and presented it to Mordecai; and Esther appointed Mordecai over Haman's estate. ³ Then Esther again spoke to the king, collapsing at his feet and crying and begging him to frustrate the evil intention of Haman the Agagite, and the scheme which he had devised against the Jews. ⁴ When the king extended his gold scepter to Esther, Esther got up and stood before the king, ⁵ and said, "If it please the king, and if I have found his favor, and the request is proper in the king's opinion, and if he really likes me, let a decree be written to revoke the letters—ᵃthe scheme of Haman, son of Hammedatha the Agagiteᵃ—which he dictated for the extermination of the Jews in all the king's provinces. ⁶ How can I bear to see this calamity overtakeᵇ my people? How can I bear to see the destruction of my own relatives?" ⁷ "Now look here," said King Xerxes to Queen Esther ᶜand Mordecai the Jewᶜ, "I have given Haman's estate to Esther, and he has been hanged on the gallows because he attacked the Jews. ⁸ But you yourselves write in the king's name whatever you want concerning the Jews; then seal it with the royal signet." (For an edict written in the king's name and sealed with the royal signet cannot be revoked.)

⁹ So the king's secretaries were summoned on the twenty-third day ᵈof the third month (which is the month of Sivan)ᵈ; and

ᵃ⁻ᵃ LXX omits; see NOTE.
ᵇ Reading *timṣā'*, instead of *yimṣā'*; see NOTE.
ᶜ⁻ᶜ All ancient versions except Vulgate omit; but see NOTE.
ᵈ⁻ᵈ LXX "of the first month, which is Nisan." See NOTE.

the edict concerning*e* the Jews was written exactly as Mordecai had dictated, to the satraps, governors, and officials of the provinces from India to Ethiopia, one hundred and twenty-seven provinces, each province in its own script, each people in its own language, including the Jews, in their own script and language. 10 He wrote in the name of King Xerxes and sealed it with the royal signet; and he sent the dispatches by mounted couriers riding *f*on swift horses, the royal coursers bred from the mares*f*, 11 to the effect that the king had given permission to the Jews in every single city to organize themselves and to defend themselves, to wipe out, slaughter, and annihilate every armed force of any people or province that was hostile to them, along with their children and women, and to plunder their personal property 12 on one day in all King Xerxes' provinces, namely, on the thirteenth day of the twelfth month, which is the month of Adar.*g* 13 The contents of the edict was to be promulgated in each province, to be published to all peoples, that the Jews were to be ready on that day to take revenge on their enemies. 14 So, urged on by the king's command, the couriers riding on swift horses, the royal coursers, galloped away. Meanwhile, the decree had been published in the acropolis of Susa. 15 When Mordecai left the king's presence in a royal robe of violet and white, wearing a big gold turban and cloak of fine linen and purple, then the city of Susa cheered and was happy.

16 For the Jews there was light and joy, rejoicing and honor. 17 Likewise, in every province and in every city, wherever the king's command and edict reached, the Jews had joy and gladness, feast and holiday. Moreover, many of the pagans professed themselves Jews, for they were afraid of the Jews.

e Reading *'al,* instead of *'el,* "to"; see NOTE.
f-f Here, as in viii 10, LXX omits these obscure, technical terms. "Hexaplaric" manuscripts erroneously(?) transliterated *hārammākîm* as *ramacheim* or *rachein;* see NOTE.
g The Greek introduces at this point Addition E: "The Second Letter of King Artaxerxes."

NOTES

viii 1. In terms of content, the seven verses in the AT that correspond to viii 1–12 are *quite* different from both the MT and the LXX. This fact is a major argument in Torrey's interesting but ultimately unconvincing view that the *original* text of Esther ended with ch. vii (see his treatment in HTR 37 [1944], especially pp. 16–17). Actually, only the most dramatic part of the story ends with ch. vii, since the journalistic style which characterized the story up through ch. ii is now resumed.

Xerxes gave. Since Haman was a traitor, his entire estate automatically reverted to the crown (cf. Herodotus III. 128–29; Josephus *Antiquities* XI. 17). The king, in turn, gave it to Esther, apparently as compensation for her suffering. Although a generous gift, it was nothing compared to what Xerxes promised his mistress Artaynte if she would release him from an embarrassing promise (see NOTE on *half my kingdom* in v 3).

the entire estate. Literally "the house"; includes all his property, that is, his real estate and other holdings (see Gen xxxix 4, xliv 1; I Kings xiii 8; Job viii 15).

was presented to. Literally "what he was to her"; the author probably intended to convey more than is suggested by the translation of either the LXX ("that he was related to her") or even of the Vulgate ("that he was her father"). Since Mordecai was appointed prime minister, Esther must have indicated not only their blood relationship but also the quality of that relationship and the character of the man.

2. *presented it to Mordecai.* Thereby investing Mordecai with the powers which he had previously conferred on Haman (iii 10), a fact which the AT explicitly states in viii 17 ("and the king entrusted to him the things concerning the kingdom"). Then Esther appointed Mordecai over the extensive estate of Haman (iii 9, 11, v 11) so that he might have wealth commensurate with his new post of prime minister (cf. viii 15, x 3).

3. *Esther again spoke.* Literally "and she added (*wattôsep*) and said." Failing to understand *wattôsep* as an idiomatic expression meaning "to do something again" (cf. Gen xxv 1; I Sam xix 21), the LXX translated it quite literally. The universal view that this phrase introduces a new scene is incorrect: the text does not say "Esther again *came*" but "Esther again *spoke*" (see COMMENT). For a discussion of paragraphing in Esther and other books of the Old Testament, see Bardtke, pp. 268–70.

collapsing. Not "bowed down" or "did obeisance" as many translators have it; the verb here is *npl* as in vii 8, not *kr‘* or *hšthwh*, the standard words in Esther for "doing obeisance"; see iii 2 and 5.

4. *extended his gold scepter.* A sign of encouragement rather than clemency. There is no reason to limit the use of the king's scepter to only one function, that is, to saving the life of one who enters the throne room unsummoned (iv 11, v 2). See Plate 2 for a Persian king holding his scepter during an audience.

5. In this verse of the LXX and the next, Esther uses the informal second person form of direct address instead of the third; and although the former would probably have been more effective under the circumstances, there is no reason to think that the author of Esther used it.

proper (kāšēr). Cf. Eccles ii 21, iv 4, v 10, x 10, xi 6. In post-Biblical Hebrew, the word is used in the familiar ritualistic sense, that is, *kosher.*

and the request is proper . . . really likes me. Some scholars delete this phrase with the LXX as being needlessly repetitious and hence a gloss; but although admittedly repetitious, these two courtly phrases, which have not been used by Esther earlier, underscore the pressure she feels and applies to the king. She is by no means certain of gaining her request; thus she must apply every pressure and persuasion at her disposal to avoid failure.

and if he really likes me. Literally "if I am good in his eyes"; Esther is being coy and coquettish here.

the scheme . . . Agagite. Some scholars delete with the LXX, but they are then forced to posit "Haman." While "son of . . . Agagite" may very well be a gloss, the phrase "the scheme of Haman" is probably original since it fulfills a definite purpose: by using it, Esther shrewdly absolves the king of all personal responsibility for the pogrom by focusing the blame on Haman who, being dead, cannot defend himself.

dictated. Literally "he wrote."

6. Esther now goes back to what she had passionately started in vii 3–4, when she was interrupted by the king's outburst against Haman (vii 5). In the AT, Esther's request is quite direct and brutal: "And she said to the king, 'Grant me to deter my enemies with slaughter!' "

How (‘êkākâ). A contraction of *’ay* and *kākâ;* the form occurs only here and in Song of Sol v 3.

How can I bear to see. Literally "how am I able that I should see."

overtake. Reading *tmṣ’* instead of *ymṣ’*, to agree with feminine noun *rā‘â*, "calamity"; *ymṣ’* was probably written under the influence of Gen xliv 34 (see Rosenthal, ZAW 15 [1897], 281).

my own relatives (môladtî). The LXX misunderstood the Hebrew here, and thought Esther referred to her own personal destruction:

"And how shall I be able to survive in the destruction of my father's house?"

7. *and Mordecai the Jew.* This phrase is crucial for the correct understanding of vss. 1–8. Many scholars, following the ancient versions, have erroneously deleted this phrase (see especially Bardtke, p. 367); the presence of the plural verbs, however, as well as the most emphatic plural pronoun *'tm* in vs. 8, argues against its deletion. Mordecai has been in the king's presence since vs. 1, where he was made prime minister (vs. 2), and has watched Esther make her very moving plea for her people (vss. 3–6).

Moreover, that only the Vulgate agrees with the MT in including "and Mordecai the Jew" is not surprising since Josephus, the OL, and the Ethiopic were translations based upon the LXX, whereas the Vulgate was a translation of the Hebrew. Thus unanimity among ancient versions does not automatically establish the correctness of an LXX reading, especially in this particular case; see NOTE below.

"Now look here (hinnēh)." Literally "behold!" Unlike the LXX, which adds "and I have shown favor to you . . . What do you still want?", sounding very much like a rebuke by the king, in the MT the king seems to encourage Esther, indicating his favorable disposition toward both her and the Jews by citing what he has already done for them.

he has been hanged on the gallows. Literally "Him they hanged"; emphatic usage. The OL erroneously adds "with all his house"; and the AT has "Queen Esther even conferred with the king about the sons of Haman so that they might also die with their father."

because he attacked ("laid his hand upon") *the Jews.* This phrase may reflect some editorializing on the part of the author, for earlier he had suggested that Haman's execution grew out of his threat to Esther's life (vii 3–4) and honor (vii 8).

8. *you ('tm).* The pronoun is very emphatic, both by its presence and its position, that is, preceding an imperative; cf. Gen xlii 16.

cannot be revoked. The parenthetic aside here is made by either the author or a glossator rather than by the king, since Esther would have known about the law's irrevocability. On this problem, see NOTE on i 19.

9. Although the longest verse in The Writings, the third major subdivision of the Hebrew Bible, it is hardly the most important, differing from iii 12 and i 1 only in three partculars: the date, originator, and intent of the edict.

Sivan. Siwān is the Hebrew cognate of the Bab. *simanu* (May–June). According to the MT, Mordecai's letter went out two months and ten days after Haman's (iii 12), a significant time lapse which can in no way be precisely accounted for.

concerning the Jews. Reading *'al,* instead of *'el;* the preposition is con-

nected with "dictated" rather than with "was written." There would be
no point in stating here what is more clearly stated at the end of the
verse, i.e., "including the Jews in their script and language." Because
the LXX read *'el* instead of *'al*, it omitted altogether the phrase "including the Jews in their script and language." The LXX also omits
"exactly as Mordecai had dictated."

10. *swift horses* (*hārekeš*). A collective term denoting some special
type of horse, presumably fast (see Mic i 13; I Kings v 8). *H'hštrnym*,
"the royal coursers," is the hebraized form of the Pers. *khshatra*,
"lordship," plus the Persian adjectival suffix *ana*, "belonging to." A
hapax legomenon, *hārammākîm*, tentatively translated here as "the
mares" (but see Striedl, pp. 173 f.), at least cannot have the meaning
that it has in post-Biblical Hebrew, namely, "mules." Whatever may be
the precise meanings of these technical terms (the LXX omits all of
them; see also Paton, pp. 277–78), their general meaning is clear
enough: these were fast, strong horses which could carry the important
message throughout the far-flung empire in good time.

11. *to the effect that* (*'šr*). *'šr* introduces the text here, as in i 19, ii
10, iii 4, iv 11, vi 2. The LXX has here "he commanded them to
observe their own laws in every city, and to assist them, and to pursue
their adversaries and those who opposed them as they wished" while
the AT has at one point "Let a copy of the letter be posted in every
place: for the Jews to practice their own laws, and to strengthen them so
that in the time of oppression they may defend themselves against those
who attack them."

to organize themselves. Cf. II Sam xx 14. Literally "to assemble
themselves." Had the Jews not assembled until the day of slaughter,
such action would have come too late and availed them little; rather
they were to begin right away making plans and preparations.

to defend themselves. Literally "stand for their lives"; the phrase is a
technical term and should not be taken too literally, for the Jews
must have played an aggressive, offensive role rather than a stubborn,
defensive one (cf. ix 13 and 15) since 75,000 of their enemies fell in
battle.

to wipe out . . . property. Significantly, this paraphrase of Mordecai's
edict is almost identical with the paraphrase of Haman's letter in iii
13. Hoschander (p. 240) would delete the shocking phrase "children
and women" as a gloss, while Haupt insisted that only the right of self-
defense was granted and that the phrase refers just to those children
and women who would themselves attack Jews. Somewhat closer to the
truth is Anderson (p. 866) who wrote "This is truly measure-for-
measure retaliation, patterned after the sanguinary terms of Haman's
original decree and recalling the ancient ban (*hērem*) vowed against all

'Amalekites' (cf. I Sam xv 3)." It is highly unlikely, however, that a
Persian king would have sanctioned such wholesale and indiscriminate
slaughtering and plundering of any minority group within his empire,
let alone among all his citizens. Actually, the central issue here is not
historicity but theology, for it is the Wisdom doctrine of retributive
justice which best explains the parallel between the phrase under discussion here and in iii 13, that is, Haman and his supporters are to receive what they had intended to give. Mordecai's letter confirms the
adage "as a man sows so shall he reap."

12. At this point the LXX, the AT, Josephus, and the OL have Addition
E (Vulg. xvi 1–24), the King's Second Letter.

thirteenth. The OL has "fourteenth," an error which could easily have
happened if a Latin scribe misread a Greek abbreviation for the number;
for example, in this same verse one Greek manuscript has *iƃ,* the short
alphabetic abbreviation for the very long word *dōdekatos,* which would
not easily have been misread.

13. *contents (patšegen).* Cf. NOTE on iii 14.

take revenge. So the MT; the LXX has "fight against," which nicely
eliminates the baser element of revenge.

14. *galloped away (yāṣᵉ'û mᵉbōhālîm).* Literally "they went out with
haste." The LXX omits the participle which is also not found in iii 15
of the MT, a parallel passage, but the author used "with haste" here to
emphasize the importance of speed in this matter.

15. *left.* Bardtke (p. 373) and others erroneously see this verse as
introducing a new scene rather than the conclusion to Mordecai's
audience with the king, which began with vs. 1; see also NOTE on vs.
3, and COMMENT.

turban (ᵃṭeret). Cf. II Sam xii 30; a headdress to be distinguished
from the royal crown *(keter)* of i 11, ii 17, vi 8.

cloak (takrîk). Occurring only here; from the Aram. *kᵉrak,* "to sur-
round."

the city . . . cheered. Literally "the city . . . shouted." "City" here
would include the Gentile majority and not just the Jews. The cheering
of the Gentiles may have been more of an expression of their dislike
and rejection of Haman than of their approval of Mordecai.

16. *light ('ôrâ).* A symbol of prosperity (Pss xxvii 1, xxxvi 10) and
well-being (Pss xcvii 11, cxxxix 12; Job xxii 28, xxx 26).

17. *holiday.* Literally "a good day"; cf. ix 19, 22. Here, as in later
Jewish usage, the phrase represents a religious festival.

pagans ('ammê hā'āreṣ). Literally "peoples of the land." A technical
term for non-Jews or Gentiles; cf. Deut xxviii 10; Josh iv 24; I Kings
viii 53; I Chron v 25; II Chron vi 33; Ezra x 2; Neh x 31; Ezek xxxi 12.

professed themselves Jews (mityahᵃdîm). The Hithpaʻal denominative of *yᵉhûdî*, "Jew"; a *hapax legomenon*. While the LXX and the OL clarified *their* understanding of the word by adding "they were circumcised," they do not necessarily interpret it correctly. Actually, the term may mean the Gentiles identified themselves with the cause of the threatened Jews and pretended to be Jews (see C. H. Gordon, *Introduction to Old Testament Times* [Ventnor, N.J.: Ventnor Publications, 1953], p. 279), or actually and sincerely converted to Judaism. If the last interpretation be correct, one is hard pressed to find a historical point in either the Persian or the Greek period when such wholesale conversions to Judaism occurred. D. N. Freedman is probably correct in suspecting that it "does not refer to a real conversion at all but is part of the enhancement of the story."

they were afraid. Literally "fear had fallen on them." There is no justification for the view of Hoschander (p. 247), Ringgren (p. 140), and Dommershausen (p. 110), that "fear" is here a veiled allusion to God. In light of the subsequent statistics concerning the slaughter of the Jews' enemies (ix 16), their fear of the Jews was quite justified.

COMMENT

Esther is safe; Mordecai has been rewarded. But although Haman is dead, his evil influence reaches out even from the grave; for the Jewish people are still under his death sentence (iii 13). So Esther must again offer her petition to the king. In this connection, two misconceptions are generally held. First, virtually all commentators err in regarding vs. 3 as the beginning of a new scene; rather, vs. 3 is best understood as continuing the scene introduced by vs. 1 (see NOTES on "Esther again spoke" in vs. 3 and on "and Mordecai the Jew" in vs. 7). Second, both Esther's conduct in vss. 3–5 and the king's response in vs. 4 argue against the universally held view that Esther risked her life a second time by appearing before the king as before, that is, unsummoned and thus subject to immediate execution. Rather, having just entrusted Haman's estate to Mordecai, Esther immediately takes up anew her real task, namely, saving her people. Thus she collapses at the king's feet (see NOTE on "collapsing" in vs. 3), and through her tears, begs the king to revoke the pogrom. As a sign of encouragement rather than clemency, the king motions with his scepter for her to rise (vs. 4).

As in vii 3–4, Esther's presentation in vss. 5–6 is quite passionate and personal, but here she pleads not for herself but for her people with whom she is now so completely identified.

The material from vss. 8 through 17 is strikingly parallel in both sequence and phraseology to that of iii 9 – iv 3, except that here the roles have been reversed: the Jews will be victors, not victims. This parallelism results, of course, from the crucial and determining role played by the "fact" of the irrevocability of the Persian law (vs. 8), that is, the provisions of Mordecai's letter in vs. 11 must at least duplicate, if not exceed, the harsh terms of Haman's letter (iii 13) in order to nullify the latter's disastrous effect upon the Jews and to deter their enemies (see also NOTE on "to wipe out . . . property" in viii 11). This must be remembered when one considers Mordecai's admittedly heartless directive "to wipe out, slaughter, and annihilate every armed force of any people or province that was hostile to them, along with their children and women, and to plunder their personal property" (vs. 11). While one may argue that the phrase "children and women" was necessary to underscore the dramatic reversal in the king's policy, the phrase is still just as embarrassing for present-day Jews as the Crusaders' cry "to the greater glory of God," used in certain tragic situations, is embarrassing today to Christians. The author does make it clear, however, that although given explicit permission to plunder, the Jews did not do so (cf. ix 10, 15, 16; see, however, NOTE on ix 15). Given the contents of the king's new decree, one can easily understand both the joy of the Jews (vs. 16) and the fear of the pagans (vs. 17).

11. THE JEWS ARE VICTORIOUS OVER
THEIR ENEMIES
(ix 1–19)

IX 1 On the thirteenth day of the twelfth month, which is the month of Adar, when the king's command and edict were about to be enforced (on that day when the enemies of the Jews had hoped to destroy them, the opposite happened: the Jews destroyed their enemies), 2 the Jews had gathered in their cities throughout King Xerxes' provinces to kill those who sought their ruin. No one, however, was successful against them since everyone feared them. 3 Moreover, all the provincial officials, satraps, governors and *a*those who conduct the king's affairs*a* aided the Jews; for they feared Mordecai. 4 For Mordecai was very influential in the royal house, and his reputation was spreading to all the provinces as the man Mordecai grew more and more powerful. 5 So the Jews defeated all their enemies, slaughtering and annihilating them, and treating their enemies as they pleased. 6 *b*The Jews slaughtered five hundred men in the acropolis of Susa itself*c*. 7 They also killed Pharshandatha, Dalphon, Aspatha, 8 Poratha, Adalia, Aridatha, 9 Parmashta, Arisai, Aridai, and Vaizatha, 10 the ten sons of Haman, the son of Hammedatha*d*, the enemy of the Jews; they did not*e*, however, lay a hand on any plunder.

11 That same day the number of those killed in the acropolis*f* of Susa was reported to the king; 12 and the king said to Queen

a–a MT "those who do the king's business," which Greek erroneously translated as "the king's secretaries"; cf. iii 9.
b OL omits vss. 6–19.
c "Itself" is not in MT, but necessary to emphasize "Susa the acropolis," which is in the emphatic position in the MT.
d Greek adds "the Bougaion"; see NOTE on iii 1.
e Greek "they did plunder"; see NOTE on ix 15.
f LXX omits "the acropolis"; see NOTE on vs. 6.

Esther, "In the acropolis of Susa alone^g the Jews have slaughtered five hundred men, as well as Haman's ten sons. What, then, must they have done in the rest of the king's provinces! But, what do you still want? It will be granted you! What is your petition? It will be done!"

13 ^{h}"If it please the king," said Esther, "allow the Jews in Susa to act again tomorrow according to the terms of today's edict. And let Haman's ten sons be exposed on the gallows!"^{h}

14 So the king commanded this to be done: a decree was issued in Susa; and Haman's ten sons were exposed^i.

15 So the Jews in Susa reorganized themselves again on the fourteenth of Adar and killed three hundred men in Susa; but they did not lay a hand on any plunder. 16 Now the rest of the Jews in the king's provinces had organized and defended themselves, gaining relief from their enemies and killing seventy-five thousand of those who hated them (they did not, however, lay a hand on any plunder) 17 on the thirteenth of the month of Adar. Thus, they rested on the fourteenth day, making it a day of feasting^j and rejoicing. 18 But the Jews in Susa had organized themselves on both the thirteenth and the fourteenth; and so they rested on the fifteenth, making it a day of feasting and rejoicing. 19 (This is why the Jewish villagers^k who are living in unwalled towns celebrate the fourteenth day of the month of Adar as an occasion for rejoicing and feasting, for holiday-making and exchanging delicacies.)

^{g} "Alone" not in the MT but necessary because *byrh*, "acropolis," is in the emphatic position.
$^{h-h}$ AT is more direct and brutal, "And Esther said to the king, 'Allow the Jews to destroy whomever they wish, and to plunder!' And he consented."
^{i} Haller, after Syriac and three Hebrew manuscripts in BH^3, adds "on the gallows."
^{j} LXX has "pleasure" here and in vs. 18.
^{k} Reading *hprzym*, with *Qrê*, instead of *hprwzym*.

NOTES

ix 1. *king's command and edict.* That is, the first one (iii 13) which was still in effect.

to destroy them. Literally "to be master over them."

the opposite happened. Literally "it (*hû'*) was changed"; the pronoun is used impersonally. Here, as elsewhere (cf. iv 3, 14, 16; vi 1), the author goes out of his way to avoid any reference to God (see COMMENT on § 5, iv 1–17).

2. *to kill.* Literally "to send the hand against"; cf. ii 21, iii 6, ix 16.

who sought their ruin (*bimbaqšê rāʿātām*). This phrase, which apparently was synonymous in the author's mind with *haṣṣārîm 'ōtām* of viii 11, refers to those who would actually fight the Jews (cf. Num xxxv 23; I Sam xxiv 10, xxv 26) and not those who were merely hostile. Such an interpretation does not preclude the Jews taking the offensive in some instances rather than waiting to be attacked, since the Jews would have known who their more implacable enemies were.

was successful against them. Literally "stood before them." The phrase was misunderstood by the LXX which rendered it "for no one resisted them, being afraid of them." No one could *successfully* sustain his attack against the Jews.

since . . . feared them. Literally "for the fear of them had fallen upon all the peoples."

3. *aided.* Cf. Ezra i 4. The author does not indicate what type of support was given, whether moral, military, financial, or all three. More significantly, he acknowledges the help of mortal men but says nothing about the Lord God of Israel, an omission which is certainly deliberate, see Introduction, pp. XXXII–XXXIII.

4. *was very influential.* Literally "was great." Although wealthy, it was Mordecai's power that people feared (cf. vs. 3).

royal house. Literally "king's house"; in the sense of the entire capital, not just the palace or acropolis; cf. NOTE on ii 8.

grew more and more powerful (*hwlk wgdwl*). Literally "was growing and was great." *Gdwl* may be read as *gādēl*, a participle, or as *gādôl*, an adjective; but most likely, it is an infinitive absolute, see Joüon, GHB, § 123*s*.

5. *defeated . . . annihilating them.* Literally "they struck with the sword a slaughter, a killing, a destruction."

as they pleased. Cf. Neh ix 24; Dan xi 16. This phrase could include anything from punishment and enslavement to indiscriminate slaughter. Although probably an exaggeration, see the appalling statistics in vs. 16. As Anderson has so aptly observed, "This is a case of do unto others as they would have done unto you" (p. 828). The LXX omits the verse.

6. *slaughtered*. Literally "killed and annihilated." So also ix 12; the LXX omits "and annihilated."

acropolis. Possibly a copyist's expansion (but see vss. 11–12). It is highly improbable that the king would have allowed fighting within the palace complex itself; moreover, vs. 15, in contrast to vs. 11, says that the Jews in Susa, meaning "the city," acted on the fourteenth as they had on the thirteenth.

7. The names of Haman's sons are as uncertain as the names of the seven eunuchs (cf. NOTE on i 10) or the seven advisers (i 14). The difficulties in establishing even the original Greek form, let alone the Hebrew, is well illustrated by the fact that just for the first Hebrew name (*pharšandātā'*), LXX^א has *Pharsannestain*, LXX^A has *Pharsanestan*, while LXX^B treats the name as two persons, *Pharsan* and *Nestain*, thus giving *eleven* names for Haman's ten sons. The AT has five names instead of ten, but its editor erroneously regarded them as five men hanged in addition to Haman's sons! Haupt (pp. 164–66) thought he could trace all the seemingly irreconcilable divergences to the same Hebrew text; and Gehman (pp. 327–28) argues that at least seven of the ten names are clearly Persian; see also Paton, pp. 70–71. Nonetheless, their origins and their meanings are still uncertain.

These names are printed in the MT in a peculiar fashion, similar to Josh xii 9–23, in that each name is printed under the other on the right-hand side of the page, and the *w't* ("and" with the sign of the accusative) accompanying each name is printed one under the other on the extreme left-hand side. The reason for these orthographic peculiarities is unknown. Masoretic explanations range all the way from the liturgical and mechanical, for example, that all the names be read with one breath, to the pictorial and theological, for example, the column of empty space between the names and the definite articles reminds the reader that there is no resurrection for the sons of Haman (for further details on this and other orthographic peculiarities, see Bardtke, pp. 383–84).

10. *not . . . lay a hand on*. Literally "not send their hand on." Though given permission to plunder (cf. viii 11), the Jews did not do so, a fact which is obviously of great importance to the author since he will make the same point two more times (vss. 15, 16). The reason for his concern in this matter is not clear. If the terrible slaughter on the thirteenth of Adar has some historical basis, then the author may have been at pains to clear the name of the Jews by emphasizing that they fought for their survival, not plunder. Possibly the author, or a glossator, was influenced here by remembering that other great destruction

of the Amalekites (see I Sam xv), when the taking of spoil brought
Yahweh's terrible wrath upon King Saul. Such self-restraint as the
Jews expressed here is quite prudent in a situation where a minority is
essentially defending itself from its enemies rather than initiating the
conflict; but Streane argues: "Their desire was deliverance and also
vengeance, but not material gain" (p. 45); see also William McKane
"A Note on Est IX and I Sam XV," JTS 12 (1961), 260–61. Possibly
the Jews also remembered Abraham's wise logic: he took no loot lest
later on the people resentfully say, "I have made Abram rich" (see
Gen xiv 22–24).

12. Although some of those killed had probably been guests at the
king's parties (cf. i 3, 5), he is concerned only with pleasing Esther,
who, he detects, is still not entirely satisfied.

slaughtered. See NOTE on ix 6.

13. *If it please the king*. As D. N. Freedman has observed, this phrase
is identical with the phrase in v 4, and serves as an *inclusio* for the whole
series of episodes hinging on the king's good will.

exposed. Literally "be hanged"; they were, however, already dead.
It is Esther's request for the exposure of Haman's sons and an extension
of the fighting, as well as her "failure" to intercede for Haman in vii
9, that has been primarily responsible for her reputation as a sophisticated Jael, i.e., a deceitful and bloodthirsty woman (see Judg iv 17–22).
Such a reputation certainly has some justification (see her request in the
AT, textual note *h–h*), but unless one is willing to judge Esther's outward
act in complete isolation, without any real knowledge of her inner
motives and without full knowledge of the external circumstances (see
COMMENT), then one's judgment must be tentatively made. Then, as now,
what the vanquished call "the villains" the victors regard as "the
heroes."

14. *this to be done*. Refers to the king's permission for the Jews
in Susa to fight again the next day, not to the exposure of Haman's sons.

15. *reorganized themselves again*. Literally "they gathered themselves
also"; see NOTE in viii 11.

According to both the MT and the LXX, the Jews did *not* plunder in
Susa itself on the fourteenth, but unless the Greek in ix 10 has accidentally lost its negative (which may very well be the case), the Greek
editor maintains that the Jews *did* plunder in the acropolis on the thirteenth. It is interesting that almost twice as many were killed in the
acropolis as in the city, although the city was larger; this fact may
justify exposing Haman's sons as a deterrent action. If revenge was
the primary reason for the second day's fighting, the author gives no
hint of it. He does not glory in details of the battle; concerning the
fighting itself he simply states the time, place, and casualty figures.

16. Verses 16–19, which the AT omits, are not so much a continuation as a summary of the preceding events and "facts." Again the narrator is interested only in the final results, not in the gory details. *gaining relief* (*w^enôah*). Cf. ix 22. Rudolph (VT 4 [1954], 90) would amend to *w^enihôm*, "and avenging themselves," and many other commentators amend to some form of *nqm*, which they erroneously translate as "avenging themselves" (cf. Isa i 24, where *nhm* is parallel to *nqm;* see also G. E. Mendenhall, "God of Vengeance, Shine Forth," *The Wittenberg Bulletin* 45 [December 1948], 37–42).

seventy-five thousand. An enormous casualty figure reduced in the LXX to 15,000—a reduction that must have come much later in the transmission of the Greek text, since 75,000 is supported by both Josephus and the Syriac, two versions based upon the Septuagint. As is to be expected (see first NOTE on viii 7), the Vulgate agrees with the MT. The AT has 10,107 men.

19. This verse, which implies a distinction between Jews living in walled and unwalled cities, is certainly a gloss, because it contradicts vss. 21–22 (see § 12, below), and breaks the continuity of vss. 18 and 20. To the MT the LXX adds "and those living in the metropolitan centers [walled cities] celebrate also the fifteenth of Adar with good cheer, sending out gifts to the poor," which is a valid inference to be drawn from the Hebrew; this verse is possibly a gloss from vss. 21–22.

villagers. Hprzym occurs only here, I Sam vi 18 and Deut iii 5. In the Talmud, where *pārûz* meant the inhabitant of an unwalled place, extended and involved discussions centered around the meaning of the related word *happerāzôt*, "unwalled cities"; see also Ezek xxxviii 11, Zech ii 4 (8H). Hoschander's reading (p. 275, n. 50) *hprsym*, "the Persians," is both forced and unnecessary.

are living. The use of the present tense here suggests that the fourteenth of Adar was the date observed for Purim in the villages and towns in the author's, or more likely a glossator's, own day. It implies either that the villages did not celebrate the fifteenth or that walled cities did not celebrate the fourteenth, and yet in verses 21–22, Mordecai commanded that both days be observed by all. The latter was the practice observed in Josephus' day; cf. *Antiquities* XI. 292. According to II Macc xv 36, the fourteenth of Adar was called "the Day of Mordecai"; cf. Inroduction, p. LVIII.

exchanging delicacies. Literally "to send portions, each to his neighbor." Infinitive with performative *mem*, as in Aramaic; cf. Joüon, GHB, § 49e.

COMMENT

In the first eight chapters of Esther the author's main concern
has been to tell an interesting story, filled with drama and suspense;
from this point on, however, the demands of law and the cult completely outweigh any dramatic considerations. Content to establish the
barest facts concerning the fighting itself (cf. vss. 1–10), the author
wants to illustrate two things: the "historical" basis for observing
Purim on different dates (vss. 11–19), and the steps whereby the
events narrated in Esther were commemorated and institutionalized
in the festival of Purim (vss. 20–32, in § 12).

The author gives no clue as to what happened in the nine-month
interval between the publication of the king's second edict (viii
9) and the day of the pogrom (ix 1). But judging from vss.
2, 5, and especially 16, we must conclude that Haman's letter
(iii 13) had either created or fanned the flames of anti-Semitism
throughout the empire and that, whether motivated by Haman's
propaganda or their own greed, thousands of "enemies of the Jews"
(cf. vs. 16) were eagerly awaiting the appointed day. If so,
they were rudely disappointed; when that fateful day arrived, no
one could successfully sustain his attack against the Jews (vss. 1–2).

Undoubtedly some pagans were defeated before they started, in
part because they feared the Jews' reputation (vs. 2), and in part
because government officials clearly favored the Jews (vs. 3). Many
pagans, however, did fight, and even if the battle statistics of vs.
16 be enormously inflated (75,000 killed!), they still attest to the
battle's scale and ferocity. The boast in vs. 5 that the Jews did
"as they pleased" suggests that some Jews, at least, were given a
free hand by the authorities and did not confine themselves to self-
defense; they may very well have sought out and destroyed those
who were hostile to them, that is, their clearly established implacable
foes. While the Jews took many lives (cf. vss. 6, 16), they took no
spoil (see NOTE on vs. 10).

The execution of Haman's sons (vss. 6–10) was, of course,
inevitable. They had lost their inheritance (viii 1), but as long as
they were alive they could still cause trouble for the Jews. Esther's

request, however, that their corpses be publicly displayed and the Jews in Susa allowed to fight again the next day (vs. 13) is much more problematic. If we were dealing with an actual historical event, then one would wonder whether Esther were being vindictive and vengeful here (so Paton, Anderson, Bardtke, and many others), or just practical and realistic (Hoschander). If the enemies of the Jews had been decisively defeated and were willing to leave the Jews alone, then Esther's request would certainly be vengeful. If after the thirteenth, however, there were still in Susa pockets of resistance looking forward to a second round with the Jews, then Esther's request would be realistic and necessary, and the exposure and desecration of Haman's sons could be understood as a deterrent (cf. I Sam xxxi 10; Herodotus III. 125, VI. 30, VII. 238) and not, as Paton has argued on p. 287, a case of her malignant spirit of vengeance pursuing them even after death.

But since we are not dealing with a strictly factual historical account (see Introduction, p. LII), Esther's request is best regarded simply as a literary device by the author to provide a "historical" basis for the conflicting dates (cf. vss. 17–18, and NOTE on vs. 19) of celebrating Purim in his own day. Thus Paton has rightly observed that "History here arises from custom, not custom from history" (p. 288). For the author of Esther the "historical" basis for observing the fifteenth of Adar was of overriding concern, the morality of Esther's request in vs. 13 being of secondary importance. Then as now, the vanquished rather than the victors usually saw the immorality of war.

On one crucial point the author seems quite clear if not explicit: men, not Yahweh, delivered the Jews. It was the influence of Mordecai (vss. 3–4) and the preparations and prowess of the Jews themselves (vs. 2) that turned the tide of battle in their favor. If Yahweh was at all responsible for that victory, the author does not indicate it here; see, however, the discussion of the role of Yahweh in the Book of Esther in the Introduction, pp. XXXII–XXXIV.

12. HOW PURIM BECAME AN ESTABLISHED FESTIVAL
(ix 20–32)

IX 20 Then Mordecai recorded these things[a], and sent letters to all the Jews throughout the king's provinces, regardless of distance, 21 enjoining them to continue to celebrate annually both the fourteenth and the fifteenth of the month of Adar 22 as the days when the Jews got relief from their enemies and as the month which had been changed for them from sorrow to joy and from mourning to a holiday, and that they should make them [b]days of feasting[b] and rejoicing, and for sending delicacies to one another as well as alms to the poor. 23 So the Jews made customary[c] what they had started doing, just as Mordecai had written to them.

24 [d]For Haman, son of Hammedatha, [e]the Agagite[e], the enemy of all Jews, had plotted against the Jews to destroy them and had cast *pur* (the lot, that is) to discomfort and destroy them. 25 [f]But when Queen Esther came[f] before the king, the king gave orders in writing that the wicked scheme which Haman[g] had devised against the Jews should come upon his own head, and that he and his sons should be hanged on the gallows. 26 That is why these days are called "Purim," from the word *pur*.

Therefore, because of all that was written in this letter and because of all that they had experienced and because of what had happened to them, 27 the Jews agreed and made it customary[h]

---

[a] Greek adds "in a book."
[b-b] LXX "holidays of marriage."
[c] Reading w^eqibb^elū, as the *Qrê* of vs. 27, and not w^eqibbēl.
[d] AT omits vss. 23–26; OL omits vss. 24–27; see NOTE.
[e-e] LXX "the Macedonian."
[f-f] MT "but when she came"; see NOTE.
[g] MT "he."
[h] Reading, with *Qrê*, the plural, instead of singular.

for themselves, their descendants, and all future converts to continue to celebrate annually, without fail[i], these two days, as
specified in their letter and on the proper dates; [28] that these
days should be remembered and celebrated by every single generation, family, province, and city; that these days of Purim
should never be abrogated among the Jews; and that the memory
of them should never die among their descendants.

[29] Also Queen Esther, the daughter of Abihail, along with
Mordecai the Jew, wrote with full authority, thereby ratifying
this second letter of Purim. [30] Friendly and sincere letters were
sent[j] to all the Jews throughout the one hundred and twenty-
seven provinces of Xerxes' kingdom [31] to establish these days of
Purim on their proper date, just as Mordecai the Jew[k] had en-
joined them and as they had agreed for themselves and their
descendants, [l]with respect to their fasting and lamentations[l].
[32] So Esther's word fixed these practices for Purim, and it was
preserved in writing[m].

[i] Reading the plural, *y'brw*, instead of *y'bwr*, the singular, with plene spelling;
r and *w* are easily confused in the Hebrew script.
[j] Reading *wᵉnišlōaḥ*, as in iii 13, instead of *wayyišlaḥ*, "and he sent."
[k] MT adds "and Queen Esther"; see NOTE.
[l-l] LXX "concerning their health and their plan," which presupposes *dbry*
šlwm w'mt k'ṣtm (so Hoschander, p. 286, n. 61).
[m] Reading *bᵉsēper* instead of *bassēper;* see NOTE.

NOTES

ix 20. *these things.* A most ambiguous phrase; probably it refers
neither to the entire Book of Esther (so Rashi) nor even to the story
of Esther and Mordecai, which in the nine-month interval between the
king's second letter and the thirteenth of Adar would have been well
known to the Jews, but to the most recent events, and especially to the
two different dates on which the Jews had celebrated their victory
(cf. vs. 19).

regardless of distance. Literally "to those near and those far," referring to the Jews, not the provinces.

21. *enjoining them.* Cf. ix 27, 29, 31, 32; an Aramaism, cf. Joüon,
GHB, § 80*h*.

celebrate annually . . . of Adar. Literally "keep the fourteenth day
of the month of Adar, and the fifteenth day with it, in every single
year." Both days, not one or the other, must be kept by all; cf. vs. 19.

22. *alms to the poor.* The OL adds "and orphans and widows." If such charitable acts occurred during the first, spontaneous victory celebration of Purim, no mention of it was made in the text. The appropriateness of these expressions of gratitude, however, need not be justified.

23. *as Mordecai had written to them.* That is, to keep *both* days of Purim (vs. 21); and yet, according to vs. 19, the villagers started out by keeping only the fourteenth.

24. Briefly, and needlessly, recapitulating the events of chs. iii through vii, vss. 24–26 differ sufficiently in detail to be regarded either as earlier (Hoschander), later (Haupt), or, at least, independent (Paton) of the material in those chapters. Although the lacunae in the AT and the OL (see textual note *d*) somewhat support Haupt's view, Bardtke argues convincingly (p. 393) that the summary character of these verses is responsible for their contradictions, not their being taken from a different source.

to discomfort. Whether *lᵉhummām* represents an intentional play on the name Haman as scholars have sometimes suggested is quite suspect and, in any case, cannot be proved.

25. *But when Queen Esther came* (*wbb'h*). Literally "but when she came," which the Vulgate, Syriac, Targums, and many commentators have understood to refer to Esther. The LXX read *wbb'*, and understood it to refer to Haman. Many modern commentators regard it as neuter, referring to Haman's "scheme" (*maḥᵃšābâ*), which is feminine in gender. The reading adopted here follows the brilliant suggestion of G. R. Driver (*Textus* 1 [1960], 128), who sees *wbb'h* as a corrupt abbreviation, *bbw' ˢ ḥ*, "when Queen Esther came."

the king. Literally "he."

in writing. Literally "in a book." The king did not express in writing that Haman (cf. vii 9) or his sons (cf. ix 14) be hanged. As with all difficult and obscure readings, many have called this a gloss. But the telescoping of events here is responsible for the contradiction, even as it is responsible for a contradiction later on in the verse which suggests that Haman and his sons were hanged at the same time rather than nine months apart (cf. NOTE on ix 6).

that he and his sons should be hanged. Emphasizes not the time but the fact of execution; that is, retributive justice, not chronology, is the author's concern here.

26. *That is why.* Literally "therefore."

This verse tries to explain the seemingly unimportant and even irrelevant mention of the *pûr,* or lot, in iii 7 and ix 24. For a detailed discussion of *pûr,* see Introduction, pp. XLVI–XLIX.

letter. That is, Mordecai's festal letter of vss. 20 and 23, not the Book of Esther itself. *'iggert* is probably a late loan word (cf. Assyr. *egirtu*); cf. ix 29; Neh ii 8, 9, vi 17; II Chron xxx 1.

experienced. So the LXX; literally "seen"; cf. Exod x 6.

27. *all future converts.* Literally "all who should join themselves to them"; cf. viii 17.

without fail. Reading, instead of *wl' y'bwr, wl' y'brw,* "they shall not pass over."

two days. Although it is an open question whether this verse agrees with vss. 21–22, that is, that both days were celebrated by all, or with vs. 19, that is, that both days were not celebrated by all, the former possibility is the more likely.

as specified in their letter. Literally "according to their writing," that is, Mordecai's letter of vss. 20 and 23.

on the proper dates. Literally "according to their time," that is, the fourteenth and fifteenth of Adar.

28. *every single.* The distributive use of the nouns here (see NOTE on i 8) emphasizes that there are to be *no exceptions:* all Jews must observe both days. The LXX, however, is not so explicitly sweeping here, for it has "These days of Purim should be observed by all times; and their meaning should not be omitted from the generations"; (see Introduction, pp. XLVI–XLIX, for the LXX's position on Purim).

29. Verses 29–32 are either a variant tradition or, more likely, a later addition to ch. ix, since they lack the support of both the AT (which lacks vss. 28–32) and the OL (which lacks vss. 30–32), while the LXX is also somewhat different; see, however, Striedl (pp. 101 f.) and Ringgren who defend their authenticity.

Esther is mentioned here by name for the first time since ix 13. That she had to send out a form letter to the Jews clearly suggests that, whatever their reasons may have been (see Introduction, pp. XXXI f.), some Jews had not complied with all, or possibly even with any, of the stipulations in Mordecai's festal letter. Exactly when her letter was written is not stated; it could have been ten days or ten years after Mordecai's.

Abihail. See NOTE on ii 15.

along with Mordecai. Since the verb "wrote" in this verse is feminine singular, agreeing with Esther, this phrase is probably an early gloss from verse 31.

with full authority. Literally "with all power"; *tōqep* occurs only here, in x 2, and in Dan xi 17. In Nabatean inscriptions *tqp* suggests validity or legitimacy (see C. F. Jean and Jacob Hoftejzer, *Dictionnaire des Inscriptions Sémitiques de L'Ouest* [Leiden: Brill, 1965], p. 333). Esther lends all her authority and influence as queen and heroine to confirm Mordecai's festal letter. Unwilling to minimize Mordecai's im-

portance, the author regards Esther's letter as a joint letter written
with him; cf. vs. 31. The suggestion of Haupt, Haller, and others that
the phrase "Mordecai the Jew" has been dislocated in the text and
should be read "Esther described all the power of Mordecai the Jew"
has no support in the versions and is strained and unconvincing.

this second (hz't hšnyt) letter. A most troublesome phrase. Following
the LXX and the Syriac, many scholars delete it as a gloss. Rudolph
sees it as a corrupted dittography of *yšlḥ* in vs. 30 (VT 4 [1954], 90);
and Torrey (HTR 37 [1944], 31–34) believes it refers to the Hebrew
translation of Esther, the first letter being "the original" story of Esther
composed in Aramaic. Most likely, it refers to Esther's own letter (vs. 29)
reaffirming Mordecai's festal letter.

30. *Friendly and sincere.* Literally "words of peace and truth"; cf.
Isa xxxix 8; Jer xxxiii 6; Zech viii 19. The Vulgate has for this verse
"and they sent to all the Jews who were upset in the one hundred and
twenty-seven provinces of King Asuerus that they might have peace
and might assume righteousness." Circumstances apparently dictated
that Esther's corroborating letter be neither hostile nor imperious. Since
Mordecai had not succeeded in compelling his coreligionists to obey,
Esther was trying to persuade them. Even as late as the third century
A.D., however, there were still Jews who did not regard the Book of
Esther as canonical; see Introduction, pp. xxiv–xxv.

31. *on their proper date.* Literally "in their times." Apparently the
main thrust or intent of Esther's letter was to establish the days of Purim
on their proper date.

Mordecai the Jew. After this phrase the MT has "and Queen Esther,"
but this must be a gloss if, as seems most likely, vs. 31 indicates the
contents of Esther's letter (vs. 29); for Mordecai alone had sent out the
first Purim letter (vss. 20–22).

with respect to their fasting and lamentations. Literally "the things/
words of fasts and their lamentations." (In an unpublished paper H. L.
Ginsberg has suggested the translation "the obligation of the fasts with
their supplications," relating it to Jewish practices recorded in Zech vii
5 and viii 19.) In the MT this phrase is syntactically unrelated to the
rest of the verse. The passage implies that matters of fasting and
lamentation had already been taken care of in Mordecai's first letter;
but if so, no mention of a memorial fast was made in the summary of
Mordecai's letter to the Jews (vss. 20–23), unless it be implied in the
phrase "from sorrow to joy, and from mourning to a holiday" (vs. 22).
Nor is there any mention of a fast in the summary of their response in
ix 23–28. More likely, especially since the element of a memorial fast
is also missing from the LXX, AT, Josephus, and the OL, it represents
a later feature or tradition which was finally introduced into the MT at

some later point. *Ṣômôt*, the plural of *ṣôm*, "fast," is quite late, appearing nowhere else in the MT. In any case, no specific date is given for the fast, although the thirteenth of Adar naturally suggests itself since that was the date originally set by Haman for the pogrom (iii 13). By the ninth century A.D., the thirteenth was the date on which Jews observed the fast of Purim.

32. *word* (*ma'ᵃmar*). Used for the king's command to Vashti in i 15.

was preserved in writing. Literally "it was written in *a* book"; reading *bᵉsēper*, rather than *bassēper*, "in *the* book," the latter implying a very specific book. The author of Esther undoubtedly got some of his material from written sources; see Introduction, pp. LI–LII.

COMMENT

Having provided in vss. 1–19 the "historical" basis for the first celebrations of Purim on the fourteenth and/or fifteenth of Adar (see NOTE on ix 19), the author outlines in vss. 20–32 the three major steps whereby Purim, although a festival not sanctioned by the Pentateuch (see Exod xxxiv 18–27), became an important part of the Jewish religious calendar, namely, by (1) Mordecai's festal letter (vss. 20–22); (2) the Jews' deliberate intention to celebrate annually the events of Purim (vss. 23, 27–28); and (3) the confirmatory letter of Esther and Mordecai (vss. 29–32).

Although scholars of both present and past centuries have sometimes regarded this entire section as being independent of i 1 – ix 19 and derived from a different source (for the most detailed defense of this position, see Paton, pp. 57–60), the evidence for this is far from conclusive (see NOTES on vss. 24, 25). To be sure, certain elements or traditions probably do represent subsequent historical customs and developments which were read back into the author's original composition, for example, see NOTE on "fasting and lamentations" in vs. 31.

There can be little doubt, however, as to the author's overriding concern in this section, which was that Jews of "every single generation, family, province, and city" (vs. 28), without exception or distinction, observe Purim—both days (see vss. 21–22, 27–28).

13. THE CONCLUSION OF THE BOOK OF ESTHER
(x 1–3)

X 1 Now King Xerxes*ᵃ* levied*ᵇ* taxes on both the mainland and the islands; 2 but as for all the achievements *ᶜ*and might of King Xerxes*ᶜ*, as well as for an exact account of the influence of Mordecai whom the king had promoted, is not all this recorded in the *Annals of the Kings of Media and Persia?* 3 For Mordecai the Jew ranked next to King Xerxes and was influential *ᵈ*among the Jews*ᵈ* and acceptable to the mass of his own countrymen. He sought the best interests of his people and was concerned for the welfare of his kinsmen.*ᵉ*

ᵃ '*ḥšrš*, "Xerxes," is somewhat closer to the Pers. *khshayarsha* than '*ḥšwrwš*, the standard transliteration in Esther.
ᵇ Greek "he wrote."
ᶜ–ᶜ MT "and his might"; see NOTE.
ᵈ–ᵈ Reading *byhwdym*, instead of *lyhwdym*.
ᵉ Greek adds at this point Addition F: "The Interpretation of Mordecai's Dream."

NOTES

x 1. *taxes.* Literally "a forced payment"; a later usage of the word; elsewhere in the MT *mas* means a *corvée* or "serfdom." Unfortunately, the author does not say why this tax was imposed, and many scholars have had difficulty seeing its relevance to the theme of Esther. It may, of course, be a piece of information which the author has taken from another source. In the nineteenth century many scholars, following G. H. Rawlinson, saw an allusion to Xerxes' efforts to recoup his losses after the debacle in Greece. With greater merit Hoschander argues that even as Haman, Mordecai, and Esther had been rewarded according to their just deserts, so here Xerxes who was after all "the main factor in the deliverance of the Jews" (p. 292) receives his just reward, namely, a fuller treasury. D. Daube (JQR 37 [1946–47], 139–47) sees Mordecai's final victory over Haman who had, in effect, counseled the king to "Kill the Jews, and take their wealth!" Although the crown presumably had not gained the ten thousand talents promised by Haman in return for the pogrom, Mordecai convinced the king that peaceful taxation rather than plundering was the best way to fill the royal coffers. But, most likely, we should understand the allusion to taxes as an expression of Xerxes' later power and success—a situation in large part attributable to, and at the same time, increasing the stature of his prime minister, Mordecai the Jew. (This view of Xerxes does not accord with that of Olmstead, who thinks that Xerxes did not live up to his early promise of success and that his character gradually disintegrated [HPE, pp. 266–67].)

islands. Literally "regions of the sea"; cf. Isa xi 11, xxiv 15. The possible scope of the king's taxation program may be seen from the fact that the *kittîm*, or Romans, in 1QpHab iii 11, came from "the islands of the sea" (see Géza Vermès, *Discovery in the Judean Desert* [Tournai: Desclee, 1956], p. 125); the term here, however, may refer only to islands immediately adjacent to the eastern Mediterranean coast; cf. Josh xv 12.

2. *achievements*. Literally "deed of his power"; cf. Jer xlviii 7.

and might of King Xerxes. Literally "and his might," referring clearly to the king, not as Ringgren contends, to Mordecai; the Greek does not even mention Mordecai in this verse.

exact account (*pārāšat*). Occurring only here and in iv 7, its meaning is uncertain. Among the suggested translations are "exact statement" (BDB), "the degree," that is, "patient nobility" (Driver, VT 4 [1954], 237), and "explanation" (Hoschander, pp. 294–95). Although Hoschander is quite right to insist on the unlikelihood of a Jewish prime minister being extensively treated in the royal annals of the Median and Persian kings, it is highly unlikely that the work cited here is either the royal diary (ii 23, vi 1) or the official royal archives. More likely, imitating the standard formula for citing historical sources in the Books of Kings and Chronicles (cf. I Kings xiv 19, 29; II Chron xxv 26, xxxii 32), the author of Esther is probably referring here to a popular historical account of the Persian kings, possibly written from a Jewish point of view, something like the midrashic source cited by the Chronicler in II Chron xxiv 27 (see COMMENT ad loc. in J. M. Myers, *II Chronicles*, AB, vol. 13).

influence. Literally "greatness."

3. *ranked next to*. Literally "was second to"; cf. II Chron xxviii 7 and II Kings xxiii 4.

influential. Possibly "popular"; literally "was great."

acceptable to the mass of his own countrymen. Literally "liked by the multitude of his brothers." Ehrlich's emendation (p. 125) w^{e}rāṣ *l^erîb 'ehāyw*, "a zealous fighter for the cause of his brethren," is imaginative and a suitable parallel to "sought the best interests of his people"; but it is quite unnecessary since the consonantal text makes perfect sense in itself and is suitably parallel to "was influential among the Jews."

was concerned for the welfare of his kinsmen. Literally "speaking peace to all his seed." Cf. Zech ix 10 and Ps lxxxv 8(9).

COMMENT

The author ends his story in the same way that he began it: by speaking of the powerful and fabulous Xerxes (cf. i 1–8 with x 1–2). He not only cites his source of information but even invites his readers (i.e., "is not all this recorded in the *Annals of the Kings of Media and Persia?*") to check the facts for themselves, thereby tending to establish in their minds his trustworthiness and the essential veracity of his account of Purim's origins.

No Saturday hero, Mordecai was remembered not only for what he had once done for his people but also for what he continued to do for them (vs. 3). What more could be said about a people's hero! An editor of the Greek translation, however, was unwilling to leave the matter there, and so he introduced at this point Addition F, "The Interpretation of Mordecai's Dream," to show that all of this was "God's doing" (F 1).

APPENDIXES

APPENDIX I:
THE GREEK ADDITIONS TO ESTHER

ADDITION A
1. MORDECAI'S DREAM
(A 1–11; AT i 1–10; Vulg. xi 2–12)

A 1 In the second year of the reign of Artaxerxes the Great, on the first day of Nisan, Mordecai the son of Jair, son of Shimei, son of Kish, a Benjaminite, had a dream. 2 He was a Jew living in the city of Susa, a prominent man who served in the king's court. 3 He was one of the prisoners whom Nebuchadnezzar, king of Babylon, had brought down from Jerusalem with Jeconiah, king of Judea. 4 And this was his dream:

> See! Cries and clamoring, thundering and earthquake, and confusion upon the earth! 5 And two great dragons advanced, both of them ready for battle; and they roared loudly. 6 And at their roaring every nation got itself ready for battle that it might fight against the righteous nation. 7 A day of gloom and darkness, affliction and distress, oppression and considerable confusion upon the earth! 8 And the entire righteous nation was alarmed, dreading their ill-fate; and they were prepared to die; 9 and they cried out to God. And from their crying there arose, as though from a tiny spring, a mighty river, a veritable flood. 10 Light and sun arose; and the humble were exalted, and devoured the eminent.

11 Now when Mordecai, who had seen this dream and what God had resolved to do, awoke, he puzzled over it all day, and wanted to understand it in every detail.

2. MORDECAI UNCOVERS A CONSPIRACY
(A 12–17; AT i 11–18; Vulg. xii 1–6)

A 12 And Mordecai was dozing in the court with Gabatha and Tharra, two of the king's eunuchs who kept watch in the court; 13 and he overheard their discussion, and investigated their nervousness, and learned that they were getting ready to assassinate King Artaxerxes. So he informed the king about them. 14 The king then interrogated the two eunuchs; and after they had confessed, they were executed. 15 The king wrote a memorandum of these things, and Mordecai also recorded these things. 16 The king ordered Mordecai to serve in the court, and rewarded him for these things. 17 But Haman, son of Hammedatha, a Bougaion, enjoyed great favor with the king; and he sought to do harm to Mordecai and his people because of the two eunuchs of the king.

ADDITION B
TEXT OF THE KING'S FIRST LETTER
(B 1–7; AT iv 14–18; Vulg. xiii 1–7)

B 1 The text of the dispatch was as follows:

The great king Artaxerxes writes these things to the governors of the one hundred and twenty-seven provinces from India to Ethiopia, and to their immediate subordinates. 2 After I had become ruler of many nations and had conquered the whole world, I was determined—not out of any power-madness but always acting with restraint and gentleness —to see to it that my subjects lived untroubled lives; by making the kingdom more civilized and by ensuring unhampered travel throughout the entire land, I was determined to restore that peace which all men want.

3 When I asked my advisers how this end might be accomplished, Haman, who is conspicuous among us for his balanced judgment and is recognized for his consistent kindness and unwavering devotion and has attained next to the highest rank in the kingdom, 4 informed us that there is scattered among the nations of the world a certain antagonistic people, whose laws make it hostile to every nation and who habitually ignore the royal ordinances, so that that government, demanded by us with the best of intentions, cannot be achieved.

5 Realizing, therefore, that this nation, and it alone, consistently stands in opposition to all men, perverting society with its own laws, and that it is hostile to our interests, and does all the harm it can so that the well-being of the land is threatened, 6 we have, therefore, commanded that those designated to you in the communications of Haman, who is the one responsible in this matter and is a second father to us, shall all—wives and children included—be wiped out by the sword of their enemies, without pity or restraint, on the thirteenth day of the twelfth month of Adar, in the present year, 7 so that they, who have always been hostile, may on a single day go violently down into Hades, thereby making our government secure and untroubled for the future.

ADDITION C
1. THE PRAYER OF MORDECAI
(C 1–11; AT v 12–17; Vulg. xiii 8–18)

C   1 Then, remembering all the deeds of the Lord, Mordecai prayed to the Lord, 2 saying,

"Lord, Lord, King who rules over all, the universe is subject to you; and there is no one who can oppose you when you desire to save Israel; 3 for you have made heaven and earth, and every marvelous thing under heaven. 4 And you are Lord of all, and there is no one who can resist you, who are the Lord.

5 You know all things; you know, Lord, that it was not because of insolence or arrogance or vanity that I did this, that I did not bow down before arrogant Haman; 6 for I would have been quite willing to have kissed the soles of his feet for Israel's sake. 7 But I did it in order that I might not put the glory of a man above the glory of God.

8 And now, Lord, God, and King, the God of Abraham, spare your people! For they are plotting our ruin; and they desire to destroy your ancient heritage. 9 Do not neglect your portion which you ransomed for yourself from the land of Egypt. 10 Hear my prayer, and be merciful to your inheritance, and turn our mourning into feasting, that we may live to sing praises to your name, Lord, and do not stifle the mouths of those who praise you."

11 And all Israel cried out as loud as they could because their end was near.

2. THE PRAYER OF QUEEN ESTHER
(C 12–30; AT v 18–29; Vulg. xiv 1–19)

C 12 Queen Esther was terrified and sought refuge in the Lord. 13 She took off her stately robes and put on clothes appropriate for distress and mourning; and instead of extravagant perfumes, she covered her head with ashes and dung. She debased her body completely; and she covered with her disheveled hair those parts which she ordinarily loved to adorn.

14 Then she prayed to the Lord God of Israel, saying,

"My Lord, only you are our king! Help me who am alone and have no helper except you; 15 for I am risking my life. 16 All my life I have heard in my family's tribe that you, Lord, chose Israel from all the nations, and our fathers from all their predecessors, for a perpetual inheritance; and you treated them just as you had promised. 17 But now, we have sinned against you;

and you have handed us over to our enemies, 18 because we extolled their gods. You were in the right, Lord. 19 Nevertheless, they are not satisfied that we are in galling slavery; but they have made an agreement with their gods 20 to nullify the promise you made, to blot out your inheritance, to silence the lips of those who praise you, to quench the glory of your house and your altar, 21 to open the mouths of the pagans for the praise of idols, and to idolize forever a mere mortal king. 22 Do not relinquish your scepter, Lord, to non-existent gods. And do not let them laugh at our downfall! Frustrate their plot and make an example of him who started it all!

23 Remember, Lord, reveal yourself in this time of our affliction! Give me courage, King of the gods and Lord of all governments! 24 Make me persuasive before the lion and dispose the king to hate the one who fights against us, so that there may be an end of him and of those who agree with him. 25 Rescue us by your hand, and help me who am alone and have no one except you, Lord.

You know everything; 26 and you know that I hate the pomp of the wicked, and I loathe the bed of the uncircumcised—and of any foreigner. 27 You know my dilemma: that I loathe that symbol of my exalted position which is upon my head when I appear at court—I loathe it like a menstruous rag—I do not wear it when I am not at court. 28 Your servant has not dined at Haman's table; nor have I extolled the royal parties nor drunk the wine of libations. 29 From the day that I arrived here until now, your servant has not delighted in anything except you, Lord, the God of Abraham. 30 God, whose might prevails over all, hear the voice of the despairing, and save us from the hands of the wicked! And, Lord, protect me from my fears!"

ADDITION D
ESTHER APPEARS BEFORE THE KING UNSUMMONED
(D 1–16; AT vi 1–12; Vulg. xv 4–19)

D 1 On the third day, when she had finished praying, she took
off the clothing of a suppliant, and dressed herself in splendid
attire. 2 After she had called upon the all-seeing God and savior,
she, looking absolutely radiant, took with her two maids, 3 leaning
daintily on the one, 4 while the other followed carrying her train.
5 She was radiant, in the prime of her beauty, and her face was
assured as one who knows she is loved; but her heart was pounding
with fear.

6 When she had passed through all the doors, she stood before the
king. He was seated on his royal throne, arrayed in all his splendid
attire, all covered with gold and precious stones—a most formidable
sight! 7 Raising his face, flushed with color, he looked at her in
fiercest anger. The queen stumbled, turned pale and fainted, keeling
over on the maid who went before her. 8 But God changed the
king's spirit to gentleness. He sprang from his throne in alarm, and
took her up in his arms until she revived. He comforted her with
reassuring words, 9 saying to her, "What is it, Esther? I'm your
brother. Be brave. 10 You're not going to die! This practice applies
only to our subjects. 11 Come here!"

12 Then he raised his gold scepter and tapped her neck; he hugged
her and said, "Now tell me all about it." 13 "My lord," she said, "I
saw you like an angel of God; and I was upset by your awesome
appearance. 14 For you are wonderful, my lord, and your face is
full of graciousness." 15 And as she spoke, she sagged with relief.
16 The king was upset, and all his attendants tried to reassure her.

Addition E
TEXT OF THE KING'S SECOND LETTER
(E 1–24; AT viii 22–32; Vulg. xvi 1–24)

E 1 The text of the dispatch was as follows:

The great king Artaxerxes to the governors of the one hundred and twenty-seven provinces from India to Ethiopia and to our loyal subjects, greetings! 2 Honored repeatedly by the very great generosity of their benefactors, many men become more arrogant. 3 Unable to bear success, they not only endeavor to injure our subjects, but they even resort to scheming against their own benefactors! 4 Puffed up by flattery of the foolish, they not only deprive men of gratitude, but even assume that they will escape the evil-hating justice of God, who always sees everything. 5 And often many of these who are in positions of authority have been made accomplices in the shedding of innocent blood by the persuasiveness of those "friends" who, having been entrusted with the administration of public affairs, have involved them in irremediable misfortunes, 6 beguiling the good faith of their rulers by the deceptive fallacies of the malicious.

7 Now, all this can be seen, not so much from the ancient records which have come down to us, as from an examination of what has recently been perpetrated by the destructive behavior of worthless officials. 8 (In the future we will make every effort to make the kingdom quiet and peaceful for all men, 9 both by not paying any attention to slanders, and by always judging the matters which are presented to us with more considered attention.) 10 For Haman, the son of Hammedatha, a Macedonian—without any Persian blood and quite devoid of our goodness—was treated by us as a guest, 11 and enjoyed the benevolence which we have for every nation, to the extent of his being called in public "our father" and of being continually bowed down to by all as second only to the

king. 12 Unable, however, to contain his arrogance, he schemed to deprive us of both kingdom and life. 13 By involved deceptions and arguments he asked for the destruction of both Mordecai, our savior and constant benefactor, and Esther, our blameless partner in the kingdom, as well as their nation. 14 By this strategy he thought he would leave us helpless and could transfer the hegemony of the Persians to the Macedonians.

15 We, however, find that the Jews who were consigned for destruction by this blackguard are not criminals, but are governed by very just laws, 16 and are sons of the Most High, the most great and living God, who has directed the kingdom for us and our forefathers in the most successful way.

17 You are well advised, therefore, not to act upon the letters sent by Haman, the son of Hammedatha, 18 since that man who contrived these things has been hanged with all his family at the gates of Susa (an appropriate sentence which the omnipotent God promptly passed on him).

19 Post a copy of this letter in every public place, and allow the Jews to observe their own customs, 20 and support them so that on that same day (the thirteenth of the twelfth month, which is Adar) in the hour of trial they may defend themselves against those who attack them. 21 (For the omnipotent God has made this a day of joy for his chosen people instead of their day of destruction. 22 Therefore, you must celebrate it with joy as a special day among your commemorative festivals, 23 so that both now and in the future it may represent deliverance for you and sympathetic Persians, but be a reminder of destruction for your enemies.) 24 Every city or province, without exception, which does not act according to the above, shall be furiously devastated by fire and sword; it shall be made not only inaccessible to men but also most hateful to wild animals and birds forever.

ADDITION F
THE INTERPRETATION OF MORDECAI'S DREAM
(F 1–10; AT viii 53–58; Vulg. x 4–13)

F 1 Then Mordecai said, "This is God's doing, 2 for I remember the dream I had about these things. None of it is unfulfilled— 3 the tiny spring which became a river, as well as the light and sun and veritable flood! The river represents Esther, whom the king married and made queen. 4 The two dragons represent myself and Haman. 5 The nations represent those who gathered to destroy the name of the Jews. 6 And my nation—this is Israel who cried out to God and was saved. (The Lord has saved his people. The Lord has rescued us from all these evils. God has worked great signs and wonders, such as had never before occurred among the pagans.) 7 The Lord made two lots, one for the people of God, and the other for all the nations; 8 and these two lots came to the appointed time, to the day of the trial before God and among all the nations. 9 And God remembered his people, and acquitted his inheritance. 10 Therefore, they shall celebrate these days on the fourteenth and fifteenth of the month of Adar, by getting together in joy and gladness before God, throughout all generations—forever—among his people Israel.

APPENDIX II:

THE COLOPHON TO THE GREEK ESTHER
(F 11; AT viii 59; Vulg. xi 1)

F [11][a] In the fourth year of the reign of Ptolemy and Cleopatra, Dositheus, [b]who claimed[b] to be a priest and a Levite, and Ptolemy, his son, brought the above letter of Purim, which [c]they claimed[c] was authentic and had been translated by Lysimachus the son of Ptolemy, a member of the Jerusalem community.

[a] Only one AT manuscript has this verse; some OL manuscripts omit it; see NOTE.
[b-b] Literally "who said"; see COMMENT.
[c-c] Literally "they said"; see COMMENT.

NOTES

F 11. Even if this colophon* to Esther be genuine (see COMMENT), it cannot be properly appended to *both* the LXX and the A-text since they are separate translations of two quite different Hebrew texts (see the writer's "A Greek Witness to a Different Hebrew Text of Esther," ZAW 79 [1967], 351–58). Thus the A-text rightly omits the colophon.

Ptolemy. A number of Ptolemies have been suggested, including the XIIth, ca. 77 B.C. (E. J. Bickerman, JBL 63 [1944], 339–62), the XIVth, ca. 48 B.C. (H. G. Ewald); but Ptolemy VII, or Soter II (ca. 114 B.C.), is probably the best identification (see B. Jacob, ZAW 10 [1890], 241 f.).

Levite. Bickerman (JBL 63 [1944], 348) reads the personal name Leveites; but see Ralph Marcus' rebuttal in JBL 64 (1945), 269–71.

* "An inscription placed at the end of a book or manuscript, often containing facts relative to its production, as the scribe's, illuminator's, or printer's name, the place and date of publication, etc.; as, from title page to *colophon*. . . ." *Webster's New International Dictionary*, 2d ed., s.v. "colophon. 2."

COMMENT

Esther is the only book of the Jewish canon which has a colophon for its Greek translation. There is no cogent reason to question its extrinsic authenticity as ancient libraries like the one at Alexandria often appended such colophons to their acquisitions (for additional examples, see Bickerman, JBL 63 [1944], 339–44). Regardless of its extrinsic authenticity, however, it cannot be appended to both the LXX and the A-text (see NOTE above).

As for the colophon's intrinsic authenticity, there is still considerable uncertainty over its possible implications. Does the phrase "who claimed to be a priest and a Levite" imply the colophonist's reservations or suspicions of Dositheus' credentials, and hence of his claims for the manuscript's authenticity? Certainly the phrase "which they claimed was authentic" implies the colophonist's awareness of another competing Greek translation of Esther, be it the A-text or a Greek version without all, or any, of the Additions. It is impossible, of course, to be certain whether the most likely date, that is, 114 B.C. (see NOTE on "Ptolemy" above), applies to the translation of Esther with or without the Additions, although the latter is more likely. All that can be said with certainty is that by Josephus' day (ca. A.D. 90) at least Additions B, C, D, and E existed, for he paraphrased them in his *Antiquities*.

For a discussion of the note appended at the end of Codex Sinaiticus by a seventh-century scribe, to the effect that the manuscript had been "corrected" by Origen's *Hexapla,* see H. B. Swete, *An Introduction to the Old Testament in Greek,* pp. 75–77; and H. J. Milne and T. C. Skeat, *Scribes and Correctors of the Codex Sinaiticus* (British Museum, 1938), p. 46.

APPENDIX III: ILLUSTRATED *MEGILLOTH*

Not only was Esther one of the most popular books among the Jews of the Middle Ages (see Introduction, p. LVI), it was also in connection with this book that the medieval art of illuminating biblical manuscripts reached its richest development. Despite the abundance of medieval manuscripts of the Book of Esther, there are many unanswered questions about the evolution of the Jewish illustrated copies. One must distinguish, of course, between the rules for illustrating a *codex,* the Hebrew text written in book form, and a *megilla,* the Hebrew text written on a leather scroll. Apart from perhaps some reluctance to represent the human form, Jewish scribes and artists of the Middle Ages were not particularly handicapped or restricted in illuminating codices of the Bible. (Some scholars believe that Christian artists influenced and may even at times have been employed to work on Jewish Bibles.*) illuminated megilla.‡ In the subsequent centuries there was a no- because the *masora* for Esther† was almost as restrictive for an artist as the masora for the Torah; for example, all columns in a megilla had to be of equal width and of equal length, with equal spaces maintained between the columns. Thus the scribe had to confine his artistic efforts to the upper and lower borders of a megilla and to the spaces between the columns (see Plate 11).

---

* So Mendel Metzger, "The John Rylands Megillah and Some Other Illustrated Megilloth of the XVth to XVIIth Centuries," BJRL 45 (1962–63), 154. Metzger attempts to establish the correct chronology of several medieval and "more modern" Megilloth as well as their iconographic sequence. For another brief introductory article on *megilla,* see R. B. Wischnitzer's article in *The Universal Jewish Encyclopaedia,* 10 vols. (Brooklyn, N.Y., 1939–43), VII, s.v. "Manuscripts."

† *Masora,* which means "tradition," refers to a collection of the notes found at the top, sides, and bottom of a book of the Hebrew Bible. The masora was designed to safeguard the traditional transmission of that particular text. For instructions given in the Talmud, see *The Masechet Soferim;* also Joel Müller, *Der talmudische Tractat der Schreiber, eine Einleitung in das Studium der althebräischen Graphik, der Masora und der altjüdischen Liturgie* (Leipzig, 1878).

Nor do we know from existing megilloth exactly when Esther was first illuminated. (The Dead Sea scrolls, of course, were not illustrated.) Whether there were illustrated Jewish biblical manuscripts in Dura-Europos* during the first and second centuries A.D., as C. H. Kraeling has suggested,† is highly questionable. In any case, the oldest extant illuminated Jewish manuscripts are the tenth-century texts of the now famous Cairo Geniza. These manuscripts, which were probably produced in the Near East under the influence of Islamic art, were illuminated but not illustrated, that is, they had floral and geometric patterns but human figures were not represented. Unfortunately, no decorated megilla was found there. In fact, not until ca. 1450 do we have even an illuminated megilla.‡ In the subsequent centuries there was a noticeable increase in pictures illustrating the text and a corresponding decline in the purely decorative art. According to Metzger, "by far the greater number of illustrated *megilloth* were not individually hand-painted; their illustrations were produced by engravings, sometimes on wood-blocks, more usually on copperplates, afterwards coloured."§

* Located midway between Aleppo and Bagdad, Dura-Europos was a thriving city in the Syrian Desert from A.D. 165 to 256, when it was destroyed by the Sassanians. A large Jewish community lived there, and its excavated synagogue has produced extensive and well-preserved murals. For a brief introduction to the subject, see M. I. Rostovtzeff, *Dura-Europos and Its Art,* Oxford University Press, 1938.

† *The Synagogue,* in *The Excavations at Dura-Europos: Final Report,* VIII, Part I (Yale University Press, 1956), pp. 394–95.

‡ According to Metzger, BJRL 45 (1962–63), 160, it is the Kirschstein-Guggenheim Megilla.

§ BJRL 45 (1962–63), 158.

APPENDIX IV: LIST OF KINGS

The Achaemenian

B.C.

550–530	Cyrus the Great
530–522	Cambyses
522–486	Darius I, Hystaspes
486–465	Xerxes I
465–424	Artaxerxes I, Longimanus
423	Xerxes II
423–404	Darius II, Nothus
404–358	Artaxerxes II, Mnemon
358–338	Artaxerxes III, Ochus
338–336	Arses
335–331	Darius III, Codomannus
336–323	Conquests by Alexander the Great

The Seleucids

B.C.

312–280	Seleucus I, Nicator
280–261	Antiochus I, Soter
261–246	Antiochus II, Theos
246–226	Seleucus II, Callinicus
226–223	Seleucus III
223–187	Antiochus III, the Great
187–175	Seleucus IV, Philopator
175–163	Antiochus IV, Epiphanes
163–162	Antiochus V, Eupator
162–150	Demetrius I
150–146	Alexander Balas
146–142	Antiochus VI

The Ptolemies

B.C.

323–285	Ptolemy I, Lagi
285–246	Ptolemy II, Philadelphus
246–221	Ptolemy III, Euergetes
221–203	Ptolemy IV, Philopator
203–181	Ptolemy V, Epiphanes
181–145	Ptolemy VI, Philometer
145–117	Ptolemy VII, Euergetes II
117–108	Ptolemy VIII, Soter II

The Maccabeans
B.C.

167–161	Judas
161–143	Jonathan
143–135	Simon

The Hasmoneans
B.C.

63	Rome enters Jerusalem
135–105	John Hyrcanus
104	Judas Aristobulus I
104–78	Alexander Jannaeus
78–69	Alexandra
69–63	Aristobulus II
63	Rome enters Jerusalem

KEY TO THE TEXT

Chapter	Verse	§
i	1–22	1
ii	1–18	2
ii	19–23	3
iii	1–15	4
iv	1–17	5
v	1–8	6
v	9–14	7
vi	1–13	8
vi	14	9
vii	1–10	9
viii	1–17	10
ix	1–19	11
ix	20–32	12
x	1–3	13